D1610111

An Anthology
of Chartist Poetry

An Anthology of Chartist Poetry

Poetry of the British Working Class,
1830s–1850s

EDITED BY

Peter Scheckner

Rutherford • Madison • Teaneck
Fairleigh Dickinson University Press
London and Toronto: Associated University Presses

Associated University Presses
440 Forsgate Drive
Cranbury, NJ 08512

Associated University Presses
25 Sicilian Avenue
London WC1A 2QH, England

Associated University Presses
P.O. Box 488, Port Credit
Mississauga, Ontario
Canada L5G 4M2

The paper used in this publication meets the requirements of the American National Standard for Permanence of Paper for Printed Library Materials Z39.48-1984.

Library of Congress Cataloging-in-Publication Data

An Anthology of Chartist poetry.

Bibliography: p.
Includes index.
1. English poetry—19th century. 2. Chartism—Poetry.
3. Political poetry, English. 4. Labor and laboring
classes—Poetry. 5. Laboring class writings, English.
I. Scheckner, Peter, 1943– .
PR1195.C455A84 1989   821'.8'080358   88-45722
ISBN 0-8386-3345-5 (alk. paper)

PRINTED IN THE UNITED STATES OF AMERICA

Contents

Contents

Contents

Contents

Contents

Contents

Contents

Contents

Introduction

Weave, brothers, weave!—Toil is ours;
But toil is the lot of men:
One gathers the fruit, one gathers the flowers,
One soweth the seed again!
There is not a creature, from England's King,
To the peasant that delves the soil.
That knows half the pleasures the seasons bring,
If he have not his share of toil!
So,—sing, brothers!
—Barry Cornwall, "The Weaver's Song"

The idle poet's lay I scorn!—
The coldly reasoning brute I hate!
I feel my heart, my sour forlorn—
I cannot bear my state!
Hot indignation burns me up—
My thoughts, my words are all in flame—
I now have drained sad sorrow's cup.
And Justice now will claim!
—"The Weaver's Song, Not by Barry Cornwall"

Chartist Poetry: A National Literature

Although Chartism lasted less than twenty years, the poetry this movement produced represents one of the most passionate, clearly focused, radical and, for its time, socially influential forces in British literature. Chartist poems were read every week by hundreds of thousands of active Chartist workers and supporters throughout England, Scotland, Wales, and Ireland; the ideas and commitment behind these works were translated month by month into political action. For one intense moment in nineteenth-century English literature, the gap between politics and culture virtually disappeared. The Chartists saw little contradiction between the aims of art and the demands of politics: art was inherently political.

Unfortunately, the poetry that came out of working-class struggles in Great Britain from the 1830s to the early 1850s has been largely ignored in the United States and slighted in England. In 1956 *An Anthology of Chartist Literature*, which included a section

15

on poetry, was published in Moscow, with an introduction and notes written in Russian by Yuri Kovalev. The collection was reprinted in London, but has been out of print now for about thirty years. Occasionally one sees Thomas Hood's "The Song of the Shirt," or Ernest Jones's "The Song of the Low" and "The Song of the Gaggers" reproduced in anthologies, but this too is rare. The preface to *The Oxford Book of Nineteenth Century English Verse* begins by acknowledging that

> western man's revolutionary struggle for the basic human rights to "Life, Liberty, and the Pursuit of Happiness" had a liberating influence on the poetic imagination and on the language of poetry. . . . This influence persisted throughout the nineteenth century and made itself felt with varying degrees of emotional intensity at every level of poetic experience.[1]

But of the eighty-five anthologized by *Oxford,* not one may be called a Chartist. Chartist poetry is unique in English literature and deserves, finally, a collection of its own.

Chartist verse was primarily written by industrial or artisan workers—the great majority of whom were self-educated—and printed in Chartist magazines, journals, and newspapers. These works were read as literature, as agitation-propaganda for the Chartist cause, and as a form of poetic handbill, since many of the poems called attention to the major political events then taking place in Great Britain, Europe, and the United States. Perhaps the most enduring aspect of Chartist poetry then and now is that it represented an alternative, working-class culture. Chartist poetry expressed values, ideas, and a social system that sharply contrasted with a culture dominated by the Church, by a fading aristocracy, and by an emerging middle class—all at one time or another bitter foes of the Chartists. The content and the voice of this poetry have little in common with the Victorian writers who characterized Chartism in their novels.

Indeed, Chartist poetry articulated and extolled almost everything bourgeois writers of the time stood against: radical social changes, internationalism, an end to national chauvinism and colonial rule, Church reform, antiracism, egalitarianism and democracy, the right to rank-and-file organizing, freedom of the press, universal literacy and education, and a more equitable distribution of profits. Certainly not every Chartist worker or writer shared all these views, but thousands did, and huge numbers of Great Britain's population read and debated these ideas. In 1841, out of a total adult population of about ten million, perhaps as many as two or three million working people read *The Northern Star,* the most popular and longest-lasting Chartist publication.[2]

The middle-and upper-class monopoly on literature was broken. For the first time on a large scale, worker-poets wrote for fellow workers and their radical sympathizers, British and non-British, and not only for the well-educated, well-heeled reader. Chartist poets often boasted that before they had become writers they were workers and Chartists. Thomas Cooper, perhaps the most prolific prison poet besides Ernest Jones, made sure he added the epithet, "The Chartist," on the title page of his monumental ten-thousand-line poem, *The Purgatory of Suicides: A Prison-Rhyme in Ten Books.* William Thom, a Scottish Chartist who died impoverished, called his work, *Thymes and Recollections of a Hand-Loom Weaver.* Ernest Jones could not hide his own middle-class background, but he liked to say that during two years in solitary confinement he had "written *four* books with the aid of blood and memory, the evidence of which I gave to the Executive, when they welcomed me out of my gaol."[3]

In 1856 a Frenchman named Etienne, in a work called *Revue des Deux Mondes,* observed that nowhere else but in Great Britain was there so much working-class poetry, which constituted a recognizable national literature; this verse was attributable to certain political events in England, notably radicalism and Chartism.[4] A reviewer boasted in *The Star of Freedom:* "Never till the present time has the poetry of the people been written. . . . It is humanising Humanity on the hearth of England's cottage-homes . . . ringing out the people's political, moral, and social aspirations, and elevating the standard of Humanity for all."[5] The Chartists were hardly less reserved about what they had accomplished. A literary review in *The Labourer: A Monthly Magazine of Politics, Literature, and Poetry,* said confidently:

> Chartism is marching into the fields of literature with rapid strides. . . . Its poetry is, indeed, the freshest and most stirring of the age; as in England, thus in France, America, Ireland, and Germany, the poetic spirit has struck the chords of liberty; and the fresh vigour of its production contrasts proudly with the emasculated verses of a fashionable school.[6]

The editors, Feargus O'Connor and Ernest Jones, ask if Tennyson can "do no more than troll a courtly lay?" And, "What is Robert Browning doing? . . . has he nothing to say for popular rights? Let him eschew his kings and queens,—let him quit the pageantry of courts—and *ascend* into the cottage of the poor."

Their great strength, the Chartists believed, lay in their ties to ordinary people. Poetry should be true to the struggles and to the lives of workers. The editors conclude: "We say to the great minds of the day, come among the people, write for the people, and your fame will live for ever. The people's instinct will give life to your philosophy. . . ."

One major Chartist historian, Dorothy Thompson, argues that "an important part of the definition of Chartism [is] to see it as the response of a literate and sophisticated working class. . . . Much of the Chartist propaganda took the form of argument, a dialogue with the middle classes."[7] Chartist poetry was a class-based literature, with its own language, and based on its own social and political struggles. It may be regarded as a literate and sophisticated rebuttal to a middle-class view of the world, a view reflected in the literature of such writers as Disraeli, Dickens, Gaskell, Kingsley, and Eliot.

Before their smash-up in the wake of the 1848 uprisings, the Chartists made ingenuous but inspiring claims about the value of poetry. A column called "The Politics of Poets" in *The Chartist Circular* stated:

> Poetry is a lever of commanding influence when it grasps the subject that interests, or the elements that move the popular will. It penetrates to every nerve and fibre of society, stirring into irresistibility its undermost currents, and spiriting into life and activity the obscurest dweller of the valley, as well as swaying the insignia of its power amongst the loftiest altitudes of genius. . . . Statesmen would do well to feel the throb thus swelling from the pent-up breast of society. It matters, little, however rude the strain; like the feather, it tells the way the wind blows. . . . Ever since the French Revolution mere sentiment in poetry has been giving way for that of principle. . . . Poetry needed, and received, a higher and firmer tone; if it has lost in feeling, it has gained in power.[8]

The Chartists described the "chief, if not the sole theme of poetry amongst democratic nations" to be the destinies of mankind, the rise and fall of empires, the uprooting of prejudice, the overthrow of despotism, and man himself standing in the presence of Nature and of God, with all his passions, his doubts, his rare properties, and inconceivable wretchedness."[9]

They could make these hyperbolic claims because for a brief moment the Chartists were convinced that they and their political allies in insurrectionary Europe were shaking the Western world.

In the mid-1830s, Chartism tapped a huge reserve of worker-generated literature of all sorts. Scores of unknown, uneducated workers as well as nationally recognized political leaders, publicists, and writers like Feargus O'Connor, James Bronterre O'Brien, George Julian Harney, Ernest Jones, William James Linton, Gerald T. Massey, Ebenezer Elliott, and Thomas Cooper, published thousands of poems and essays in various Chartist publications during the insurrectionary period of the late 1830s and 1840s. Perhaps for the first time a mass social and political struggle—which by the 1870s had succeeded in democratizing British political institutions—simultaneously produced a huge volume of working-class literature.

The most influential and widely read of the Chartist poets were Linton (1812–97), Jones (1819–68), Massey (1828–1907), and Cooper (1805–92). Ebenezer Elliott (1781–1849), the "Corn-Law Rhymer") is the most important, pre-Chartist "poet of the people" in the 1830s.

These poets had a wide range of political perspectives, which was correspondingly reflected in their poetry, though each in his time spoke for a particular segment of the Chartist movement. Linton ("Spartacus") believed that an alliance with the middle class was possible and necessary to defeat the Church, the aristocracy, and ruling-class privileges. Of the four, his was the longest-lived commitment to the Chartist cause. Linton had an internationalist outlook, and many of his poems, particularly the long poem, "The Dirge of the Nations" (1849), shows the connection between the struggle in England and the revolutions in Europe. The theme of Linton's cycle of poems, "Rhymes and Reasons Against Landlordism" (1850–51), is the social relationship between the working and ruling classes. In his short poem, "Try again" (1851), Linton tries to sustain the movement after the defeat of the Chartists during the 1848 rebellions.

O Hope forlornest, masked like Despair!
Truth must some day succeed.
Thy failure proves—What?—thy once failing there.
Fail yet again if there be martyr need!
Try again!

Like most of the Chartists, Linton had no long-range program to remedy the injustices he fought so long against. Therefore, his poetry, like most of the poetry in this collection, adheres in open-ended fashion to rather utopian democratic and republican ideals.

For a time Massey subscribed to the radical left of the Chartists.

During the revolutionary 1840s, he worked with Julian Harney—
the editor of *The Red Republican*—who, on 9 November, 1850,
brought out the first English translation of the *Communist Manifesto* in his magazine. Massey's poem, the "Song of the Red
Republican," was the weekly's banner poem.

Nevertheless, Massey's poetry was characteristic of all of the
conflicting strains of the Chartist movement as it neared its demise in the early 1850s. Among the Chartist writers, religious
strains clashed with the "red republicanism" of militants like
Harney and Jones, and political idealism clashed with the emergence of Marxism. The language, for example, of Massey's most
"seditious" verse, as in so much of Chartist poetry, is clearly
marked by biblical imagery. An example is "The Red Banner,"
appearing in a regular column called "Poetry for the People" in
The Red Republican. The second stanza of this work reads as follows:

> Fling out the Red Banner! its fiery front under,
> Come, gather ye, gather ye! Champions of Right!
> And roll round the world with the voice of God's thunder
> The wrongs we've to reckon—oppressors to smite;
> They deem that we strike no more like the old hero-band—
> Martyrdom's own battle-hearted and brave;
> Blood of Christ! brothers mine, it were sweet, but to see ye stand
> Triumph or tomb! welcome! glory or grave![10]

In other works, Massey compares the Chartists with the Is-
raelites emerging from Egyptian slavery.

Ernest Jones is Chartism's most important poet and writer. He
supported the physical force wing of the Chartists, internationalism, national liberation in imperial Europe, and O'Connor's
land scheme. His association with Marx and Engels began after
the 1848 revolution and continued into the 1850s, during which
time he was continually imprisoned for his subversive activities.
Jones's work during the 1840s and 1850s is a combination of
socialist and utopian sentiments. His long poem, *The New
World*,[11] written in prison between 1848 and 1850, is set alle-
gorically in Hindustan and is about class struggle in England. The
work is revolutionary—the people ultimately overthrow bourgeois rule—but also utopian: somehow a classless society results.
Of the four poets, Jones was most consistently an internationalist
and a spokesman for the British worker against the middle and
aristocratic classes.

As a major Chartist poet, Thomas Cooper illustrates a contradiction inherent in Chartist verse: how to fit working-class goals and ideas into traditional forms not accessible to self-educated workers. Cooper was by trade a shoemaker who taught himself six languages, as well as science and mathematics. His major work is the ten-volume, *The Purgatory of Suicides*, written while Cooper was imprisoned in 1843 for sedition. The epic is composed in Spenserian stanza—eight lines in iambic pentameter, followed by a line of iambic hexameter. It had few working-class readers, though Cooper was thereafter endeared to a liberal section of the middle class.

Cooper is an extreme example of a Chartist who wrote more for middle-class recognition than for the class he championed. By 1848 he had caught the attention of the Christian humanist writer Charles Kingsley, whose 1850 novel, *Alton Locke*, is based on the life of Cooper and Gerald Massey—two of the most famous worker-poets of the Chartist era. In at least one major respect, the story of Alton Locke parallels that of Cooper and Massey. The fictional Locke, like both Cooper and Massey, eventually breaks decisively with the English working classes. At the end of Kingsley's novel, Locke embraces a strange mixture of democracy and Christian mysticism. By the mid-1850s Massey and Cooper abandoned their former working-class militancy and wrote for the now-dominant middle class. With the imprisonment and forced exile of most of the Chartist leaders after 1848, men like Massey and Cooper had no deep ideological commitment that would sustain their sympathy with the Chartist struggles.

The Roots of Chartist Radical Politics

Times are altered; trade's unfeeling train
Usurp the land, and dispossess the swain;
Along the law, where scattered hamlets rose,
Unwieldly wealth and cumbrous pomp repose;
And every want to opulence allied,
And every pang that folly pays to pride.
—Oliver Goldsmith, "The Deserted Village"

Goldsmith's eighteenth-century poem rues the passing of a time when the land and the English peasantry could sustain the nation. Now the "tyrant's hand is seen, / And desolation saddens all [England's] green. . . . / Ill fares the land, to hastening ills a prey, / Where wealth accumulates and men decay." As radical and militant as the Chartists seemed to be in the 1830s, and as subversive as many of them became by 1848, they clearly had not sprung

out of a barren political soil. The Chartists were part of a tradition
of radicalism that went back at least to the 1640s—to the English
Revolution, at least two hundred years before the term *Chartism*
was coined in 1837. The historian Christopher Hill observed that
"popular revolt was for many centuries an essential feature of the
English tradition, and the middle decades of the seventeenth
century saw the greatest upheaval that has yet occurred in Britain."[11]

Such political factions as the Levellers, the Diggers, and the
Ranters played very much the same political and ideological role
that the Chartists assumed two hundred years later. These earlier
groups threatened all the traditional forms of social and political
institutions, class structure, and property in ways quite resembling the Chartists. In many ways the Levellers, who were a force
for democracy during the mid-seventeenth century, were forerun-
ners of the Chartists.

Although neither the Levellers, the Diggers, nor the Ranters
ever achieved anything as ambitious as a national press, various
national associations, conventions, petitions, or demonstrations
involving hundreds of thousands of England's disenfranchised,
they represent Chartist prototypes. In some respects, the resemblance is obvious. As described by Hill, "the physical force
Levellers," were

> less concerned with constitutional issues, more with economics, with
> defending the poor against the rich, the common people against great
> men—which one suspects were the chief issues in the minds of the
> poorer classes in the late 1640s. Its spokesmen may also have reflected
> agrarian communist ideas which had long circulated in England.[12]

The general list of democratic reforms put forward by the Levellers during the 1640s was as radical in its day, as was the six-point
Charter drafted by William Lovett and first published in London
on 8 May 1838: redistribution of the franchise; abolition of the
monarchy and the House of Lords; the election of sheriffs and
justices of the peace; law reform; abolition of tithes, and thereby
the abolition of a state Church; and abolition of conscription,
excise, and the privileges of peers, corporations, and trading
companies.[13] The six demands of the Charter were: equal elec-
toral districts, abolition of property qualifications for M.P.s, universal manhood suffrage, annual parliaments, vote by ballot, and
payment of M.P.s.

The radical wing of the Levellers, made up mostly of Londoners
and antiroyalist soldiers, demanded male suffrage, arguing that

"the poorest that lives hath as true a right to give a vote as well as the richest and greatest."[14] In December 1648, a local group of Levellers produced a pamphlet entitled *Light Shining in Buckinghamshire*, which called for equality of property, a demand the Chartists considered too radical for their national petitions. The "True Levellers," as the Diggers called themselves, were the most consistently republican and equated monarchy with landlordism. The Diggers advocated a communist land program and began communal cultivation of land at St. George's Hill near London in 1649. The Chartist Land Plan advocated by Feargus O'Connor certainly owed a debt to the Levellers and Diggers. The basic assumption, as originally articulated by the Diggers, was that land ownership freed workers from political oppression and economic exploitation.

The next great mass movement in England that resembled the mass character and some of the ideology of the Chartists was led by the Luddites. They were most active in the year of Dickens's birth—1812. Luddism had its own roots in machine-breaking in the eighteenth century, but the difference between this movement and the ones before it, is rather like the difference between trade unionism in the 1830s and the physical force wing of the Chartists in 1848: they were both potentially insurrectionary movements. E. P. Thompson's description of Luddism is true for the militant wing of Chartism: the Luddite movement, he writes, "continually trembled on the edge of ulterior revolutionary objectives. This is not to say that it was a wholly conscious revolutionary movement; on the other hand, it had a tendency towards becoming such a movement."[15] The Luddites, like the Chartists twenty-five years later, "revealed the highest political content, as well as the greatest spontaneity and confusion."[16]

The critical moment for the Luddites occurred around March 1812. It was a period, in Thompson's words, of "insurrectionary tension." The reasons were many: the unpopularity of the Napoleonic war, the economic crisis of 1811–12, poor harvests, food shortages, soaring inflation, depressed wages, and the introduction of power-looms in the mills that displaced weavers. Secret committees of weavers were formed, riots broke out in various districts for higher wages or against the displacement of workers by machinery, and mills and warehouses were attacked. On 11 May the prime minister, Spencer Perceval, was assassinated in the House of Commons. "In the summer of 1812," Thompson reports, "there were no fewer than 12,000 troops in the disturbed counties, a greater force than Wellington had under his command in the

Peninsula."[17] Of this period, Thompson concludes, "Sheer insurrectionary fury has rarely been more widespread in English history."[18]

Thereafter, until the 1840s, riots for bread or food were evident
"in almost every town and county" in England.[19] G. D. H. Cole
writes that "socialism was born on the morrow of the Peace [with
France] of 1815.[20] The European war shifted, in effect, to the class
war in Great Britain. Military barracks were constructed in rebellious workers' and peasants' districts of England. In 1816—as
in most of the violent years of Chartism—the English working
classes were held down by force. To the rulers of Great Britain,
every decade after the 1815 peace in Europe must have seemed
more dangerous than the previous one.

The period before the formation of the London Working Men's
Association—the parent body of the People's Charter—has been
described as "the decade of silent insurrection, when a specific
working-class consciousness was developing, in education, political action, trade organization, even cultural aspiration."[21] From
the 1820s on, workers shared a sense of identity based on class
and a radical culture based on mutual class interests. Perhaps the
dominant forces keeping radical class consciousness alive
throughout the years preceeding the Chartist movement were
education and a growing radical press.

From the 1810s onward, one of the major contributions of
Robert Owen and Owenism to the development of working-class
consciousness and identity was in the era of education. "The
future father of English Socialism"—as Engels called Owen—
assumed that by banning ignorance and establishing rational
thought, society could be perfected. The education of society
would take place through cooperative organizations. During the
1820s and continuing into the Chartist period, this is the Owenite
message adopted most vigorously by the British working class.
Naturally this belief in self-education lent a great impetus to a
working-class press and, ultimately, to the fight for a free radical
press. As one historian described this period: "Radical politics
were never far away from some form of adult education. . . .
Education and the press were . . . the main unifying forces of
radical movements."[22]

When the London Working Men's Association was born in
1836, one of its first steps was to fight for a cheap press, and one
of its outstanding features was "the detailed educational pro-
gramme to which it committed itself."[23] A year later, when the

People's Charter emerged, it was no less concerned with combining political, social, educational, and cultural objectives.

If anything, the Chartists heightened the Owenite push toward intellectual and cultural enlightenment. The evolution of Chartist literature and especially its poetry, should be understood in this context: Chartist politics was inextricably tied to its interest in education and culture. The Chartist press and its literature played a central role in enabling working people to identify themselves as a class and in defining their political and cultural objectives. Dorothy Thompson emphasizes this point by arguing that despite the low levels of literacy among many workers, "written and printed material was an essential part of the lives of them all."[24]

Why Poetry?

> Poetry is impassioned truth, and why should we not utter it in the shape that touches our condition the most closely—the political?
> —Ebenezer Elliott

That the Chartists should so naturally be drawn to poetry as a specific literary form is certainly related to the street literature of the ballads and broadsides of the eighteenth and nineteenth centuries. Long before the Chartists began to regularly publish their own poems in the 1830s, an older, plebian culture existed among workers who already had a strong sense of class identity. One form of popular literature was the broadside ballad, hawked, sold, and read in the streets. This ballad, or tale, consisted of a sheet of verses printed on one side of a piece of thin paper usually decorated with a crude woodcut, and sold for one or twopence.[25] Chartist poems often resembled the format of these ballads when they appeared in the Chartist press. These broadsides were sung or read aloud and gave a very large number of people access to current events, trade customs, local legends, and culture.[26]

Stock themes of the broadsides included the humorous treatment of love, sex, and romance. Topical events like the advent of steam, the crowning of Queen Victoria, new finery and fashions, crime, murder, and execution, were also popular. Nonetheless, Ashton concludes, "Despite the principal concern with the immediate and worldly, some of the ballads which were overtly political in title and content, tell us something about the developing state of consciousness amongst the laboring classes in early Victorian Cheltenham"[27]—a center of Chartist activity involving working-class institutions and customs. In the early decades of the century, these ballads were prototypes of Chartist poetry insofar as the broadsides "reached to the roots of the harsh realities in the laboring life [and] were the popular literature par excellence of the working classes."[28] Along with the unstamped press, the broadsides apparently were the closest the poor had to newspapers before the advent of the popular press in the 1850s.

The broadsides gave the working class large doses of scandal, sensation, violence, crime, and romance. But when the broadsides were connected to various traditions connected with trade customs and the work of artisans, this form of street literature represented the emergence of a working-class culture. At certain trade ceremonies, especially among coalminers or textile workers, verses were composed. Other songs praised particular occupations: ploughmen, shoemakers, builders, grocers, and cutlers.[29] Many of the poems in this anthology are by such workers and were originally intended to be sung at trade gatherings. Over a period of decades, a working-class culture developed into poetry, essays, fiction, and autobiographies.

Chartist poetry was emblematic of an age that saw in poetry both a way to escape and a way to emancipate. As Charles Kingsley illustrated in *Alton Locke* (1850), loosely modeled on the life of Thomas Cooper, poetry and literature was another form of the political and social struggle of workers who were trying to liberate themselves from the drudgery of labor. When Alton, a tailor and for a while a Chartist militant, begins "to crave for some means of expressing these fancies" to escape "the soulless routine of mechanical labour," he "turned instinctively to poetry." He begins to write and shows his first verse to his mentor, Sandy Mackaye, a radical Scottist bookseller. "Hech, sirs, poetry! [Mackaye responds] I've been expecting it. I suppose it's the appointed gate o' a workman's intellectual life—that same lust o' versification."[30] In *Alton Locke* it seems quite natural, if not inevitable, that a self-educated Chartist worker should turn to poetry both for his own salvation and for that of his class.

Mackaye introduces Alton to a tradition of democratic and radical poetry educated workers were familiar with: Robert Burns; William Thom (1798–1848); Thomas Hood's "The Song of the Shirt"; Thomas Cooper's "The Purgatory of Suicides"; Tennyson; and, above all, Byron's *Childe Harold*, *Lara*, and *The Corsair*. Inspired by these models, Alton has little trouble finding a canvas for his verse. "I must do my duty therewith in that station of life to which it has pleased God to call me, and look at everything simply and faithfully as a London artisan."[31]

Citing such worker-poets as Hood and Charles Mackay, Alton concludes that "the London poets have always been greatest" who labored in tears, who heard not the "voices of singing men and singing women," but who cried "about the walls of Jerusalem." Alton hopes that he too can "weep for the sins of my people," and turns to the realities of his class:

> crime and poverty, all-devouring competition, and hopeless struggles against Mammon and Moloch, amid the roar of wheels, the ceaseless stream of pale, hard faces, intent on gain, or brooding over woe; amid endless prison-walls of brick, beneath a lurid, crushing sky of smoke and mist. It was a dark, noisy, thunderous element, that London life; a troubled sea that cannot rest, casting up mire and dirt; resonant of the clanking of chains, the grinding of remorseless machinery, the wail of lost spirits from the pit.[32]

This describes much of the content of Chartist poetry, as well as the concerns of the social-condition novels written during this period by Dickens, Gaskell, Disraeli, and others. The ideological differences between these Victorian writers on the one hand, and the Chartists themselves on the other, are dealt with in another section.

The atmosphere breathed by Alton and Chartist poets generally was a heady one, intoxicating in its complexity of political ideas, social struggles, and avalanches of mainstream and unstamped literature. With the rise of weekly and monthly periodicals, cheaper publishing, and thousands of self-taught workers eager to read "subversive" ideas, far more common people were reading poetry. The politics and economics of the day and a spirited cultural climate seemed to feed on one another. Workers found self-expression in poetry, a meager chance at economic improvement (William Thom for a brief moment was popular in literary circles in London—before dying in poverty at age fifty), an occasion to ply a middle-class trade for which no special training was necessary, and a way to introduce class politics to thousands of readers.

Furthermore, hardly anyone questioned the inherent public nature of poetry. Authentic poetry, the Chartists and their sympathizers would argue, was not the expression of a private state of mind. Matthew Arnold had observed in his *Preface to Poems* (1853) that the "eternal objects of Poetry, among all nations and at all times . . . are actions; human actions; possessing an inherent interest in themselves."[33] The Chartists thought this action was a social struggle against all forms of oppression and exploitation, though certainly Arnold had no such idea in mind. Poetry had a much higher purpose than simply to please and delight. As articulated by Arnold in "The Study of Poetry" and illustrated by the poets collected here:

> We should conceive of [poetry] as capable of higher use, and called to higher destinies, than those which in general men have assigned to it hitherto. More and more mankind will discover that we have to turn to poetry to interpret life for us, to console us, to sustain us. Without poetry, our science will appear incomplete; and most of what now passes with us for religion and philosophy will be replaced by poetry.[34]

For a brief moment in the eighteen thirties and forties, these worker-poets saw in their verse a form of elixir. As Arnold and so many of these poems implied, poetry should not only interpret the world, but change it. Ernest Jones's "The Poet's Mission" makes this ambitious claim for the poet.

Who is it, with age-vanquished form,
  Treads death's ascending path:
Yet stronger than the fiery storm
  Of tyrants in their wrath?

Whose voice, so low to human ears,
  Has still the strength sublime
To ring thro' the advancing years—
  And history—and time?

Who is it in love's servitude,
  Devotes his generous life,
And measures by his own heart's good
  A world with evil rife?

The Bard—who walks earth's lonely length
  Till all his gifts are given;
Makes others strong with his own strength,
  And then fleets back to Heaven.

The Roots of Chartist Poetry

It now becomes a matter of the highest necessity, that you all join hands and head to create a literature of your own. Your own prose, your own poetry . . . would put you all more fully in possession of each other's thoughts and thus give you a higher respect for each other, and a clearer perception of what you can do when united.

  —Thomas Cooper, "To the Young Men of the Working Classes"

As it evolved, developed, and declined during a quarter of a century, Chartist poetry reflected a multiplicity of influences and nuances. Music was of principal and early significance. Many of these works were meant to be sung. Ernest Jones recited his *Chartist Songs* (1846) at political meetings. "The Song of the Low" is perhaps the most notable example of a Chartist poem set to music; John Lowry was the composer. Other important influences included Christian hymnology, communal hymn-singing, the Bible, and radical hymn books, for example, Robert Owen's *Social Hymns* (1840) and *Democratic Hymns and Songs* (1849).

By far the greatest single cultural debt the Chartist poets owed was to earlier poets, political theorists and philosophers, and essayists. Based upon his stay in England during the early 1840s, Friedrich Engels observed:

> No better evidence of the extent to which the English workers have succeeded in educating themselves can be brought forward than the fact that the most important modern works in philosophy, poetry, and politics are in practice read only by the proletariat. . . . it is the workers who are most familiar with the poetry of Shelley and Byron. Shelley's prophetic genius has caught their imagination, while Byron attracts their sympathy by his sensuous fire and by the virulence of his satire against the existing social order.[35]

The Chartists modeled themselves on such poets as Milton, Marvell, Pope, Burns, Shelley, Byron, Scott, Southey, and Longfellow. In his own way, each of these writers had been rebels. Milton was admired both for his verse and for his radical views on the licensing and censorship of the press, monarchy, clerical corruption, and marriage and divorce. Milton's defense of the execution of Charles I in 1649 had only increased his popularity among the Chartists.

Byron and Shelley were especially appealing to Chartist readers and poets. Shelley's *Queen Mab* was called the "Chartist Bible." The 2 January 1847 issue of *The Northern Star and National Trades Journal* described Byron's "Don Juan" as "a record of free thought and an eloquent vindication of democracy, which every republican, every lover of his species, should have in his library." *The Chartist Circular* wrote about Byron, "Of all the poets who have directed their minds to the study of the social condition of man, none has sympathized more deeply with the sufferers, none shewn a more determined spirit of resistance and retaliation to the oppressor."[36] Byron's "The Prisoner of Chillon" inspired Jones's poem, "Bonnivard."

In 1809 Byron had written in *English Bards, and Scotch Reviewers* that zeal for his country's honor "bade me here engage / The host of idiots that infest her age." The Chartists felt that they were similarly honor-bound; they too had a host of idiots to expose. The Chartists might have thought that Shelley was addressing them personally in his 1819 poem, "Song to the Men of England."

> Men of England, wherefore plough
> For the lords who lay ye low?
> Wherefore weave with toil and care
> The rich robes your tyrants wear?

"Forge arms,—in your defense to bear" struck an immediate chord in 1839, when the poem was published in Shelley's *Poetical Works.* "Sonnet: England in 1819," in the same collection, might have been found in *The Chartist Circular* when both the poems and the periodical appeared in 1839.

> Rulers who neither see, nor feel, nor know,
> But leech-like to their fainting country cling,
> Till they drop, blind in blood, without a blow,—
> A people starved and stabbed in the untilled field,—
> An army, which liberticide and prey
> Makes as a two-edged sword to all who wield. . . .

The works of these poets were regularly reprinted in Chartist publications. The Chartists believed they were carrying on a democratic tradition begun by Marvell. In addition, they were raising the literacy of working people who had no formal education. For the first time in a mass way, the Chartists were using poetry— their own and their predecessors—to continue the political struggle between themselves and the ruling classes.

The major Chartist publications regularly brought to the attention of their readers reviews and reprints of the "Radical" poets. In its 20 January 1838, edition, *The Northern Star* included the following advertisement: "To the Public: With this week's number of *The Northern Star,* every Lancashire Purchaser will be presented with a splendid portrait of Andrew Marvell (copied expressly from a Painting in the British Museum)."

Later issues included reprints of Byron's and Shelley's poetry, reviews of American and British fiction, poems by fellow Chartists, and a regular column called "Poetry and Review." *The Chartist Circular* ran a regular column called "The Politics of Poets," in which the writers called Wordsworth's poems "deeply, essentially, entirely Radical." Wordsworth chose his themes, like the Chartists, "from the lowest and simplest walks of life—who associates himself in spirit, if not in person, with the poor and the suffering—whose heroes were waggoners, strollers, pedlars, beggars, hedgers and ditchers, and shepherds. . . ."[37] The *Circular* said of Milton, "Altar, sword, and pen, that is, the church, the army, the law (and the press), all are corrupt to the very core, and require the application of reform. And no man but Milton for this work."[38]

By the time the Chartists produced their own literature in the late 1830s, they found a tradition in verse rich in revolt—primarily that of the middle classes against an aristocratic class in decline. The principal goal of the Chartist poets was to create a culture and a verse uniquely working-class in character. Chartist literature had to move beyond the bourgeois culture of the Romantics to continue the radical tradition of such giants as Milton, Burns, Shelley, and Byron. These poets had been rebels in their time and in their way, but they were not fighting for an end to the exploitation of labor and for the social and political emancipation of agricultural and industrial workers. They had not preached for an end to imperial rule; they did not have an internationalist perspective. The Chartists were motivated by class interests—reflected in their verse—that no poets or writers of fiction before them had had.

The Politics of Poetry

CLASS AGAINST CLASS—all other mode of proceeding is mere moonshine. Once achieve this—nay!—*once turn the balance*—and who can doubt the result.
—Ernest Jones, *Notes to the People*

The 1830s was a period of radical and popular culture, a culture marked by a class consciousness shared by a large majority of the working classes. E. P. Thompson reports that "something like two out of every three working men were able to read after some fashion in the early part of the century,"[39] and what they chose to read and to write was almost always political. The Chartists debated the correct course of this or that political action or objective, but it was clear to them from the beginning that poetry, like everything else they wrote and disseminated, would be political.

Poetry was a continuation of the class battle. For most of the Chartists, the "chief, if not the sole theme of poetry amongst democratic nations" was clearly stated by this review in a regular column called "Politics of Poets" in *The Chartist Circular.* "The destinies of mankind, the rise and fall of empires, the uprooting of prejudice, the overthrow of despotism, and man himself standing in the presence of Nature and God, with all his passions, his doubts, his rare properties, and inconceivable wretchedness. . . ."[40]

Naturally, not everything produced during this period was necessarily "Radical," and the reading public was not of one class. But working-class and bourgeois audiences alike seemed to demand an engaged poetry, a *public* poetry. In 1853, toward the end of the Chartist movement (the last national Chartist Convention was in February 1858), Matthew Arnold wrote his first piece of published prose, the preface to *Poems* (1853). Although Arnold was hardly a Chartist sympathizer, he did urge poets to adhere to certain guidelines followed consciously or not by the worker-poets of this period. Arnold's first dictum was that poets portray an action rather than express a subjective feeling, and the second was that the poet concentrate on the overall subject and nature of his work rather than on details of rhetorical phrasing.

> We have poems which seem to exist merely for the sake of single lines and passages; not for the sake of producing any total-impression. We have critics who seem to direct their attention merely to detached expressions, to the language about the action, not to the action itself. . . . They will permit the Poet to select any action he pleases, and to suffer that action to go as it will provided he gratifies them with occasional bursts of fine writing, and with a shower of isolated thoughts and images. That is, they permit him to leave their poetical sense ungratified, provided that he gratifies their rhetorical sense and their curiosity.[41]

Without agreeing ideologically about what was appropriate poetic content, Arnold and the Chartists understood that fine poetics without a "fitting action" was so much fluff. In fact, Arnold criticized Shakespeare's "gift of expression" because it occasionally led him astray, degenerating sometimes into a fondness for curiosity of expression, into an irritability of fancy, which seems to make it impossible for him to use plain, simple, language.[42]

Both Arnold and these poets wanted to move away from the subjectivity of verse. The proper environment in which verse might flourish was not "the state of one's own mind." The Chartists would hardly have even understood the notion of art for art's sake, and Arnold moved with such determination toward an objective view of the world that eventually he gave up writing poetry entirely, and instead concentrated on prose and the essay format.

Arnold would never have sympathized with the principal subject of most Chartist verse—the emancipation of workers from an oppressive social and political system. Ironically, in 1847, during the height of Chartist militancy, Arnold became the private secretary to Lord Lansdowne, the president of the council in the ministry of the Chartists' most notable enemy—Lord John Russell. But on one crucial point Arnold and the Chartist poets would have agreed. The "false aim" of poetry, in the critic's words, is "an allegory of the state of one's own mind, the highest problem of an art which imitates actions. . . . No great poetical work has ever been produced with such an aim."[43]

The Chartists regarded poetry as the highest form of creative expression, "the Flower of Humanity," the *Literature Review* called it. Poetry, the *Review* continued,

> will continually be springing, in its own natural way, in the most bleak and barren byways of the world. . . . in spite of Poverty and its evil influences, in spite of Penury and its untoward circumstances, in spite of the iron heel of Oppression, and the inexorable knife of malignant Fate, the Flower of Poetry will be found springing into life . . . and the hearts of poor working men will break into singing, showing that they too possess the magic to trim the divine lamp of Poetry in the hearts and homes of the suffering poor.[44]

Poetry not only offered the poor a psychological respite from suffering, but it could "kindle the hearts of the masses, and awaken in their crushed being a sense of the beauty and grandeur of this world." In poetry the people can hear songs

> which Tyranny quakes to hear, and which the world will not willingly let die. This is one of the proudest characteristics of the age we live in, this poetry of the people, written by and for themselves. Never till the present time has the poetry of the people been written. . . . ringing out the people's political, moral, and social aspirations, and elevating the standard of Humanity for all.[45]

Never before, and perhaps never since this period, has a political-social movement of such national proportions regarded poetry in such exalted terms. Chartist poetry was more than a way to awaken the masses to struggle: it kept alive their hope for a better world.

Chartist Themes

Times will set the coldest burning,
Times that come with great events,
Like the deluge-tides returning
On decaying continents,
Sweeping worn-out wrongs before them,
Wrecks, and wrongs, and discontents.
                    —Ernest Jones, "We Are Silent"

The overriding themes of Chartist poetry did not die with the Chartist movement in the mid-1850s. Although the British working class won political representation by the end of the 1860s (or at least the men did), the more profound concerns of Chartism—working conditions, international cooperation and fraternity, and a socially equitable society—remained. Echoes of Chartist verse may be found in American black poetry during the intense social and political struggles in the 1930s and 1940s, notably in works by Langston Hughes, W. E. B. Du Bois, Fenton Johnson, Claude McKay, Jean Toomer, Melvin Tolson, Gwendolyn Brooks, Paul Laurence Dunbar, James Weldon Johnson, and Arna Bontemps. Other Americans were writing poems resonant in spirit and in content to Chartist poetry of the 1830s and 1840s. These voices included John Neihardt, Witter Bynner, James Oppenheim, Lola Ridge, Louis Untermeyer, Leonard Bacon, and Archibald Mac-Leish. Such world famous poets as Carl Sandburg, W. H. Auden, Bertolt Brecht, C. Day Lewis, Günter Grass, and Pablo Neruda, voiced similar concerns. The differences, of course, between the Chartists and these modern poets are that Chartist poetry represented a national body of work with a certain thematic coherence; that it comes out of a well-defined grass-roots political and social movement; and that the poems taken as a whole were largely intended as a means to educate workers and further the aims of the six-point Charter.

What are the principal themes of Chartist poetry? A prominent theme, like Chartism's most ambitious goal, was international brotherhood and the cessation of imperial rule and racism, which were destructive of that end. Poems expressing these sentiments were particularly in evidence by the middle and late 1840s, as most of Western Europe and Great Britain experienced revolutions or insurrections, and internationalism among the workers in Europe was in high tide. George Julian Harney wrote a song for the Fraternal Democrats—an organization that linked the Chartists to European revolutionaries in exile. Called "All Men Are

Brethern," the poem links the economic slavery of the British worker to the plundered millions of the earth, victims all of imperial rule. Ernest Jones's long poem, "The Age of Peace," is a compelling indictment of imperialism, war, and slavery.

An adjunct to the theme of internationalism and anticolonial rule is the notion that African slaves have much in common with the white workers of Great Britain—a fairly advanced view for this period. In the anonymous work, "The Black and the White Slave," the poet equates the suffering of the slave with the misery of the factory child. "The Land of Freedom" is an ironic poem about an African who goes to England, believing himself now a free man. Witnessing the oppression of British soldiers, the impoverished in poor houses, and the corruption of the press by the rich, among other "little errors [included in] our blessings," the African returns home.

Another underlying theme is the destruction of body and spirit through industrial labor. An entire generation of men, women, and children are consumed by the work they do for others. The best known of these poems are Thomas Hood's "The Song of the Shirt" and Jones's "The Song of the Low." In the former a woman works "Till the heart is sick, and the brain benumb'd, / As well as the weary hand." Season passes season, and the birds seem to "twit me with the spring." Jones's most memorable poem is simultaneously ironic, bitter, and rebellious. "We're low—we're low . . . as low as low can be." Too low to eat the bread they make, to vote the tax, or wear the clothes they make for the rich, "We're not to low—to kill the foe, / But too low to touch the spoil."

Man has been uprooted from the soil and thrust cruelly into mills, poor homes, and hovels. Nature itself, which once all men could enjoy, has now been expropriated by the owners of industry. William James Linton ("Spartacus") writes that the "earth belongeth to the whole,— / God gave it not to thee; / Nor made the meanest human soul / Another's Property" ("Rhymes for the Landlorded"). "The Factory Town" by Jones vividly describes the inhumanity of a city robbed of anything beautiful or life giving.

Chartist poetry strove not merely to be descriptive of an age rent by class oppression, the tedium of labor, and the alienation of man from nature—a world that had turned so obviously against ordinary men and women. It sought with all its untutored rhetoric to enlist the giant of labor to the cause of Chartism. These poems hail labor as the "source, thro bounteous Nature's aid / Of ev'ry blessing which sustains mankind" ("Ode to Labour"); it beseeched all men of reason to rise up against injustice. "This is

no slumb'ring age," says an anonymous poet. "Be up and doing—
for the world / With might change is rife" ("Progress"). "Oh! yes, it
is better, far better to die / In a glorious cause than to pine beneath
chains" ("Rally Again, Boys"). In 1841 Edward Mead wrote "Chartist Song," set to the music of a popular tune. The poem is far
from sophisticated, but it must have been impressive to hear
thousands of marching workers singing the lines of the chorus.
"Swear by freedom's holy name, / By her to stand or fall man, /
Spurn a coward vassal's chain, / Your watchword one and all
man." In 1846 Charles Cole wrote in his poem, "The Strength of
Tyranny, "The tyrants chains are only strong / While slaves submit
to wear them; . . . Perish all tyrants, far and near / Beneath the
chains that bind us: / And perish, too, that *servile fear* / which
makes the slaves they find us." These were some of the great
passions in the poetry of the 1840s when, at least to the Chartists,
almost anything seemed possible.

Chartist Poetry and the British Radical Press

How can we be cheerful when we are surrounded by a *reading public,* that is
growing too wise for its betters?
—Thomas Love Peacock, Mr. Flosky, in *Nightmare Abbey*

In France it was what people did that was wild and elemental; in England it
was what people wrote.
—G. K. Chesterton, *The Victorian Age in Literature*

The huge amount of verse written by self-educated workers
beginning in the 1830s may have been a first in British literary
history, but a radical press had been active since the end of the
Napoleonic wars. William Cobbett's *Weekly Political Register* had
begun a mass inexpensive printing in 1816, which sold forty
thousand copies of the first issue within a month.[46] Its readership,
like the radical periodicals that followed, consisted of the working
classes.

Three years later an act of political oppression occurred that was
a watershed in the development of the radical press. On 16 August 1819, in St. Peter's Fields, Manchester, yeomanry charged
into a crowd of 80,000 workers and their families who were
demanding reform and the repeal of the Corn Laws. Eleven
people were killed and 400, including more than 100 women,
were wounded. After this "Peterloo Massacre," the government
regarded the radical press with great seriousness. The Six Acts
were passed in November, and three of these acts dealt with "the

blasphemous and seditious press." The Libel Acts of 30 December 1819 extended the Stamp Act of 1712 to include the popular cheap press.

Thereafter, the radical movement and the radical press entered a stage of heightened activity. As Royle puts it, "The rapid spread of Chartism in the late 1830s cannot be understood unless the impact of the unstamped is fully appreciated.[47] Radical ideas, which during and immediately after the Napoleonic wars belonged largely to the intelligentsia, now became the property also of the artisans and some skilled workers, future organizers of the Chartist movement. "The impulse of rational enlightenment," writes E. P. Thompson, "was now seized upon [by workers] with an evangelistic zeal to carry it to 'numbers unlimited'—a propagandist zeal scarcely to be found in Bentham, James Mill or Keats."[48] At the height of the campaign against the stamp tax in the mid-1830s, according to Plummer, "something like 150,000 copies of the unstamped papers were defiantly distributed each week; every copy likely to be passed from hand to hand, studied in coffee-houses and taverns, and read aloud to groups of non-readers."[49] "The certainty of the existence of a working-class reading public is plain," concludes R. K. Webb. "The reading public was very probably much larger than has been generally thought. . . . Any estimation of the political and social implications of this new phenomenon must be considered in light of the fantastic multiplication of all kinds of printed material."[50]

An unstamped press came into being, and with it an organized and working-class culture. The fight for a free radical press was not merely another battle along the way for British workers to achieve their own political voice: the struggle was, in Thompson's words, "a central formative influence upon the shaping movement" of the working class in Britain.[51] Henry Weisser's assessment of the link between the press and the radicalization of the British working class is similar. "Undoubtedly the most important instrument in creating a new class consciousness, national and international, among British workers was the cheap, popular press. Without it, concern for Europe and Europeans would not have developed."[52]

Thompson claims that "perhaps 500 people were prosecuted for the production and sale of the 'unstamped,'" a figure that included editors, booksellers, hawkers, and agents.[53] By 1832, Thompson concludes, "there is a Radical nucleus to be found in every county, in the smallest market towns and even in the larger rural villages."[54]

To radicalize so many of their numbers, these radical artisans—tailors, shoemakers, cabinetmakers, weavers, saddlers, and spinners—had to rely on self-education; they taught themselves and then become teachers. Many of these artisans turned to poetry. Huge amounts of Chartist as well as earlier radical verse were printed which, sold cheaply or given away, served as propaganda. Hundreds of working-class men and women enlisted in this war of the radical press, and the dissemination of their own poetry as well as cheap reprints of earlier subversive poetry served to raise the general level of social consciousness.

As early as the 1790s, the output of printed materials of all kinds became a flood. This literature was most influenced by the French Revolution, Thomas Paine, the Enlightenment, and the British Romantic poets. The principal audience of these writings were the urban working classes, who learned to read in innumerable societies (mechanics' institutes, temperance clubs, chapels, co-operative stores, Sunday schools, Corresponding Societies, and Chartist study groups), who had these works read to them in private if they were unable to read, or who attended public meetings and heard about these works. By the 1790s, reports Brian Simon, the Corresponding Societies

> had begun to spread the ideas of the French revolution among the artisans and smaller tradesmen of towns which were awakening to the effects of economic change. Political activity, coupled with thorough discussions at Sunday "class" meetings, in which each member participated in an organised way, provided a new form of political education, much deeper than had ever been available before. Moreover the thirst for knowledge began to be met with a literature propagating the most radical political views, a popular literature addressed to the common man which was read in ever widening circles.[55]

One of the most significant effects of the war of the unstamped and the radical press was the political education of thousands of workers during the period. In 1816, William Cobbett, perhaps the most important radical publisher of his day, issued the *Political Register* at just over one shilling. By November of that year he had reduced the price to twopence and claimed that forty-four thousand copies of the first cheap number had been printed and sold.[56] A Colonel Fletcher wrote to the Home Office that "there is scarcely a street or a post in the Land but that is placarded with something seditious."[57]

Even by our own standards of literacy, the level of political and social consciousness acquired through literature and the press among factory and craft workers was high. In 1826 a public dinner was held to celebrate Thomas Paine's birthday and to welcome the release of Richard Carlile, the radical writer, from a six-year prison term. Toasts were drunk to Paine, Robert Owen, Rousseau, Voltaire, Diderot, Benjamin Franklin, Byron, Shelley and "all Englishmen who have written to the end of human improvement."[58] The *Northern Star* described a successful Chartist Sunday school in the Carpenters' Hall, Manchester, in 1844. Chartist parents and children were in attendance. They began this "democratic academy" with the singing of Chartist hymns. Later the children recited poems called "The Downfall of Poland," "Byron's Dream," "The Factory Slave's Last Day," "The Charm of Freedom," and "The Democratic Working Man."[59] Engels observed that during this period "no better evidence of the extent to which the English workers have succeeded in educating themselves can be brought forward than the fact that the most important modern works in philosophy, poetry, and politics are in practice read only by the proletariat."[60] By the forties it had become clear that the overriding objective of the Chartist movement was to combine political work with self-education; one was ultimately impossible without the other. "We are called *ignorant*," a Chartist lecturer wrote, in an attempt to secure a Trades Hall where workers could meet, "by those who . . . happen to be uppermost; be it so, we will remove that ignorance by teaching one another, by discussing politics day after day, and by an interchange of thoughts and sympathy."[61] A few months later another Chartist organizer wrote in a letter from Nottingham: "This is a famous radical town. Reading rooms and libraries abound, though some of them are unfortunately held at public houses."[63]

Throughout the forties, local Chartist organizations set up their own libraries, reading rooms, and discussion classes as "essential to the progress of Chartist principles."[63] The *Northern Star* reported that a delegate meeting at Birmingham in September 1848, suggested to the Chartist Executive "the establishment of mutual instruction societies throughout the Chartist ranks, as the dispelling of ignorance is the only means of obtaining the Charter."[64]

Such instruction was hardly limited to politics. Every major Chartist publication contained scientific and cultural information as well. All the major Chartist publications—*The Labourer, The Red Republican* and *The Friend of the People, McDouall's Chartist Journal and Trades' Advocate*, and of course the most influential of all, *The Northern Star*—included original Chartist poetry as well as the masters—Shelley, Byron, Wordsworth, Marvell, and Milton. The

Northern Star not only included a poetry section; it also ran a column called "Literature and Review," which ran reviews of contemporary novelists, poets, and essayists, including Charles Dickens. The analyses were often fairly provocative, as one letter, signed by Engels and Marx to the editor Feargus O'Connor, illustrates. Their letter, from the German Democratic Communists of Brussels, attacked "such disguised bourgeois" (for example, the poet Thomas Cooper) who, "while they show off with the name of Chartist for popularity sake, strive to insinuate themselves into the favour of the middle classes by personal flattery of their literary representatives" (such as Charles Dickens) "and by propounding such base and infamous old women's doctrines as that of 'non-resistance.' "[65]

A final example of the British radical press shows its sophistication and its independence from any rigid ideology. The 4 July 1846 edition of *The Northern Star* celebrated the American Revolution, but, true to the Chartists' critical reading of world events, such editorial praises were qualified. "It must be admitted that as yet this declaration of a great principle has not been fully carried out even amongst the people who pride themselves upon having given birth to that declaration," a reference to slavery. Nevertheless, an original encomium in verse follows, signed, "an English lady." "The Star-Spangled Banner" and Longfellow's "The Arsenal at Springfield" are reprinted.

Chartist Representations in Mainstream Victorian Literature

It's almost enough to make one think, if one didn't know better, that at times some motion of a capsizing nature was going on in things, which affected the general economy of the social fabric.
—Charles Dickens, Alderman Cute, in "The Chimes"

The literature of Chartist workers, particularly its poetry, bears little resemblance to Victorian representations of the Chartist movement. Disraeli, Dickens, Kingsley, Gaskell, and George Eliot loosely based much of their subject matter on the Chartists, but rarely with sympathy. Chartist poetry symbolized the heart of working-class culture from the 1830s to the 1850s, and it had little in common with a substantial body of Victorian fiction that is set during this period. As a body of work, Chartist poetry represents a set of class interests contrary to the social values appearing in conventional prose fiction of the time.

Perhaps the most compelling reason to compare Victorian literature of the 1830s, 1840, and 1850s, to that of the Chartists is that without Chartism there probably would not have been the "condition-of-England" or social novel in the first place. Novels like *Sybil, Mary Barton, Alton Locke,* and *Hard Times* would be unimaginable if Chartist-led struggles had not existed. The character of the novel in the early Victorian period developed as a direct result of Chartism. Disraeli and Dickens, writes Jack Lindsay, had brought the mass movement of workers "right into the forefront; and 1848 saw the reliance of a series of important novels on the basic social question. . . . These works were directly the result of Chartism whether they overtly dealt with the Chartist theme or merely drew on the new clarified atmosphere of struggle."[66]

These novels, standards of Victorian fictional prose, include *Sybil* (1845) by Benjamin Disraeli, *Alton Locke, Tailor and Poet* (1850) by Charles Kingsley, *Barnaby Rudge* (1841) and *Hard Times* (1854) by Charles Dickens, and *Mary Barton* (1848) and *North and South* (1855) by Elizabeth Gaskell. A somewhat later work, *Felix Holt, the Radical* (1866) by George Eliot, is set around the time of the first Reform Bill of 1832. From them we get the principal contemporary—and, one might add, middle-class—portrait of Chartist workers in British literature. These novels are concerned about the social condition of England in the insurrectionary forties; they are generally liberal and sympathetic toward the plight of workers and recognize that, historically, the reign of the aristocratic class was mercifully over. *Alton Locke* illustrates the artistic potential of a Chartist worker. It is impossible to imagine these books had the Chartists never existed.

As Dorothy Thompson points out in her book called *The Chartists,* "A very great deal of our information about the 1830s and the 1840s must come, by definition, from middle-class sources."[67] Even though these Victorians attacked British social and political institutions, they are unmistakenly bourgeois. Disraeli was twice prime minister (1868 and 1874–1880). Kingsley was the Regius Professor of Modern History at Cambridge University in 1860 and the next year became a history tutor to the Prince of Wales. Both he and Gaskell had deep connections to the Church: Kingsley was the rector of Eversley when he was twenty-five, and Gaskell was the daughter of a Unitarian and married to a Unitarian minister.

By the mid-1850s Dickens was the most successful novelist and publicist (his weekly magazine was called *Household Words*) in England. Curiously, he managed to achieve his popularity without having created any fully developed working-class heroes—with the exception of Stephen Blackpool in *Hard Times.* As critics have pointed out, Dickens's characters are lawyers, clerks, artisans, small or large businessmen, tradesmen, innkeepers, and servants. His world is that of the middle class, rarely if ever that of industrial or agricultural labor.

To these middle-class writers, Chartism had all the fascination and attractiveness of a serpent. The workers exploited in factories and on farms were to be pitied. But when they organized, they were portrayed as intoxicated, irrational, uncivilized, unpredictable, violent and, except for *Alton Locke,* uncultured. In Victorian novels workers are characterized as self-destructive and semiarticulate when they riot, and abject and pathetic when they do not. In *Alton Locke* and *Mary Barton* they are given to religious epiphanies. The lower orders are too abused by poverty to verbalize their exploitation, as are the Hands in *Hard Times* or the insurrectionary farm workers in *Alton Locke* and *Sybil,* and they are misled by seditious leaders—*Sybil, Alton Locke, North and South,* and *Barnaby Rudge.*

In some ways, George Eliot's *Felix Holt* articulated a radical conservatism that spoke for all these writers. Eliot completed her novel, subtitled *The Radical,* in May 1866. By December of the following year she added an appendix called "Addresses to Working Men" in which, through the *persona* of Felix Holt, Eliot set out the political philosophy of the novel. The address, in effect, stated the class view of all five writers. She begins by saying that "the only safe way by which society can be steadily improved and our worst evils reduced, is not by any attempt to do away directly with the actually existing class distinctions and advantages . . . but by the turning of Class Interests into Class Functions or duties." From then on Eliot talks about the need to preserve "the supreme unalterable nature of things," that is, class and social order.

> The fundamental duty of government is to preserve order, to enforce obedience of the laws. . . . It is only by disorder that our demands will be choked, that we shall find ourselves lost amongst a brutal rabble, with all the intelligence of the country opposed to us, and see government in the shape of guns that will sweep us down in the noble martyrdom of fools.

"The security of [the] treasure" of society—knowledge, science, poetry, intelligence, manners, and "the interpretation of great records"—demands "not only the preservation of order, but a certain patience on our part with many institutions and facts of various kinds, especially touching the accumulation of wealth, which from the light we stand in, we are more likely to discern the evil than the good of it." Overall, Felix Holt's address articulates the class outlook of *Sybil, Barnaby Rudge, Mary Barton,* and *Alton Locke:* social order, not justice, is primary.

Each of these novels makes the discovery that workers must not be entrusted with political power. Good sense, social generosity, and rational government are the province of the middle classes. The ethically minded hero—the aristocratic Charles Egremont and the Chartist Walter Gerard in *Sybil,* the Chartist-poet Alton Locke, the mill worker Stephen Blackpool in *Hard Times,* and the "radical" Felix Holt—learns not to trust rebellious workers. The novels begin with a genuine sympathy for the plight of the industrial and agricultural laborer in the 1830s and 1840s. Rebellion and class antagonism are understandable given the misery of workers' lives, but only the ruling middle classes, sympathetic Churchmen, and a handful of paternal aristocrats and wealthy businessmen can be the custodians of the state. Social injustice is a matter for those in power to alleviate. Economic and political ills have no genuinely democratic solution. Although secondary ideological differences exist among Disraeli, Dickens, Gaskell, and Kingsley, they fundamentally share Alton Locke's view of rioting workers who, in this particular case, are literally starving to death.

> Then I found out how large a portion of rascality shelters itself under the wing of every crowd; and at the moment, I almost excused the rich for overlooking the real suffers, in indignation at the rascals. But even the really starving majority, whose faces proclaimed the grim fact of their misery, seemed gone mad for the moment. The old crust of sullen, dogged patience had broken up, and their whole souls had exploded into reckless fury and brutal revenge. . . .[68]

Compassion for the poor and exploited turns quickly to scorn, fear, and paternalism whenever the mob appears. Rather than allow workers to decide their own fate, participate in government, or democratize the government—which was the spirit of the six-point Charter—these Victorian voices opt for government intervention, in the form of physical suppression if necessary, benevolence whenever possible.

Of these novels, *Sybil* is by far the most ideologically complex. Although it begins by presenting a sympathetic Chartist leader, Walter Gerard, it dismisses Chartism by identifying it with the Hell-cats of Wodgate—workers who are led by a drunken blacksmith called the Bishop. Subtitled, "Or the Two Nations" as a way of presenting the two worlds of labor and the ruling classes during the 1840s, *Sybil* reflects a paradoxical vision. With one eye

on the future led by his own Tory party, and one eye looking back
to an idealized feudal world dominated by the Church, Disraeli
argues that only an alliance of an enlightened aristocracy, represented here by Egremont; a benevolent Church, under the leadership of a St Lys; good industrialists, like Mr. Trafford; and the
People, cleansed of their Chartist misleaders, can heal a deeply
divided nation.

Every sign of worker militancy is ridiculed. Devildust, the
novel's most radical and class conscious character, whose pro-
nouncements on capitalism would be quite appropriate for the
Chartist paper, *The Northern Star,* at the end becomes a successful
capitalist. Devildust is the only working-class character in these
novels who has an answer to the Chartist debate on the question
of physical versus moral force. "I never heard that moral force
won the battle of Waterloo," he tells his comrades. "I wish the
Capitalists would try moral force a little, and see whether it would
keep the thing going. If the Capitalists will give up their red-coats,
I would be a moral force man to-morrow."[69]

Toward the end of *Sybil* a coalition of workers calls for a general
strike and thousands march on the Mowbray Castle. The loyal
Mowbray workers help to defeat the Wodgate Hell-cats who are
leading the assault because they consider the Hell-cats intruders
and foreigners. In the final battle, the loyalists, allied with middle-
class yeomanry and commanded by local aristocrats, defeat the
Chartist Hell-cats. Disraeli's message is that at least a section of the
British working force is rational enough to reject the Chartists.

Mary Barton offers a fuller and somewhat more sympathetic
account of labor's case against capital during the revolutionary
forties. Whereas Dickens and Disraeli tend to be more patronizing
toward workers—that is, the masters need to be more benevolent
and provide a more enlightened rule—Gaskell argues something
else. Assuming her own narrative voice, Gaskell says that John
Barton, Mary Barton's father, became a Chartist and a Communist
because he was a visionary, which reveals "a creature who looks
forward for others, if not for himself."[70]

Gaskell gives the case for both capital and labor. "I am not sure
if I can express myself in the technical terms of either masters or
workmen, but I will try simply to state the case on which the latter
deliberated." She states that the owners' incentive is to "buy
cotton as cheaply, and to beat down wages as low as possible."
Her conclusion, and the thrust of the book generally, is to suggest
that both classes have valid interests. "And in the long run the
interests of the workmen would have been thereby benefitted.

Distrust each other as they may, the employers and the employed must rise and fall together. There may be some difference as to chronology, none as to fact. . . . So class distrusted class, and their want of mutual confidence wrought sorrow to both."[71] The result is a strike in Manchester that benefits neither labor nor capital.

Unlike Disraeli or Dickens, Gaskell's intention is not merely to get more relief for workers, but to mediate between the classes, to effect a sympathetic understanding between the middle class and labor. It is therefore vital that, at the novel's conclusion, the dying Chartist, John Barton, be forgiven by the factory owner, Mr. Carson, for the murder of Carson's only son. At the end, while Carson holds the dying man in his arms, worker and master pray to be forgiven their various sins.

Gaskell's second great novel about social unrest is *North and South,* which appeared between September 1854 and January 1855 in Dickens's *Household Words.* The book's publication coincides with the demise of Chartism, and is more about the relationship between John Thornton, a mill owner, and Margaret Hale, the daughter of a rural minister, than it is about the struggle between Thornton and his striking workers. The book makes the plea heard in *Mary Barton:* for domestic tranquillity to prevail, worker and employer must respect one another. Gaskell does, however, make it clear that whatever the provocation, workers must not take matters into their own hands. As in *Sybil,* decent workers are peaceful; the militants are troublemakers. The more loyal workers complain to Margaret that the employers have unfairly brought in scab Irish workers to break the strike. But, they continue, "the most cruel cut of all was that of the Milton workmen, who had defied and disobeyed the commands of the Union to keep the peace whatever came; who had originated discord in the camp, and spread the panic of the law being arrayed against them."[72] Because of the militants the strike is lost.

Gaskell's publisher and mentor was Dickens. He knew far less about industrial or agricultural labor than she did, and as the events of the 1830s and 1840s exploded around him, Dickens reacted by raging against social injustice on the one hand, and by pleading for social peace on the other. As late as 1855, after he completed *Hard Times,* Dickens revealed his deep stake in social and political tranquillity. During a scandal involving Sir Austen Henry Layard, twice under secretary for foreign affairs, Dickens feared that this political "mistake," in his words, would be beyond the endurance of the English people. In a 11 May 1855 letter to his long-time friend, the Baroness Burdett-Coutts, Dickens articulated perhaps the most intense ideological conflict in his thinking: his detestation of the economic and social oppression of the poor, and his fear that workers might actually upset the entire political edifice.

> The people will not bear for any length of time what they bear now [he wrote]. I see it clearly written in every truthful indication that I am capable of discerning anywhere. And I want to interpose something between them and their wrath.
>
> For this reason solely, I am a Reformist heart and soul. I have nothing to gain—and everything to lose (for public quiet is my bread)—but I am in desperate earnest, because I know it is a desperate case.[73]

Dickens saw that "there are two great classes looking at each other in this question."[74] Rather than choose sides on this occasion between the "popular" and "aristocratic" class, Dickens played the peacemaker and donated twenty pounds to a City Administrative Reform Meeting.[75]

Dickens made these statements after having lived through about fifteen years of revolutionary events throughout Western Europe and in Great Britain. By the late 1830s, Dickens's world exploded about his head—or so it must have seemed to him. After October 1838, when the last monthly issue of *Nicholas Nickleby* was published, the political and social world of Great Britain was never quite the same. The London Working Men's Association drafted a petition, including the Six Points of the Charter, in January 1837—which became the basis for the Chartist movement. On 8 May, the next year, the People's Charter was published, marking the formal beginning of Chartism. It was also the first year of a decade of revolution in Europe.

On 20 April 1839, George Julian Harney, the editor of the *Democratic Review* and the *Red Republican,* wrote in *The London Democrat,* "France is on the eve of revolution, Belgium pants to be free, in Germany liberty is awake, the patriots of Spain are ready to send Isabella and Carlos to the devil together, the Italian lifts his head, and the exiled Pole again dreams of the restoration of his fatherland."

His speech seemed to herald a social upheaval in his own country. The Rebecca Riots erupted in Wales (May 1839) and the Bull Ring Riots began in Birmingham (July); the first National Petition was rejected by the House of Commons (July); mass arrests of the Chartists occurred (summer 1839); Chartist-led uprisings exploded in Sheffield and Bradford (January 1840); and the trials of the arrested Chartists began (March 1840).

How did Dickens, the most sympathetic of the Victorian novelists to England's lower classes, react to all these upheavals and, in particular, to the laboring classes who made up these struggles? Of the nine novels Dickens wrote between 1837 and 1853, years roughly corresponding to the Chartist era, only one, *Barnaby Rudge,* is a historical novel whose theme is that of a social revolt. Dickens began writing it in January 1839; it was published in one volume in December 1841. *Barnaby* is only by implication about the Chartists. The workers who all but overran London for six days, from 2 June to 9 June, did so seventy years before Dickens started his novel in 1780 during the so-called Gordon Riots.

The rioters are shown as having some legitimate grievances. Dickens portrays a rigid social system that is characterized by oppressive criminal laws, degrading prisons, negligent and stupid rulers, and a distant and uncaring government. But *Barnaby* sent a clear message to Chartist England during the critical years 1839–41: a bad system has produced a savage and out-of-control lower class. Insurrection and revolution are evils more greatly to be feared than the exploitation of the poor.

In *Hard Times* (1854) workers do not understand the class nature of their exploitation. Workers like Stephen Blackpool and Rachael suffer in silence and reject their striking comrades. Blackpool tries to come to terms with the strike by telling his master Bounderby, "We are in a muddle." He seems never to have heard of the Chartists or read a single radical statement. When the mill owner asks Blackpool how he would set this muddle to rights, Dickens's most outspoken proletarian character replies, "I dunno, Sir. I canna be expectenn to 't. 'Tis not me as should be looken to for that, Sir. 'Tis them as is put ower me, and ower aw the rest of us. What do they tak upon themseln, Sir, if not to do 't."[76] Arnold Hauser, the art historian, calls this obtuseness on the part of such innocents as Stephen Blackpool, Dickens's "dog's morality." "The further removed an attitude is from the mature, critical, intellectual approach of a serious-minded man, the more understanding and sympathy [Dickens] has for it."[77] Leaving the great political solutions to the enlightened middle class was a sentiment from which Dickens never departed.

Given Dickens's patronizing, petty bourgeois attitude toward workers and their rebellions, it is no wonder he had little sympathy with the Chartists. His formula for social peace—as reflected in *Barnaby Rudge* and in *Hard Times*—is the renunciation of vio-

lence and insurrection by workers on the one hand, and the
patriarchal, philanthropic good wishes of the masters on the other
hand.

Alton Locke unfolds as a reactionary and religious attack against
the Chartists and their absence of rationality, culture, and re-
straint. The novel is a challenge from within, since Kingsley was
himself inspired by such Chartist writers as Thomas Cooper,
William Lovett, and Gerald Massey. The story, in the form of an
autobiography, is told by a reformed Chartist. Alton Lock is by
trade a tailor, and in turn a revolutionary, a poet, and finally a
Christian visionary, who sees the evil of his Chartist ways. The
more one gives way to political passions, to violence, to insurrection, in short to the Chartists themselves, the more one turns
away from God. At the end, Alton discovers for himself and for
the honest workers of England that politics is at best irrelevant.
Restored to Christian spiritualism by the aristocratic Lady Ellerton, Alton learns that "Chartism has sinned—has defiled itself in
the eyes of the wise, the good, the gentle."[78] Ellerton cautions
Locke: "Without the priesthood there is no freedom for the people. . . . The people can never be themselves without the cooperation with the priesthood."[79] Disraeli argues much the same
in *Sybil*.

Kingsley's *Alton Locke* illustrates the ambivalence and fascination these writers had with Chartism and with the workers who
participated in this movement. Kingsley himself helped organize
the Christian Socialist tailors' cooperative, and this apparent di-
chotomy—sympathy with labor and a strong clerical orientation
that deeply mistrusts all political parties—does battle throughout
the novel. But in the end, like Disraeli, Dickens, and Gaskell,
Kingsley gives in to a deep mistrust of workers.

These writers were fully conscious of the social importance of
the Chartists; their works are a reaction to Chartism. But none of
them would make the leap from their genuine idealism to faith in
the laboring classes. As G. B. Shaw observed in his 1912 introduction to *Hard Times*, Dickens

> turns his back frankly on Democracy, and adopts the idealized
> Toryism of Carlyle and Ruskin, in which the aristocracy are the mas-
> ters and superiors of the people, and also the servants of the people
> and of God. . . . [He] appeals again and again to the governing
> classes, asking them with every device of reproach, invective, sar-
> casm, and ridicule of which he is master, what they have to say to this
> or that evil which it is their professed business to amend or avoid.

Nowhere does he appeal to the working classes to take their fate into their own hands and try the democratic plan.

Shaw's statement applies to all five novelists.

Chartist Internationalism

I am not an Englishman alone—I am a man. I—we all—have a wider and a greater country than these narrow isles. It embraces the Frenchman and the German—it includes the Hungarian, the Italian and the Pole—my country is the world, and the nation I belong to is the most numerous of all; the nation of the oppressed. I acknowledge but two nationalities in existence, the tyrant and the slave . . . the rich and the poor—and in the latter I am a soldier.
—Ernest Jones, "On Internationalism"

Chartist poetry distinguished itself in many ways from conventional early Victorian fiction and from the various representations of the Chartists in these writings. From the start, Chartist poetry articulated a high degree of class consciousness and an internationalist outlook. Ties with international revolutionary figures were never a uniform Chartist policy, and such powerful leaders as Feargus O'Connor consistently opposed any attempt of such internationalists as James Bronterre O'Brien, George Harney, and Ernest Jones to break decisively with middle-class radicals. Nevertheless, internationalism was always on the Chartist agenda, however passionately debated. The same cannot be said of any of the well-known bourgeois writers of this period.

Prior to the formation of the London Working Men's Association in March 1836—the parent body of the People's Charter—Thomas Paine's writings on internationalism, the French Revolution, and rationalism left its mark on a generation of British working-class leaders. As described by Weisser, because Paine's writing centered on the French Revolution, "it is no wonder that after a quarter of a century of French revolutionary turmoil British workers should continue to be very strongly influenced by those Gallican events. Principles, issues, examples, vocabulary, songs, heroes, and villains, were all drawn wholesale from that era."[81]

In the period from 1815 to 1829, the two main themes in the ultra radical press were the aftermath of the French Revolution and the possibility of enlightened politics both in Europe and in England. In 1820 a revolution erupted in Spain. By the year's end rebellions had spread to Portugal, Naples, Sicily, Piedmont, and Greece, and a preoccupation with revolution dominated the radical press.

Many Chartist leaders enthusiastically embraced this radical heritage, and from the very beginning major Chartist publications endorsed an internationalist outlook. In July 1831, the leading publisher of the unstamped press, Henry Hetherington, issued the *Poor Man's Guardian* in defiance of the new "Blasphemous and Seditious Libels Acts." He hired the Irish lawyer, James Bronterre O'Brien, who consistently advocated global class consciousness and who put the British struggle within a European context. O'Brien sent in many of his articles from Paris, a logical choice since the French revolutions of 1789 and 1830 had a profound effect upon the British working class. In Paris, O'Brien published the first volume of his *Life of Robespierre*, concentrating on the revolutionary and Jacobin groups of the French Revolution.

The chief organizer of the London Working Men's Association (LWMA), William Lovett, was himself greatly influenced by Paine, Robert Owen, and the rationalist traditions of London artisans. "As the heart of the organisation," Weisser writes, "he was the person most responsible for the remarkable flurry of working-class contacts with European workers in the thirties."[82] Lovett spoke for a generation of his fellow Chartists when he wrote the following words to the "Citizens of the American Republic":

> We address you in that spirit of fraternity which becomes working men in all the countries of the world; for, as the subjugation and misery of our class can be traced *to our ignorance and dissensions*—as the knaves and hypocrites of the world live by our follies, and the tyrants of the world are strong because we the working millions are divided—so assuredly will *the mutual instruction and united exertions* of our class in all countries rapidly advance the world's emancipation.[83]

On 13 November 1836, in the *London Dispatch*, the LWMA published its "Address to the Working Classes of Belgium," in response to the imprisonment of a Flemish working-class leader, Jacob Katz, for holding a public meeting of workers. In the words of the *London Dispatch*, "This was high treason in the eyes of the wealth consumers."[84] The November address made the following points:

> We are of the opinion that those who produce the real wealth of any country . . . have in reality but *one great interest.* . . . We believe, therefore, that our interest—nay, the interests of working men in all countries of the world—are identified, and consequently that principles of fraternal friendship should lead us to cultivate peace, industry, and the mutual interchange of kind feelings and benevolent actions.

Ignorance has caused us to believe that we were "born to toil," and others to enjoy—that we are naturally inferior, and should silently bow to the government of those who call themselves superior. . . . The existence of their power depending on the ignorance, the instilled prejudice, the cupidity of the multitude, they have formed their institutions for hoodwinking and keeping them in subjection—their laws have been enacted to perpetuate their power, and administered to generate fear and submission towards self-constituted greatness, hereditary ignorance, or wealth, however unjustly acquired.[85]

By the early forties the Chartists began to formalize their ties with European workers. The first international meeting in London was organized by the German Workers Education Society on 22 September 1844, and exactly a year later, at a banquet to celebrate the French Republic's constitution of 1792, the Society of Fraternal Democrats was founded. George Julian Harney—a leader of the left wing of the Chartists, editor of the *Northern Star* (from 1845 on), the *Democratic Review,* and the founder of the *Red Republican*—was a driving force behind the Fraternal Democrats. Basically, the Fraternal Democrats hoped to expand Chartist internationalism through education and propaganda rather than through a European-wide insurrection. Their motto—All Men Are Brethren—was the same motto of the Polish and German democratic societies and was printed in twelve languages on their membership cards.[86]

As 1848 got closer, the links between the *Northern Star,* the Fraternal Democrats, and such Chartist leaders as Harney and Ernest Jones were strengthened. Harney met Karl Marx in London in November 1847. Engels had been writing for the *Northern Star* since the spring of 1844, and Harney and Jones went to Paris on 4 March 1848 to deliver a congratulatory address to the Provisional Government.[87] A major step toward internationalizing the Chartist movement was taken when the *Red Republican* appeared on 22 June 1850. The shibboleth of the French Revolution—Equality, Liberty, Fraternity—appeared under the paper's title, together with these lines of poetry by the British poet laureate, Robert Southey: "If it be guilt / To preach what you are pleased to call strange notions: / That all mankind as brethren must be equal . . . I plead me guilty." Louis Blanc, Ledru Rollin, and Guiseppe Mazzini frequently wrote for the *Red Republican.* The weekly urged its readers to

recollect how they have been betrayed by princes, nobles, and diplo-matists—that they may always bear in mind that these men are the allies of the Jesuits, who never forget nor forgive. All nations must act for the general benefit of mankind, and not for local advantages or national aggrandisement. The despots, regardless of nationality, assist each other against the people, having established for that purpose a League, which they blasphemously call "Holy."[88]

Harney kept reminding his readers that the British ruling class not only presided over British workers, but over an empire "seventy-four times larger than the British Isles," and over a population that "amounts to five times the number of the inhabitants of the 'United Kingdom.' " In the year of the *Red Republican*'s publication, the British Empire, Harney continued, was "nearly one-eighth larger than the Russian empire, and its population equals the united inhabitants of Russia, Austria, France, Prussia, Spain, and Holland."[89] Beginning on 9 November 1850, the first English version of the *Communist Manifesto*, translated by Helen Macfarlane, appeared in Harney's newspaper. Internationalism had gotten its first theoretical basis.

On the issue of internationalism, the contrast between the Chartists and such defenders of the Empire as Disraeli and Dickens are clear and deserve some elaboration. As a member of Parliament when he wrote *Sybil*, and later as prime minister of Great Britain twice—Disraeli was an enlightened reactionary. *Sybil* is an explicit argument for an alliance between the Church and an aristocratic and royal class cleansed of corruption and selfishness. "If we could only have the Church on our side, as in the good old days," says Sybil's father, the Chartist Walter Gerard, "we would soon put an end to the demon tyranny of Capital." *Sybil* illustrates the dangers of an armed working class separated from the Church, the monarchy, and the good aristocrats like Charles Egremont.

Disraeli had an obvious class stake in the Empire; Dickens did not. Nevertheless, on at least one occasion during the Chartist period, Dickens publicly supported British colonial policy. On 10 May 1857, Indian troops under British rule shot their officers and marched to Delhi. The Indian Mutiny had begun; it lasted until 8 July 1858, fourteen months later. According to one historian, in defense of British civilization, "A Gallows was set up in a city square and hundreds of innocent Indians were hanged as drunken British soldiers laughingly watched."[90] Not until the Jamaican colony erupted in the so-called Governor Eyre controversy in 1865 did such an international political crisis touch a raw nerve in England, especially among the intelligentsia. In an October 1857 letter to the Baronness Burdett-Coutts, Dickens expressed his reaction to the mutiny. He sounded like Kurtz in *The Heart of Darkness*. There, Kurtz had uttered his final solution to the Native Problem: "Exterminate the brutes." Dickens wrote to his confidant:

> I wish I were the Commander in Chief of India. The first thing I would do to strike that Oriental race with amazement (not in the least regarding them as if they lived in the Strand, London, or at Camden Town), should be to proclaim to them in their language, that I considered my Holding that appointment by the leave of God, to mean that I should do my utmost to exterminate the Race upon whom the stain of the late cruelties rested; and that I begged them to do me the favor to observe that I was there for that purpose and no other, and was now proceeding, which all convenient dispatch and merciful swiftness of execution, to blot it out of mankind and raze it off the face of the earth.[91]

After 1848

> Chartism means the bitter discontent grown fierce and mad, the wrong condition therefore or the wrong disposition, of the Working Classes of England. It is a new name for a thing which has had many names, which will yet have many.
> —Thomas Carlyle, "Chartism: Condition-of-England Question"

The beginning of the end of Chartism came in 1848. In March there were riots in London and Manchester. On 10 April the petition was delivered to Parliament by Feargus O'Connor where it was openly ridiculed three days later. In May riots broke out in Bradford, followed by rioting in London. By then Chartist leadership had split over the issue of physical force, with Jones and Harney leading the left wing in support of the February 1848 revolution in France against Louis Philippe. Jones was arrested in Manchester on 6 June and in July Chartist leaders were arrested for planning an Irish insurrection. Chartism swayed under police action, mass arrests, and by the infiltration of police spies and *agents provocateurs*. On 5 August 1848, Samuel Kydd wrote in *The Northern Star:*

> The region of terror progresses, and grows more searching and dreadful. . . . So close has our political atmosphere become, that we are almost suffocated. So crowded are rumours followed in quick uncertainty: so fearful the thrilling doubts and stifled fears of every man we meet, that it requires courage even to think steadily and boldness and nerve to direct order from this motley chaos. . . .

"By the end of September 1848," writes John Saville, "the Chartist left had been beaten. Their leaders, except Harney, were in prison, transported or awaiting trial, and the movement in the country was disorganised and dispirited. Among the majority who remained politically active there tended to be a sharp turn to the Right."[92] Chartist poetry written after 1848 had to face the prospect of the defeat of Chartism and workers' struggles in England and Europe. The three giants of late Chartist poetry—Linton, Massey, and Jones—did not go down quietly, although others surely did.

In 1849 Linton published his long poem, "The Dirge of the Nations." Recalling Shelley's "Prometheus Unbound," Linton's poet-hero is chained to the rock of his despair, while "Yet the gory-headed Vulture / Teareth the Promethean heart; / Yet dead Hope, denied sepulture, / Roams a weary ghost apart." Should he "care to struggle" in a world of political reaction? The poem might have been written in the dark days of the 1940s, when the "heavy tread / Of the Nations with their Dead, / And their voices call to me / Through the mist of agony" would have referred to Nazi-occupied Europe. But Linton's Prometheus refuses to be buried alive. "Our shout / Hath o'er-ridden Fate's decree; / And the thunder of our glee / Yet shall roll through Heaven's gates / On the western clouds of Doom."

Gerald Massey emerged as a major Chartist poet in the 1850s when the movement was coming to an end. Like Linton and Jones he tried to fan what militancy was left. His "Men of 'Forty-Eight,' " written in 1851, invokes the spirit of the fallen heroes of 1848. "When the world wakes up to worst, / The tyrants once again;— / And Freedom's summons-should shall burst / In music on the brain. / With heart to heart and hand in hand, / Ye'll find them all elate,— / And true as ever Spartan band!" Massey's "Song of the Red Republican" introduced the Chartists' last great militant and internationalist hurrah, *The Red Republican*, a journal that lasted for twenty-four issues, the final one dated 30 November 1850. By the time Harney changed its name to the *Friend of the People* (it ran from 14 December 1850 to 26 July 1851) the remaining Chartists, as the rather ambiguous name of the journal suggests, were no longer part of a mass movement.

In certain respects Massey's "Song of the Red Republican" is emblematic of the many contradictory strains in Chartist poetry and, with hindsight, helps explain its demise. Massey's verses are full of biblical images, a common tendency among the Chartist poets. In his poem, Chartist leaders and workers are identified with Christ ("The herald of our coming Christ leaps in the womb of Time; / The poor's grand army treads the Age's march with step sublime") or with Christ's work ("I see the toiled hath become a glorious, Christ-like preacher, / And as he wins a crust shines proudly forth the great world teacher"). With religious and political images so discordantly placed side by side, it is no wonder that Massey, like Linton and Jones, should be so ill-prepared to offer any kind of unifying guidance once the events of 1848 erupted. The ideological struggle reflected in the poetry between, for example, the secular and the religious trends and between violence and moral force, finally made itself felt in the movement. At the end, Chartist poets, like the British working class itself, had no clear notion as to where and how to lead the movement.

After 1848, Chartist poetry in general lost its militancy and its mass character. Most of the poetry published in the following decades was by Ernest Jones, William Linton, and Gerald Massey. Although there were no more calls to arms, and fewer and fewer poems heralded Chartist struggles and martyrs, at least one echo remained, loud enough to be heard throughout the nineteenth century and into our own: heroic men may become passive from generation to generation, but oppression rarely slumbers. To remain free, men must continually do battle. In 1889, when Chartism was a memory and most of the Chartist leaders were dead, Massey's collection, *My Lyrical Life: Poems Old and New* was published. Included was "The Awakening." The poem speaks to all ages.

> To see men awake from the slumber of ages,
>   Their brows grim from labour, their hands hard and tan,
> Start up living Heroes, long dreamt-of by Sages!
>   And smite with strong arm the Oppressors of man:
> To see them come dauntless forth 'mid the world's warning. . . .
>
> Show how the Eternal within them is stirring,
>   And never more bend to a crowned clod:
> Dear God! 'tis a sight for Immortals to see,—
>   A People up-girding its might to be free.

"Earth has no sight half so glorious to see, / As a People up-girding its might to be free!" the poem ends. Perhaps this is the most enduring message Chartist poetry has bequeathed.

As a purely literary phenomenon, Chartist poetry cannot pretend to compete with the best of English Romantic verse. Given, however, its unique historical, social, and cultural importance in

the fight for democratic and economic rights, the most impressive
fact about this collection is that it exists.

Notes

1. John Hayward, ed., *The Oxford Book of Nineteenth Century English Verse*
(Oxford: Oxford University Press, 1964), p. v.
2. Edward Royle, *Radical Politics 1790–1900 Religion and Unbelief* (London:
Longman, 1971), p. 80.
3. *The Red Republican*, 10 August 1850.
4. Philip Collins, *Thomas Cooper, The Chartist: Byron and the 'Poets of the Poor'*
(Nottingham: University of Nottingham Press, 1969), p. 10.
5. *The Star of Freedom*, 7 August 1852.
6. *The Labourer: A Monthly Magazine of Politics, Literature, Poetry* 2 (1847): 95.
7. Dorothy Thompson, *The Early Chartists* (London and New York: Macmillan, 1971), p. 13.
8. *The Chartist Circular*, 24 October 1840.
9. Ibid., 31 October 1840.
10. *The Red Republican*, 22 June 1850.
11. Christopher Hill, *The World Turned Upside Down* (New York: Penguin,
1972), p. 13.
12. Ibid., p. 114.
13. Hill, *The Century of Revolution 1603–1714* (New York: Norton, 1961), p. 129.
14. Ibid.
15. E. P. Thompson, *The Making of the English Working Class* (New York:
Random, 1966), p. 553.
16. Ibid.
17. Ibid., p. 564.
18. Ibid., p. 570.
19. Ibid., p. 63.
20. G. D. H. Cole, *A Short History of the British Working Class Movement 1789–
1927* (London: Allen & Unwin, 1948), p. 65.
21. Gwyn A. Williams, *Rowland Detrosier: A Working-Class Infidel 1800–34*
(York: St. Anthony's Press, 1965), p. 4.
22. Harold Silver, *English Education and the Radicals 1780–1850* (London and
Boston: Routledge and Kegan Paul, 1975), p. 70.
23. Ibid., p. 73.
24. Thompson, *Early Chartists*, p. 13.
25. Owen R. Ashton, "Chartism and Popular Culture: An Introduction to the
Radical Culture in Cheltenham Spa, 1830–1848," *Journal of Popular Culture*, vol. 2,
no. 4 (Spring 1987), pp. 65–66.
26. Matha Vicinus, *The Industrial Muse* (New York: Harper, 1974), p. 9.
27. Ashton, "Chartism and Popular Culture," p. 66.
28. Ibid., p. 67.
29. Vicinus, *Industrial Muse*, pp. 12–13.
30. Charles Kingsley, *Alton Locke* (185), chap. 8.
31. Ibid., chap. 9.
32. Ibid.
33. Matthew Arnold, *Poems*, preface, p. 205.
34. Ibid., "The Study of Poetry," p. 306.
35. Friedrich Engels, *The Condition of the Working Class in England*, trans. and

eds. W. O. Henderson and W. H. Chaloner (Stanford: Stanford University Press, 1958), pp. 272–73.

36. *The Chartist Circular,* 29 August 1840.
37. Ibid., 1 August 1840.
38. Ibid.
39. E. P. Thompson, *Making of the English Working Class,* p. 713.
40. *The Chartist Circular,* 31 October 1840.
41. Arnold, *Poems,* p. 208.
42. Ibid., p. 211.
43. Ibid., p. 209.
44. *The Northern Star and National Trades Journal,* 7 August 1852.
45. Ibid.
46. Edward Royle, *Radical Politics 1790–1900 Religion and Unbelief* (London: Longman, 1971), p. 28.
47. Ibid., *Chartism,* 2d ed. (London: Longman, 1980), p. 13.
48. E. P. Thompson, *Making of the English Working Class,* p. 726.
49. Alfred Plummer, *Bronterre: A Political Biography of Bronterre O'Brien 1804–1864* (London: Allen & Unwin, 1971), p. 49.
50. R. K. Webb, *The British Working-Class Reader 1790–1848* (New York: Augustus M. Kelley, 1971), p. 23.
51. Thompson, *Making of the English Working Class,* p. 729.
52. Henry Weisser, *British Working Class Movements and Europe: 1815–48* (Manchester: Manchester University Press, 1975), p. 2.
53. Thompson, *Making of the English Working Class,* p. 729.
54. Ibid., p. 733.
55. Brian Simon, *Studies in the History of Education, 1780–1870* (London: Lawrence and Wishart, 1960), p. 129.
56. Webb, *British Working-Class Reader,* p. 50.
57. Ibid.
58. *The Republican,* vol. xiii, no. 5 (February 1826).
59. *The Northern Star and Leeds General Advertiser,* 20 April 1844.
60. Engels, *Condition of the Working Class,* p. 272.
61. *The Northern Star and Leeds General Advertiser,* 17 October 1840.
62. Ibid., 6 February 1841.
63. Simon, *History of Education,* p. 247.
64. *The Northern Star and National Trades Journal,* 30 September 1848.
65. Ibid., 25 July 1846.
66. Jack Linday, *Charles Dickens: A Biographical and Critical Study* (London: Dakers, 1950), p. 309.
67. D. Thompson, *Chartists,* p. 238.
68. Kingsley, *Alton Locke,* chap. 28.
69. Benjamin Disraeli, *Sybil, or the Two Nations* (1845), Book 6, chap. 3.
70. Elizabeth Gaskell, *Mary Barton* (1847), chap. 15.
71. Ibid.
72. Gaskell, "North and South," in Dickens, *Household Words,* chap. 28.
73. Dickens, *Letters of Charles Dickens to the Baronness Burdett-Coutts.* ed. Charles C. Osbourne (London: J. Murray, 1931), p. 140.
74. Ibid., p. 51.
75. Ibid., p. 152.
76. Ibid., *Hard Times* (1854), Book 12, chap. 5.
77. Ibid., p. 126.
78. Kingsley, *Alton Locke,* chap. 40.

79. Ibid.

80. *People's Paper,* 4 December 1854.

81. Weisser, *British Working Class Movements,* pp. 4–5.

82. Ibid., p. 67.

83. William Lovett, *The Life and Struggles of William Lovett* (London: G. Bell and Sons, 1920), p. 129.

84. *London Dispatch,* 30 October 1836.

85. Lovett, *Life and Struggles of William Lovett,* p. 80.

86. Weisser, *British Working-Class Movements,* p. 139.

87. John Saville, *The Red Republican and the Friend of the People,* 2 vols. (New York: Barnes & Noble, 1966), p. x.

88. *The Red Republican,* 17 August 1850.

89. Ibid., 24 August 1850.

90. Bernard Semmel, *Jamaican Blood and Victorian Conscience: The Governor Eyre Controversy* (Boston: Houghton, 1963), p. 21.

91. Dickens, *Letters,* 4 October 1857, pp. 188–89.

92. Seville, *Red Republican,* September 1848.

Anonymous Verses and Songs

NOTE: Throughout the anthology, superscript numbers refer to notes at the back of the volume. Superscript letters refer to notes that appeared in the original editions of the poems; these notes are reprinted at the ends of their poems.

CHESTER GAOL

When winter grim unlocked his stores
    Of wind, rain, snow, and hail,
  And nature seemed to mourn the fate
  Of patriots doomed by legal hate,
  To pine enclosed by many a grate,
    Where echoes many a wail,
These lines are found close by the doors
    Of Chester County Gaol:—

Whoe'er you be that find this scroll,
    Let our desires prevail,
  And send it to the *Northern Star*,[1]
  That our complaints may spread afar;
  Let not your politics debar
    From printing this detail,
But generous prove, and ease our souls,
    In Chester County Gaol.

The glorious cause depends on you,
    Then do not spurn our tale,
  But let this genuine story go,
  And tell the world of all our woe,
  That we our foes may overthrow,
    And with our friends regale;
Besides, good friend, they're not a few
    Outside of Chester Gaol.

You've heard how Whig and Tory knaves
     Destroy the public weal,
   And how they tax the bread we eat,[2]
   How their police pollute the street—
   How foreigners insult our fleet,
       Whene'er they meet a sail,
   How Englishmen made into slaves,
       Are sent to Chester Gaol.

You've heard of the convention,[3] too,
     How they made Russell[4] rail;
   And how they made Lord Melbourne[5] fret,
   How they made Brough'm and Lyndhurst[6] sweat,
   And how they spread their poisonous net,
To catch M'Douall,[7] and others—few
Escaped them that they had in view,
And sworn to by their perjured crew,
     Made drunk with wine and ale—
To swear that every charge was true,
Although the men they never knew,
     And sent us to Chester Gaol.

It was the Assize of thirty-nine,
     When some were held to bail,
   By traversing none were acquit,
   The Judges ne'er intended it;
   The evidence was made to fit,
     And understood their tale,
And Campbell[8] said 'twas his design
     That we should stay in Chester Gaol.

The Jury, pitiable mob,
     Looked wretched, poor and pale,
   When they were told what they should say,
   To find us guilty that same day;
   Not one poor devil dare say nay,
     Old Gurney[9] made them quail,
Well knowing they must do the job,
     Or go to Chester Gaol.

As soon as we had heard our doom,
     A melancholy tale,

For our loved wives and children dear,
　　'Twould turn them almost wide to hear,
　We had been treated so severe,
　　Besides providing bail;
Divided both from them and home,
　　And kept in Chester Gaol.

For eighteen months our sentence past,
　　While tyrants held the scale,
　Of justice, and it was decreed,
　That certain sureties we should need,
　To keep the peace five years indeed,
　　Recorded in detail;
Seven hundred pounds, a sum so vast,
　　Or stay in Chester Gaol.[10]

We all were quickly then conveyed,
　　To eat our half boiled meal,
　Into a yard, like a deep pit,
　And told we must inhabit it,
　For eighteen months, if they thought fit,
　　Which made us stamp and rail;
But the Governor must be obeyed,
　　In this cursed Chester Gaol.

Each morning when they ring the bell,
　　And never do they fail,
　We are obliged to come down stairs,
　At six o'clock; no stools or chairs,
　Are here, and to increase our cares,
　　Whatever we may ail,
We are locked up twelve hours in a cell
　　In *happy* Chester Gaol.

At nine o'clock we go to church,
　　To hear the parson's tale,
　After, we walk till dinner time,
　Then get potatoes, 'tis no crime,
　To say they're anything but prime,
　　Or even fit for sale;
For butcher's meat we're in the lurch
　　In this same Chester Gaol.

The gentry of this ancient town,
    That look both proud and hale,
  Come here each day at us to gaze,
  Which fills us all with much amaze,
  To see their ignorant, ill-bred ways,
    And impudence wholesale;
More coarse than any silly clown,
    That comes to Chester Gaol.

Instead of tea, we skilly get,
    Each evening without fail,
  Which makes us scarcely fit to stand,
  With sick head-ache and trembling hand;
  We look just like some sickly band
    (We can't buy even ale,)
Of slaves that's worn with constant fret,
    In cruel Chester Gaol.

You know our usage, Englishmen,
    You've heard our bitter tale:
  Will you neglect your sacred charge,
  Or strive to keep your friends at large?
  And arm yourselves with sword and targe,
    That you may never fail;
But for the Charter strike again,
    Or come to Chester Gaol.

Let all your powers directed be,
    Against tyrannic zeal,
  That would starve you and your neighbours too,
  Let all united be and true,
  And keep *"The Rights of Man"*[11] in view,
    And cast aside the veil;
Let all your proud oppressors see,
    You are determined to be free,
And gain your long lost liberty,
    Or die in Chester Gaol.

Let not the Poor Law[12] frighten you,
    Nor yet the diet scale,
  Nor new Police, nor Russell spies,
  Nor Brougham's schemes, nor Nosey's lies,
  Nor *Cockup,* who the law defies,

Nor even *five years bail;*
Bid all your fears a long adieu.
    And laugh at Chester Gaol.

Let every man in harness stand,
    And buckle on his mail,
To fight for freedom never shrink,
On you depends the victory, think,
To equal laws and rights come drink,
    Down with O'Connell's[13] tail;
Obey each patriot chief's command
    That's now in Chester Gaol.

Farewell brave Chartists, let no fears
    Cause your bold hearts to quail,
Prepare to fall, or gain your right,
That you and yours may rest at night,
And rise like freemen with the light,
    For to enjoy your meal;
Don't shrink, like cowards, bathed in tears,
    But come to Chester Gaol.

Farewell, brave Chartists; never dream
    Of finding any bail,
Until you have prepared the tools,
That will convince both knaves and fools,
You are determined to have rules
    To regulate the scale,
That you may tax both land and steam,
    And empty up Chester Gaol.

The Northern Star and Leeds General Advertiser, 12 October 1839

THE JUDGES ARE GOING TO JAIL

a popular song for 1840

(FROM THE JOHN BULL)

Hurrah for the masses,
The lawyers are asses,
    Their gammon and spinach is stale!

The law is illegal,
The Commons are regal,
  And the Judges are going to jail,
    Hurrah for the masses!
  The lawyers are asses,
    The Judges are going to jail.

Lord Denman's[1] been prigging,
So he'll have a wigging,
  And be hung like his wig, on a nail;
What a time to get fogles,[a]
Chains, purses and ogles,
  Now the judges are going to jail.
    Hurrah for the masses!
    We'll cut off the gasses,
      To bother the Judges in jail.

Little Johnny[2] gives orders,
All Beaks[3] and Recorders,
  The stairs without landing[b] to scale,
While we, down at Wapping,
Are drinking hot-stopping,
  To the health of the Judges in jail.
    Hurrah for the masses!
    We'll kiss all the lasses
      To the tune of the Judges in jail.

And when soundly rated,
Their goods confiscated,
  We'll *jist* keep an eye on the sale;
For the times *are* a mending,
When 'stead of *sending,*
  The Judges are *going* to jail.
  Hurrah for the masses!
    We'll fill our carcasses
      With the prog of the Judges in jail.

For old Hatton-garden,
We don't care a farden,
  The policemen look seedy and pale:
The chop-and-change Harvey,
Who plated the jarvey,

Shall follow the Judges to jail.
 Hurrah for the masses!
 We'll rob all that passes,
  As a sell for the Judges in jail.

They jaw'd us so cruel,
And fixed us to gruel,
 And sent us to grin through the rail;
But, by Goles, now we've broke 'em
They'll sit picking oakum—
 Hurrah for the judges in jail!
  Hurrah for the masses!
  We'll eat sparrow-grasses,
   While the Judges get porridge in jail.

Come feather the nests
Of the Court of Requests,
 Which we'll hold in the streets without fail,
And if any besieges
Our just privileges,
 He shall go with the Judges to jail.
  Hurrah for the masses!
  There are no upper classes,
   So reckon the Judges in jail.

 We are true British cracksmen,
 And know how to tax men,
And we won't be nobody's tail;
But we'll each use a halbert.
For the Queen and Prince Albert,
 Who have sent them old Judges to jail.

(GRAND CHORUS)

 Hurrah for the masses!
 The lawyers are asses,
 We'll cut off the gasses,
 And shiver the glasses,
 And eat sparrow-grasses,
 And fill our carcasses,
 And kiss all the lasses,
 And rob all that passes—

There are no upper classes,
    The Judges are going to jail!

The Northern Star and Leeds General Advertiser, 8 February 1840

aPocket-handkerchiefs
bTreadmill

AIR

(VIVE LE ROI)

Swearing death to tyrant King,
    Heaven guards the patriot heart;
Join'd in hand and heart we'll sing,
    Vive la Charte, vive la Charte!
Ruin seize the tyrant knave,
    Can slavery or woe impart
Aught of pleasures to the brave,
    Vive la Charte, Vive la Charte!
Bear our conquering standard high,
    Terror strikes each miscreant heart;
Onward! still our battle cry,
    Viv la Charte, Vive la Charte!
Raise the brand of liberty,
    Dare the foe, brave the smart;
Swell the chorus loud and high,
    Vive la Charte, Vive la Charte!

The Northern Star and Leeds General Advertiser, 20 June 1840

HOW TO BE A GREAT LORD

(FROM THE BEAUTIES OF THE PRESS)

Would you be a Great Lord? Let me shew you the way;
Too proud to be honest, a debt never pay;
Your fame and your fortune on prostitutes squander,
With a pimp in your coach, at your table a pander.

Or mount your own box, 'tis by far the less evil,
That pimp and that pander drive post to the devil.
Roast a child for your sport, set the hamlet on fire,
Then cut down with your sword both the sun and the fire:
A terrible Colonel now bully and swagger,
And plant in the heart of your country—a dagger.
When sharpers have done you, regard my advice,
Repair with a bribe what you lost by the dice.
Think little—drink much—your best principles barter,
And instead of a rope be preferred with a garter.
Or a mime on the stage, and becoming your part,
In character act, and be still what thou art.
Does indigence ask? shut your purse and your door;—
Distress is so shocking! God d—n all the poor!
Now job for a borough, now truck for a place,
Or stoop to a pension, and rise by disgrace;
And last to your friend let your kindness be shewn;—
Be true to his wife—and be chaste to your own.

   Now if thou art not a Great Lord, by St. Peter
Thou art a great rascal, in prose or in metre.

The Northern Star and Leeds General Advertiser, 12 September 1840

THE STATE PAUPER'S SOLILOQUY

When I was born, the child of three,
As jolly lads as you may see,
Who paid the expenses of rearing me?
               The People.

Who bonfires made, and made a fuss,
Uproarious and riotous,
And wished my mother more of us?
               The People.

For several little slips of grace,
That happened in my younger days,
I wonder who the piper pays?
               The People.

And now that I've a lawful wife,
Who makes us lead, with little strife,
A pretty comfortable life?

                    The People.

Who gives us our tax-free houses fine,
And finds us wherewithal to dine,
On turtle and on Bordeaux wine?

                    The People.

Should phaetons be worse for wear,
Or parks or temples want repair,
Who suffers when we take the air?

                    The People.

And when I'm dead, as die I must,
And these poor bones return to dust,
Ah! who will bury me?—I trust,

                    The People.

The Northern Liberator, 18 January 1840

CHARTISTS AND LIBERTY

Yes! the morning is awakening,
    When the Charter must be won—
Yes! the darkness now is breaking,
    At the dawning of the sun
            Of Liberty.

Not the countless dew-drops beaming
    All in beauty o'er the land,
When the moon's first ray is streaming,
    Shall surpass the numerous band
            Of Liberty.

Multitudes, that none can number,
    In that season of their power,
Shall arise, as from a slumber,
    Chartists wakened in an hour
            Of Liberty.

Then from the craggy mountains
   The joyful shout shall fly,
And shady vales and fountains
   Shall echo the reply
      Of Liberty.

The poor man's lowly dwelling
   Shall send the news around,
With many voices swelling
   In one continued sound
      Of Liberty.

Then shall the voice of singing
   Flow joyfully along,
And Chartists be rejoicing
   In one triumphant song
      Of Liberty.

The Northern Star and Leeds General Advertiser, 10 April 1841

THE PAUPER'S DRIVE

There's a grim one-horse hearse in a jolly round trot;
To the churchyard a pauper is going, I wot:
The road it is rough, and the hearse has no springs,
And hark to the dirge that the sad driver sings:
   "Rattle his bones over the stones;
   He's only a pauper, whom nobody owns!"

Oh! where are the mourners? alas! there are none;
He has left not a gap in the world now he's gone;
Not a tear in the eye of child, woman, or man.
To the grave with his carcase, as fast as you can:
   "Rattle his bones over the stones;
   He's only a pauper, whom nobody owns!"

What a jolting and creaking, and splashing and din!
The whip how it cracks! and the wheels how they spin;
How the dirt, right and left, o'er the hedges is hurl'd!
The pauper at length makes a noise in the world!
   "Rattle his bones over the stones;
   He's only a pauper, whom nobody owns!"

Poor pauper defunct! he has made some approach
To gentility, now that he's stretch'd in a couch!
He's taking a drive in a carriage at last;
But it will not be long, if he goes on so fast.
      "Rattle his bones over the stones;
      He's only a pauper, whom nobody owns!"

You bumpkins! who stare at your brother conveyed.
Behold what respect to a cloddy is paid,
And be joyful to think, when by death you're laid low,
You've a chance to the grave like a gemman to go.
      "Rattle his bones over the stones;
      He's only a pauper, whom nobody owns!"

But a truce to this strain; for my soul it is sad
To think that a heart in humanity clad
Should make, like the brutes, such a desolate end,
And depart from the light without leaving a friend!
      Bear softly his bones over the stones;
      Though a pauper, he's one whom his MAKER yet owns!

The Northern Star and Leeds General Advertiser, 5 February 1842

WHAT IS A PEER?

What is a peer? A useless thing;
A costly toy, to please a king;
    A bauble near a throne;
A lump of animated clay;
A gaudy pageant of a day;
    An incubus; a drone!

What is a peer? A nation's curse—
A pauper on the public purse;
    Corruption's own jackal:
A haughty, domineering blade;
A cuckold at a masquerade;
    A dandy at a ball.

Ye butterflies, whom kings create;
Ye caterpillars of the state;
    Know that your time is near!

This moral learn from nature's plan,
That in creation God made man;
   But never made a peer.

signed Midland Progressionist

The Northern Star and National Trades Journal, 25 November 1848

THE TORY SQUIRE

I am a squire of genus *"bray,"*
And oft to London I wend my way:
I leave my acres, and haws and hips,
   To list to wisdom from Tory lips.
My long rent-roll is my daily vaunt,
Where'er I go I can see no want;
And why I'm so rich, the secret I'll tell,
Who lives on the poor is sure to live well.
   What baron or friar, or knight of the shire,
   Is half such a dolt as a Tory squire.
   Is half such a dolt, half such a dolt,
      As a Tory squire?

After session, of pheasants I dream,
For shooting, I vow, is a pleasure supreme!
By self-denial I never try
   My dainty palate to mortify.
Punishing poachers I deem no sin,
But dev'lish seldom I look within;
A rousing cup and jolly good song,
Are my delight when the nights are long.
   What baron or friar, or any such *liar*,
   Is half such a dolt as a tory squire,
   Is half such a dolt, half such a dolt,
      As a Tory squire?

The Northern Star and Leeds General Advertiser, 29 October 1842

THE PATRIOT'S GRAVE

There is blood on the earth—'tis the blood of the brave
    Who have gone to their rest to the freeman's grave!
They are dead—but the spirit they kindled is here,
With the fire-breath of life, all unquenched and clear,
And strong in its might as the storm at night,
When it whirls the clouds o'er the moon so bright!

    There is blood on the earth! all wild and red—
    It cries to our God from the freeman's bed!
    It will not fade, nor be washed away—
    And the echoes are rife with this mournful lay.
    "By gilt and wrong, both reckless and strong,
    They were slain for the truth which they loved so long!"

    There is blood on the earth—in vale and glen
    It has water'd the flowers like dew—and men
    Of the noblest heart and most fiery brain,
Have fallen, like Gods, immortal though slain;
    For with death at their side, they have life for a bride,
    Whose beauty shall flourish whilst time betide.

The Northern Star and Leeds General Advertiser, 9 September 1843

Lines suggested by seeing the rank grass with its apposite and imposing colour which covers the last resting-place on Tara-Hill, of those Irishmen who loved their country "not wisely, but too well."

AMERICAN STRIPES

"With rooster-tail[a] and best gin-sling
    Fill high, them Britishers I'll wipe,
Our native flag, the only thing
    American which bears a stripe."

"Hold, not so fast," John Bull replies,
    (For though of speech a pretty figure),
There's one thing more which truth's stern eyes
    See bear a stripe—a Yankee's nigger."

The Northern Star, 30 March 1844

Miss Wickliffe, the daughter of the Postmaster-General proposed "The American flag, the only thing American, which will bear stripes."

Globe, Saturday, 23 March

NEVER GIVE UP

Never give up! It is wiser and better
    Always to hope than once to despair:
Fling off the load of Doubt's cankering fetter,
    And break the dark spell of tyrannical care;
Never give up! or the burden may sink you—
    Providence kindly has mingled the cup,
And, in all trials or troubles, bethink you,
    The watchword of life must be, Never give up!

Never give up! there are chances and changes
    Helping the hopeful a hundred to one,
And through the chaos High Wisdom arranges
    Ever success—if you'll only hope on:
Never give up! For the wildest is boldest,
    Knowing that Providence mingles the cup;
And of all maxims the best, as the oldest,
    Is the true watchword of Never give up!

Never give up—tho' the grape-shot may rattle,
    Or the full thunder-cloud over you burst,
Stand like a rock,—and the storm or the battle
    Little shall harm you, though doing their worst:
Never give up! if adversity presses,
    Providence wisely has mingled the cup,
And the best counsel, in all your distresses,
    Is the stout watchword of Never give up!

The Northern Star and National Trade Journal, 22 February 1845

[a]Cocktail; but the delicacy of the American ladies has led them to adopt the use of the word "rooster" for the hen's husband

THE HERMIT

For years, upon a mountain's brow,
A hermit lived—The Lord knows how.
Hardships and penance were his lot;
He often prayed—the Lord knows what.
A robe of sackcloth he did wear,
And got his food—the Lord knows where.
At last this holy man did die;
He left this world—the Lord knows why.
He's buried in this gloomy den,
And he will rise—the Lord knows when.

Notes to the People, 1851, vol. 1, p. 423

THE BLACK AND THE WHITE SLAVE

I had a dream of slavery,
    A vision of the night;
And methought I saw, on either hand,
    The victims—black and white.

I glanced my eye to the negro sky,
    And I looked to the spinner's room;
And one was lit with the hues of Heaven,
    And one was a hell of gloom.

There were fruitful, bright, and shining fields,
    and the sun was all above,
And there was something in the air
    That even a slave might love.

And there was the quick incessant whirl
    Of wheels revolving fast,
And there was the rank and moted air—
    Like a siroc's deadly blast.

Then the negro's shell and the factory bell
    For brief relief rang out—
Some ran to the shade where the blue stream played,
    Some raised the revel shout.

But as for yon poor sickly chyild,
  When her mid day was come,
She still abode in that region wild,
  She could not reach her home.

There was no gladdening stream for her,
  Albeit her tender years;
The stream that strayed, in that horrid shade,
  Was the factory infant's tears.

Aye! tears direct from the throbbing heart—
  Hot drops from burning brain—
Yet no relief from that shower of grief—
  Her tyrant came again.

Then I heard the crack of the sounding whip
  Ring sharply through the air;
But the slave was a huge and hardy man,
  That well the lash might bear.

The next was the dull and sickening sound
  Of the "strap" in that vale of tears;
I saw no man, save the wretch who struck
  The child of tender years.

He smote the infant o'er the face,
  The neck, the trembling breast;
And the words that fell from his brutal tongue
  But made her the more distressed.

And still as the blood came creeping down
  Towards the crime stained floor,
Still on was urged that little slave,
  Till her hateful task was o'er.

While the "man" slave sat at his cottage door,
  Or lay in the plaintain shade,
That worn-out child crept sadly home,
  Where her bed of chaff was laid,

Yet aye in her sleep the infant hears
  That every chaunting chime,
And she starts from her healthless rest and calls
  "Oh! Mother! is it time?"

Then I knelt me down, in that vision wild,
　　And raised my hands to God:
I breathed a prayer for the man and child
　　Who groan 'neath the tasker's rod.

Great God! like thy pure and balmy sir,
　　Let all thou hast made be free,
And blot from thy fair and beauteous world
　　The ban of slavery.

The Chartist Circular, 7 June 1840

THE POOR MAN'S SINS

(By the Author of "Headlong Hall.")

The poor man's sins are glaring;
In the face of ghostly warning
　　He is caught in the fact
　　Of the overt act—
Buying greens on a Sunday morning.

The rich man's sins are hidden
In the pomp of wealth and station,
　　And escape the sight
　　Of the children of light,
Who were wise in their generation.

The rich man has a kitchen,
And a cook to dress his dinner;
　　The poor, who would roast,
　　To the baker's must post,
And thus becomes a sinner.

The rich man's painted windows
Hide the concerts of the quality;
　　The poor can but share
　　A crack'd fiddle in the air,
Which offends all sound morality.

The rich man has a cellar,
And a ready butler by him;
    The poor must steer
    From his pint of beer,
Where the Saint can't choose but spy him.

The rich man is invisible
In the crowd of his gay society;
    But the poor man's delight
    Is a sore in the sight,
And a stench in the nose of Piety!

The Red Republican, 5 October 1850

ODE TO LABOUR

(From Tait's Magazine)

Hail labour! source, thro' bounteous Nature's aid,
Of ev'ry blessing which sustains mankind!—
Yea, Nature's frowns thy power hath so allay'd,
That man thro' life need scarce an evil find
From sultry sun, or piercing wintry wind.

With wonder may we view what thou'st achiev'd,
So fetter'd as thou hitherto has been;
But from thy trammels soon thou'lt be reliev'd,
And waft thy sons to happiness serene,
Which 'twere vain thought to contemplate unseen.

Amaz'd, we see thee, with a dauntless mind,
Into the bowels of the earth descend;
And Nature's boundless treasures, there confined,
From their long resting place thou dost unbend—
Upraise to light—to human use's send.

Enraptur'd view you beauteous fertile plain,
Late unproductive, desolate, and bare.
Where Nature vainly gave soil, sun, and rain,
Till thou didst ply thy vig'rous arm with care,
Nor grain, nor herbage, flower nor fruit grew there.

Delighted, yonder splendid mart behold,
Or rich bazaar, where costly treasures shine;
The glare of light therein which doth unfold
The varied wealth, too num'rous to define;
They, each and all, have sprung from hands of thine!

On yon stupendous pile astonish'd gaze,
Which seems to hurl defiance to Old Time;
Each minute part thou'st form'd, the mass did'st raise,
As 'twere from chaos to a work sublime,
To shield each inmate from the changeful clime.

On yonder stately barque look with surprise,
Which dauntless ranges o'er the ocean wide;
By thee 'twas form'd—'tis stor'd where'er she lies,
Her sails thou'lt trim, or pow'rful engines guide:
To commerce spreads thy wealth on ev'ry side!

The electric shaft propell'd by yon dark cloud,
From human habitation thou'lt convey;
Tho' lightning glares and thunder speaks aloud,
We can the elemental strife survey
Unharm'd if thou thy pow'rful aid display.

Yon gaudy, glitt'ring coach thy hands did rear,
And all the trappings which belong thereto,
The horses did supply, or steam prepare—
Produced each power, by which it onward flew:
Thy aid withdrawn, a useless-thing thou'dst view!

Yon parchment deeds compactly seal'd and sign'd,
Thro' which vain idlers have usurped the soil,
Fleec'd thee and thine, by fraud and force combin'd,
And, by mere suff'rance thereon, let thee toil:
Yea skins, seals, wax thou'st form'd but to despoil.

Yon implements of horrid war thou'st made,
With which thy sacred rights are from thee wrest;
Ay, worse than all, thy dearest sons array'd,
Have held the deadly weapons to thy breast,
By tyrants fore'd, and destitution press'd.

Thy ingrate offspring—"Capital" by name—

Who should thy strength replenish and sustain,
Doth madly join all those who'd thee defame—
Thy sturdy limbs in fetters vile who'd chain,
Or fain thy life's-blood suck from ev'ry vein.

Too long, thou all productive power, thou'st worn
Contumely's garb. Yea, destitute, uncheer'd,
Too long the bitter taunt thou'st tamely borne,
Of those who've wanton'd in the wealth thou'st rear'd:—
Hail, happy change—thy arm's now rais'd and fear'd.

But tho' thy arm's in giant strength erect,
As infants', harmless, thou its pow'r will wield;
Thy sacred rights thou'lt grasp—each wrong correct,
Then act with mercy—not to vengeance yield:—
Wisdom and worth thou'lt succour—weakness shield.

AN INDUSTRIOUS ENGLISHMAN
The Chartist Circular, 12 October 1839

PROGRESS

Up, man of reason—rouse thee up;
   This is no slumb'ring age,
Begird thy loins, unbare thine arm,
   And for the right engage;
Stern duty's voice demands thine help,
   Arouse thee for the strife,
Be up and doing—for the world
   With mighty change is rife.

Though knaves should scheme and rogues combine
   To thwart your honest aim,
Maintain your ground—press on, press on—
   Add fuel to the flame;
More and more yet, keep to the work,
   Raise, raise the pile on high,
Until its blaze in giant might
   Leaps to the very sky.

Already much has been achieved,
   There's much more to be done,

But aid the work with all your strength,
  The good shall yet be won;
O'erleap the barriers prejudice
  May set up in your way,
Hope on—take courage—persevere—
  And yours shall be the day.

Mind soars o'er matter, sordidness
  Sinks with'ring to the earth,
And wealth, that long hath claimed the bow,
  Succumbs to humbler worth;
Base systems born in ages dark
  Are falling to decay,
And soon a blast by Progress blown
  Shall sweep them all away.

And cant no longer shall be palmed
  As virtue on the good,
Nor shall pale-faced Hypocrisy
  Stands where it long hath stood;
The semi-blind shall have their sight,
  And opening their eyes
Things shall be known whenever seen,
  Whatever their disguise.

The Northern Star and National Trades Journal, 6 March 1852

THE TOILER'S DREAM

Not in the laughing bowers,
Where, by green twining elms, a pleasant shade,
At summer's noon is made,
And where swift-footed hours
Steal the rich breath of the enamoured flowers,
Dream I. Nor where the golden glories be,
At sunset, laving o'er the flowing sea;
And to pure eyes the faculty is given
To trace a smooth ascent from earth to heaven.

Not on the couch of ease,
With all the appliances of joy at hand—
Soft light, sweet fragrance, beauty at command;
Viands that might a god-like palate please,
And music's soul-creative ecstasies,
Dream I. Nor gloating o'er a wide estate,
Till the full, self-complacent heart elate,
Well satisfied with bliss of mortal birth,
Sighs for an immortality on earth.

But where the incessant din
Of iron hands, and roars of brazen throats,
Join their unmingled notes;
While the long summer day is pouring in,
Till day is gone, and darkness does begin;
Dream I—as in the corner where I lie,
On wintry nights, just covered from the sky.
Such is my fate; and barren though it seem,
Yet, thou blind, soulless scorner, yet I dream!

And yet I dream—
Dream what? Were men more just, I might have been
How strong, how fair, how kindly and serene,
Glowing of heart, and glorious of mien;
The conscious crown to Nature's blissful scene;
In just and equal brotherhood to glean,
With all mankind, exhaustless pleasure keen.
Such is my dream.

And yet, I dream.
I, the despised of Fortune, lift mine eye,
Bright with the lustre of integrity,
In unappealing wretchedness, on
And the last rage of Destiny defy;
Resolved alone to live—alone to die,
Nor swell the tide of human misery.

And yet, I dream,—
Dream of a sleep where dreams no more shall come,—
My last, my first, my only welcome home!
Rest, unbeheld, since life's beginning stage,
Sole remnant of my glorious heritage.

Unalienable, I shall find thee yet,
And in thy soft embrace the past forget!
Thus do I dream.

The Northern Star and National Trades Journal, 8 February 1851

[From a volume of "Poems by a Seamstress."]

A.L.

THE SLAVES' ADDRESS TO BRITISH FEMALES

Natives of a land of glory
Daughters of the good and brave,
Hear the injured Negroes' story,
Hear and help the fetter'd Slave!

Think how nought but death can sever
Your lov'd children from your hold.
Still alive, but lost for ever,
Ours are parted, bought and sold!

Seize, O seize, the favouring season,
Scorning censure or applause;
Justice, Truth, Religion, Reason,
Are our leaders in our cause.

Follow, faithful, firm, confiding
Spread our wrongs from shore to shore;
Mercy's God your efforts guiding
Slavery shall be known no more.

The Northern Star and Leeds General Advertiser, 17 February 1838

A.M.P.

THE LAND OF FREEDOM

Beneath Afric's hot sun, Mohab toil'd thro' the day,
   Light-hearted and glad, though a slave;
For Mohab could eat—to his God he could pray;
And at night, on his pallet, he grateful would say,
   He liv'd by the labour he gave.

But the white man had told him that there was a shore
   Where the poor and the stranger were free—
Where the stern hand of justice indignantly tore
Every fetter which man for his fellow-man bore:
   Mohab wished that that land he might see.

Soon a ship bound for Britain his native home passed,
   In whose captain a patron he found;
From his master he fled—the trim vessel sail'd fast,
And Mohab beheld England's white cliffs at last,
   And be sprung a free man—on free ground.

"What large vessels," he ask'd of his patron, "are those,"
   They fill me with feelings of wonder?"
"They are war-ships, by which we for ever oppose
All attempts of invaders; and liberty's foes
   Full well know the force of their thunder."

"And what's that dark vessel, unlike all the rest?"
   He inquired, and was told 'twas "The Tender,"
And that, when the war vessels for men were distress'd,
On board that dark hulk many persons were press'd,
   Whom their country compell'd to defend her.

"But come to the barracks," the Englishman cried,
   For our army you yet have to see:
A brave army is ever a nation's best pride,

And our soldier's in battle have often been tried,
   And are worthy the land of the free!"

And they saw a deserter dragg'd forth from his cell,
   And by force to the triangles bound,
And they heard the loud shriek, and the heart-thrilling yell,
'Till the mangled and shivering sufferer fell
   Senseless, covered with blood, on the ground.

Then the African said, "That's like slavery's thong,"
   And the Briton replied, "I confess
There are some little errors our blessings among;
But we have a relief from oppression and wrong
   In the voice of our free British Press."

"I'll examine your journals," the African thought,
   And he found, when enabled to read 'em,
That the rich man by bribes venal journalists bought,
And by libel indictments vile ministers sought
   To crush the true struggles for freedom.

And he saw a huge poor-house, "By Liberals plann'd,
   And a man with sunk eyes and parch'd tongue,
On whom famine had laid her cold withering hand;
A poor starving wretch in a plentiful land,
   But his kindred around him still clung!

They from him his wife and his little ones tore,
   And to separate dungeons conveyed:
Mohab heard him in accents most piteous implore
For a morsel of bread; he was spurn'd from the door,
   With hunger's sharp pangs unallay'd.

"Then, farewell!" Mohab cried, "to the land praised so high
   As the home of wealth, freedom, and bravery:
Tho' the truth of your boasting I dare not deny,
Yet I thank the great God of my fathers that I
   Am a child of the regions of slavery!"

Dr. Arbington

The Chartist Circular, 27 June 1840

A.R.

FRIENDSHIP AND WAR

(Forwarded to us by the Author's Son)

Ye monarchs that delight in war—
   And fight for fame and gain;
Ye only count the thousands lost,
   Ye never feel the pain.

Secure in wealth, at ease yourselves—
   No slaughtered friends ye mourn:
But I, alas! whose friends are few—
   Those few are from me torn.

My dearest friend with whom I met,
   To spend the social hour;
Lies cold and prostrate on the ground,
   To glut your sovereign power,

No Bachinalian lost I mourn—
   No venial worthless soul.
Whose only merit was a noise,
   While o'er the flowing bowl.

But manly worth, and generous deeds,
   That scorned defraud or guile—
He neither fear'd the tyrant's frown,
   Nor sought the tyrant's smile.

Nature to him, had rarely given.
   The feelings warm and strong;
And melody, in accents sweet,
   Proceeded from his tongue.

With dauntless breast he met the foe—
   The battles' rage he stood;

He saw the dreadful carnage, and
  The fields deep dyed with blood.

Till press'd at length, with toil and want—
  No friendly aid at hand
He fell beneath a load of woe,
  Amid a foreign land.

Flow! flow, these tears they are due,
  Oft has he charmed my mind;
And every coarse corroding care,
  He softep'd and refined.

No sottish selfish feasts were ours,
  But such as virtue loves;
Such as the good and great admires—
  Eren such as heaven approves.

The living manners quick he caught,
  And scan'd with reason clear.
The springs of wild *ambitious* rage,
  Or pity's melting tear.
Well did he know the passions' force—
  Each joy, each grief—he knew:
And with a master's hand expos'd
  Their every form to view.

But cold, and lifeless, now he lies,
  The noble spirit's gone:
And left in earthlings here below—
In sorrow to bemoan.

But strongly pressed upon my mind,
  His image shall abide:
Where'er I meet a social friend.
  I'll think on thee. Reside.

The Chartist Circular, 7 May 1842

A. W.

TO THE SONS OF TOIL

Ye sons of men give ear awhile,
   And listen to my prayer;
To you I ask, ye sons of toil,
   Who are press'd with want and care,

How comes it that ye toil and sweat,
   And bear the oppressor's rod;
For cruel men who dare to change
   The equal laws of God?

How comes, that man with tyrant heart
   Is caused to rule another;
To rob, oppress, and, leech-like, suck
   The life's blood of a brother?

Did Heaven's Eternal Justice say,
   Ye sons of men give ear!
Your portion's poverty and want,
   And others' loads must bear.

No! Heaven decreed all men should share
   Alike his equal laws;
That all should live, and happy be,
   And plead each other's cause.

Yes, brighter days await thee yet,
   Thy chart now meets our view;
To cheer our drooping, fainting hearts,
   And all our joys renew!

Arouse then, Britons! to your posts!
   Let cowards quit the field;

The known and right will claim the fight,
    And heaven will be our shield.

The Northern Star and Leeds General Advertiser, 3 April 1841

Crito

ODE TO LIBERTY

Devoid of Liberty what's life?
    A shadow and a name;
An undivided scene of strife,
    Of misery and shame.

A thousand worlds were void of worth,
    If liberty were lost,
A thousand to obtain it giv'n
    Were but a trifling cost.

'Tis liberty makes all things sweet,
    Its loss makes all things sad,
Where freedom reigns fond pleasure meet,
    And every heart is glad.

What are the empty dreams of wealth,
    Where thou art not a guest?
Ambition runs its mad career,
    And avarice rules the breast.

O! give me back my freedom lost,
    Or lay me in the grave,
None will survive its loss divine,
    Save he, who's born a slave.

Oldham, 25 April 1843

The Northern Star and Leeds General Advertiser, 6 May 1843

D.C.

OPPRESSION

Shall we for ever lick the dust
Or fear the tyrant's boding frown,
And cringing, pander to the lust
Of pamper'd minions of a crown?

Shall we for ever bear the scorn
    Of heartless wealth and fancied power?
Bequeath to ages yet unborn
    Our abjectness—a galling dower?

Shall we for ever be the spoil
    Of greedy avarice? and brood
O'er festering wrongs and thankless toil
    In calm and melancholy mood?

Shall we behold the festive halls,
    Where the loud laugh of revelry
Echoes along the tinselled walls
    In mockery of our misery?

Shall we a blind submission pay
    To steel'd oppression's ruthless reign?
Quiescent sigh? and meekly pray
    Of death to end our rankling pain?

Forbid it, God! the dignity
    Of manhood must awaken'd be;
Justice demands, and Liberty
    Proclaims we must and shall be free!

The Northern Star and Leeds General Advertiser, 3 September 1842

E. C. H.

ADDRESS TO THE CHARTER

"dum spiro, spero"

All hail to thy genial influences—
    The good, the just, the free—
And hail to thy bright wave rolling on
    With the tide of liberty!

The wanderer forth from early home,
    Though darkend be his lot,
Still knows he lives—still knows he hears
    Hope's voice "forget me not".

The slave, oppress'd with canker'd chains,
    O'erworn with grief and care,
He knows, he feels, there still remains
    A hope, though distant far.

The "poor man," though condemn'd and wrought,
    And crushed beneath the rod,
Hope's echoes still sound o'er his soul,
    Reflected high from God.

Then ne'er despair, but hope through all,
    Justice you still must have;
Oppression to the dust shall fall,
    Though tyrants' vassals rave.

The instrument of slavery's form
    Can flourish but an hour;
Crush'd, like the moth, before the storm,
    How transient is their power!

The floods that roll through Egypt's lands
    Are calm and small at first;

But a silent heaping from nature's hands
    Must swell them ere they burst.

So gather, yet Chartists! and all around
    Spread fast, till your foes be few;
So gather, ye Chartists, on England's ground,
    With your just rights still in view.

Chartists! still linger; but stop no more
    When your bright hands ripely wave;
Rise then, from northerly, shore to shore,
    March o'er the oppressor's grave.

As towering waves, when the seas rise high,
    So roll ye vastly on;
As the stirring breeze, when the whirlwind's nigh,
    Sweeps wide o'er the torrid zone.

A happier year, and a brighter ray,
    Shall usher a glorious morn;
How happy the poor, on that free-born day,
    Who have triumph'd o'er proud man's scorn.

The Northern Star and Leeds General Advertiser, 6 June 1840

E. P.

THE MANY AND THE FEW

AN APPEAL FOR THE RIGHT

Proud dwellers in gay palace halls—ye honoured of the earth—
Ye noble rulers of our land—oh! where have ye had birth?
With awe we own your mighty power, and humble homage pay,
For we must be, ye God-like men, of other, baser clay.

What are ye—masters of our lives—ye all enjoying few?
Why do the MANY ever live submissive slaves to you?

Why do the millions ever toil, though neither clothed nor fed?
Why has their dearest patriot blood on many a field been shed?

That you may riot in your halls in pampered, idle mirths
And trample at your lordly will the mass of baser earth!
And *is that mass of meaner clay? are* you of Heaven born?
And must the *idle* FEW but give the *toiling* MANY scorn?
Oh! "no!" ye injured million, "no!" I hear you loudly cry:
"We were not made to serve the few—to labour—starve—and
    die."
"The righteous God of all ne'er said our blood and sweat should
    be
A traffic for our fellow-men
He said that all were free."

The soil is rich with nature's fruits—with nature's bounties fair.
The earth is teeming with her stores to bless the tiller's care.
The idle revel in their halls—their costly boards are prest
With all the treasures of the land—the rarest and the best.
The gorgeous feast, the wassail loud, the wine-born lordly glee—
The dazzling joys of wealth and pride, and fashion's high decree.
All pleasures of the court and camp—the ball—the chase—the
    field,
All, all to those who labour not, the right to might must yield.

But in the wretched toiler's home, no rich repast is spread,
For wassail gay he only hears his children's cries for bread,
His days in weary cares are past, his nights in anxious fears,
And hopes of household happiness to come with other years.

But not for him the future smiles—to him the season yields,
No harvest plenty for his toils in nature's flowing fields,
Earth's gathered stores, earth's treasures vast, all, all that's good
    and fair,
Alas! for right they only swell the idle tyrant's share,

And must it be, ye many slaves, that time will longer tell
The tale of shame, that freedom's might, a dastard few could
    quell?
No! by insulted mankind's wrongs, it must no longer be.
Arouse ye! from your sleep of chains, old England's islands
    three!

Arouse! for liberty arouse! from farthest hill and glen;
Away with coward apathy, and, oh! again be men!
Your watchword, RIGHT! give thundering forth to England's
    farthest shore;
Then up, and burst these bonds accursed—for once—for
    evermore!

Paisley, 10 December 1839

The Chartist Circular, 28 December 1839

AN ENGLISH WORKMAN'S ADDRESS TO ENGLAND

"The admiration and envy of surrounding nations."!!

oh! England, how we dote on thee,
    Thou glorious land of matchless worth!
Home of the happy and the free;
    Where freedom smiles on ev'ry hearth.
The dusky slave of Afric's soil—
    The savage Indian of the West,
With food and raiment for their toil—
    Benighted fools, are blest.

But no such base ignoble lot,
    Oh! England dear, thy sons degrade;
The boon for which we've toiled and fought
    Is ours—the liberty we've made.
We starve, yet fondly to thee cling,
    Though *fed not* as we fain would be,
For art thou not, as poets sing,
    "The glorious and free."

Though foul-mouthed demagogues declaim,
    And tell, despite fame's loud parade,
Thy freedom great is but a name—
    The painted shadow of a shade.
That though thy sons thus blazon thee,
    And proudly praise the name they carve,
They have but that blessed liberty—
    The *liberty to starve.*

But, honoured land, thy name is known
   Wherever distant bondage toils;—
The first art thou to hear the groan
   Of other slaves of distant soils.
And can it be, that thou art dead
   To *native* use—to nature's cry,
By famished thousands, raised for bread,
   Beneath their native sky?

Oh no! thy rulers, nobly great,
   And very wise, and very good.
Oh! they must know a people's state
   Is ever best with scanty food;—
They know that some were made to till,
   And others must alone to feast—
God made the *few* to rule at will—
   The *many* are the least.

Afar beyond the Western Sea,
   And where arise Swiss mountains fair,
The many, meek as slaves may be,
   Must legislation's troubles share.
But, Englishmen! oh! ye are blest,
   Unstained by such ignoble thrall:
Your *kind good* masters do the best,
   And think for each and all.

Then well may England's minstrels sing
   The sweetly laudatory lay,
And well her lordly halls may ring
   With wine-cup praises loudly gay.
Ye peasant throng—ye baser brood,
   For England loud your praise should be;
Then shout, though lacking daily food,
   "The glorious and free."

23 November 1839

The Chartist Circular, 7 December 1839

F

ONE AND ALL

"One and all," is Cornwall's cry—
One and all, let us reply;
Hand to hand, and heart to heart,
Let us act a nation's part;
Let us free our native isle
From the rule of despots vile;
And send apostles o'er the world
With the Chartist flag unfurl'd.

One and all, let us proclaim
He who bears a bondman's name,
And seeketh not to cleanse its shame
Deserves to live in scorn, and die
With the vilest things that lie
Grovelling on their mother earth,
'Midst the spawn which gave them birth.
Earth will curse the dastard grave
Of the mean and cringing slave.

One and all! let tyrants quail
Now that sound is on the gale.
Who dare meet a nation's frown?
Who can keep a nation down?
Millions claim their rights as men,
Millions brave corruption's den,
Millions shout, from sea to sea,
"One and all," *we will be free!*

The Northern Star and Leeds General Advertiser, 25 June 1842

95

TO THE CHARTISTS OF SHROPSHIRE

Raise the Chartist banner high,
    Plant it in the Wrekin,[a]
Let its mottoes proudly fly,
    To the tyrant speaking.
Agitate each wooded vale,
    Agitate each village;
Show the wife and orphan pale,
    How the factions pillage.
Leave no spot in Shropshire wide
    Until it owns the Charter;
Spare the man who would divide
    Your ranks, or freedom barter.
Prove that in each vein now runs
    The British blood of old;
And that—crushing freedom's foes
    Ye dare be firm, and bold.
Cease not in your noble cause,
    Until you freedom gain;
And liberty, and equal laws,
    Are England's own again.
Then bear the Chartist flag once more,
    O'er mountain stream and vale;
A cause like your's, so bright and pure,
    Is never doom'd to fail.

8 May 1843

The Northern Star and Leeds General Advertiser, 27 May 1843

"In the spring of 1842, the colliers and iron-workers of South Shropshire were amongst the firmest and foremost advocates of our beloved Charter. Is the Spirit of Democracy dead amonst them now, or only sleepeth it? I would in the following lines call upon them to awake, arise, and again unfurl the banner of Freedom! All England is moving; will Shropshire stand alone, silent and mute?"

[a] The highest hill in the Midlands; it is situated a few miles from Wellington, Salop, and is 1320 feet above the level of the sea.

TO THE CHARTISTS OF WALES

Another soul hath winged its way,
To God's bright seat on high:
Another heart is Mammon's prey,
And ye stand tamely by!
Where is the Cambrian[1] blood that flowed in Howell's[a] veins?
Where are the men of old who burst the tyrant's chains?

Is liberty a farce?
Is justice but a name?
And must each pen, alas!
But chronicle your shame?
Oh if Llewellin[b] came from out his lonely tomb,
Would he not weep to see, his much loved Cambria's doom?

Would he not curse the slaves,
That kiss the blood-red hand?
That forms their children's grave,
And desolates their land?
Would he not wish your hills were sunk beneath the sea,
Since ye no longer are worthy of heritage so free?

Oh! can you see your children,
The innocent, the pure,
Stricken down by wicked men,
And still their yoke endure?
Can ye see your native land, beneath the despot's thrall
And not awake! arise! at freedom's earnest call?

O, Cambrians! your sires
Call on ye from their graves;
If lived their wonted fires
Ye would not long be slaves.
They bid ye to unfurl the Chartist flag again,
They bid ye bear it onward o'er mountain, hill, and plain.

Rise from your slumber!
O! rise from your sleep!
Millions in number,
Why crouch ye and weep?

England is waiting ye; tyranny flies;
Hark! hark! to the summons, awake and arise!!

3 June 1843

The Northern Star and Leeds General Advertiser, 10 June 1843

"An inquest was held upon the body of a little girl, aged five years, who died from starvation on the roadside near Llangefni, North Wales, last week. It appears that her father was unable to procure employment, and had applied to the relieving officer in the parish, who gave him one shilling, and told him to be off about his business, and not trouble him again. The consequence was that the father had nothing to give to his children, one of whom died for want of proper food.

The Northern Star, 6 May 1843

[a] A famous Welch chieftain, the friend of Llewellin.
[b] The last of the Welch princes. He was taken, bravely defending his country, by Edward I and executed in London.

J.E.

THE FACTORY CHILD

I hear the blythe voices of children at play,
And the sweet birds rejoicing on every spray;
On all things the bright beams of summer hath smil'd,
But they smile not on me the poor factory child.

The gay sports of childhood to me they deny,
And the fair path of learning I never must try;
A companion of creatures whom guilt hath defiled,
Oh! who does not pity the poor factory child.

Oh! who would not mourn for a victim like me,
A young heart-broken slave in the land of the free;
Hardly tasked, and oft beaten, oppress'd and revil'd,
Such, such is the fate of the poor factory child.

In the dead of the night when you take your sweet sleep,
Through the dark dismal street to my labour I creep;

So the din of the loom till my poor brain seems wild,
I return,—an unfortunate factory child.

The bright bloom of health has forsaken my cheek,
My spirits are gone, and my young limbs grown weak;
Oh! ye rich and ye mighty let sympathy mild,
Appeal to your hearts for the poor factory child.

Oh! pity my sufferings e'er yet the cold tomb,
Succeed my loathed prison, its task, and its gloom;
And the clods of valley untimely are pil'd,
O'er the pale wasted form of the factory child.

Aberdeen, 20 July 1841

McDouall's Chartist Journal and Trades' Advocate, 21 August 1841

J.H.

FROST

He is far from the land where his offspring sleep,
    And the waves are around him playing,
But he only turns from the view to weep,
    For his thoughts to his home are straying.

He recalls the scenes of his dear native land,
    The hearts who to life had entwined him;
And the tears fall uncheck'd by one friendly hand
    For the joys he has left behind him.

He lived for his country, for freedom he tried
    To raise up the wretched he wish'd;
Nor soon shall the tears of his country be dried,
    Nor for long shall its efforts desist.

Oh! he turns to a spot where the sunbeams rest,
    When they promise a gloomy morrow;

They shine o'er his form like a smile from the west,
   From his own lov'd island of sorrow.

The Northern Star and Leeds General Advertiser, 2 May 1840

Poor John Frost is now many a mile from us. The following Lines were
suggested to me from reading Moore's lines—"She is far from the land," &c.

J. W. C.

RALLY AGAIN, BOYS

Come rally again, boys! we must not resign,
   But each storm we encounter,[1] let's nobly brave;
It is better to perish at liberty's shrine
   And the last drop of blood in her altars to lave.

Oh! yes, it is better, far better to die
   In a glorious cause than to pine beneath chains;
For the heroes that fall there's a tear and a sigh,
   Whilst a kindred heart on the earth there remains.

Then let's rally again, boys, and never despair,
   Ev'ry onslaught of faction, we'll boldly resist,
Tho' the vaults of the dungeon we're destin'd to share,
   Yet until we've conquer'd, we'll never desist.

For awhile they may torture and murder the brave,
   But the flood of each martyr will spring into life,
Till the footsteps of every tyrant and slave
   Are wash'd out, and no longer pollute the fair earth.

Then let's rally again, boys, there's strength enough yet
   In the ranks where the embers of liberty glow;
The blood they have shed, let us never forget,
   But strike for our freedom one vigorous blow.

Tho they baffle, they cannot subdue us for long,
   When united in one mighty phalanx we be;

When our hearts they are firm as our arms they are strong,
   The tyrants will tremble, "the oppress'd will go free."

Then let's rally again, boys, we never will rest,
   For the tyrants who bind us no peace shall there be,
Till each slave us unfetter'd and freedom has bless'd
   The land of our birth, and proclaimed "we are free."

   Oppressors may put to the rank the oppress'd,
      Their murderous hands in our blood they may drench;
   But the fire that burns in each patriot's breast
      For glorious freedom, they never can quench

   Then let's rally again, boys, proscription we'll brave,
      Until liberty's banner on high is unfurl'd,
   And the standard of freedom o'er tyranny's grave
      Shall be planted in triumph all over the world.

Bristol, 5 December 1842

The Northern Star and Leeds General Advertiser, 17 December 1842

M. K.

WE MAY, WE WILL, WE MUST, WE SHALL BE FREE

We *may* be free! 'tis ours the mighty power
   To speak in tones both terrible and loud,
Nor will we crouching and obsequious lower
   To worship baubles and adore the proud;
The titled tyrants, who, with plunder'd might
Have thrones erected on the grave of *right.*

Ah! no; we seek for *freedom,* and our claim
   Is bas'd upon our birth. Our native land!
The land of glory and of butchering fame
   We seek to rescue from the bloody brand
With which proud conquerors have its name begor'd,
Those meek vice regents of a righteous Lord

M.K.

We *will* be free! applauding reason smiles
   Her simple acquiescence; and the just,
The patriot noble, need no courtier's wiles
   To shroud the truth within a hideous crust
Of black perversion; such as priests and knaves
Have used to model and to mould us slaves.

We *must* be free! for all the varied springs
   Of dark oppression, now would seem to lose
Their potency; as on her bliss-imparting wings
   True knowledge soars abroad, disturbing the repose
Of ancient error, and diffusing light
Where nought existed but the gloom of night.

We *shall* be free! aloud the truth proclaim,
   From east to west let freedom's name be heard;
Let tyrants hear it! that her virtuous fame
   Will shine unsullied, though they would retard
With puny effort her majestic sway,
A nation wills it and who dare gainsay?

Then hark! O countrymen! awake ye dead!
   Ye who have slept in apathy profound,
Arise! arise! by freedom's pole star led,
   March nobly onward till with success crown'd
You reap the comforts which your deeds have gain'd,
And cease to struggle as do slaves enchain'd.

The Northern Star and Leeds General Advertiser, 3 December 1842

R

THE CAPITALIST

On the glittering piles of wealth he gaz'd,
   (His heavy coffers hold;)
Till his giddy brain with the sight was daz'd,
   His heart was chang'd to gold.

Soon all human feelings sickening died
    Crush'd by that passion's pow'r;
As the life-parch'd flow'rs of the morning fade
    Scorch'd by noon's blazing hour.
And the blood that cours'd through his portly frame,
    Forgot its crimson dye—
To the glowing gold pour'd through every vein
    It ow'd vitality.

He dwells in a mansion whose splendour mocks
    Noble or regal state;
Like a bloated spider their life he sucks
    Whose toils his wealth create
He throws round his victims the iron net,
    Which want has wove for him
And he joys to see on their pale cheeks set
    The seal of hunger grim.
And he hath search'd out what was never known,
    To Alchymists of old—
He taketh his brothers sinew and bone
    And melts to yellow gold!

The dawn looks forth where his plundered serfs
    Their weary labours ply;
While the latest star which the midnight gives,
    Quits, ere they cease, the sky.
See the bloodshot eye and the haggard form,
    The idiotic stare,
And consumption's slow insidious worm,
    Are brauds his servants bear.
Stern manhood o'erpowered his sturdy strength
    Bows in the deadly strife;
And the throbbing brow of opening youth
    With cares of old is rife.

A hale old age, save in ancient song
    To workers is unknown—
(But a sleepless angel each blighting wrong
    In God's day book writes down!)
Bravely, O bravely, the golden flood,
    The rich man quaffs the while;
And little he recks if his brothers blood
    Its lustre somewhat soil;

Honours and titles await his call
    With aught earth's confines hold.
For the nations (like they of Dathan) all
    Adore this calf of gold.

O fell is the noble's insane misrule,
    When trampled nations obey;
And blackest of all the plagues of hell,
    Is the priest's unbounded sway.
But this goodly earth is more deeply curst
    By mammon's blacker slaves.
Who answer the anguished cry for bread
    By digging pauper graves.
O quail ye not lest that skeleton host
    May turn and their tyrants slay?
For the hunter feareth that hour the most,
    When the hunted stand at bay.'

Say paled not your cheek when that dying howl
    Of hunger past your doors,
Lest your children's clutch of your hoarded spoil
    Should prove less firm than yours?
For the time draws neigh when the reck'ning due
    With brigands shall be made
And the long arrears and interest too,
    In full shall be repaid!
And O when that day of maddening strife,—
    Of long-pent justice comes.
When the people's watchword is—"Life for life"
    God help the guilty ones

The Red Republican, 26 October 1850

"Gold and gold and nothing but gold,
He had gold to give and gold to lend,
Gold to lay by, and gold to spend."   Hood

R. M. B.

NURSERY RHYMES

"LITTLE JACK HORNER SAT IN A CORNER"
New Reading

Little Jack R-ss-ll sat on his bustle,
    Counting his sal-a-ry;
Then into his fob he popp'd every bob,
    Saying "What a great man am I."

Jack loved sal-a-*ry*, and thought he would try
    To keep in his place while he could;
So to Parlia*ment*, in a fidget he went
    To work for his livelihood.

Thinks he, without doubt, he must shortly go out
    If we don't find the Commons a *job;*
And a thought that was bright, came like a Bude light,
    To illumine the depths of his nob.

Then he bounced from his seat in a mighty heat,
    And said, "Mr. Speaker, I rise
To move that all other grave business we smother
    While I whisper a word to the wise.

"There's a judge who alleges that our privileges
    Are not worth a straw or a fig;
And asserts with contempt, that we are not exempt
    From the arm of the law—dash his wig!

"But I mean, Sir, to state that we can't legislate
    (And the judges must see their mistake),
If we mayn't give a sample, by way of example,
    Of a breach of the laws that we make.

105

"Sir, are we to be talked to, insulted and baulk'd too,
    By fifteen old codgers in gowns,
Who to dull special pleading confine all their reading
    To decide upon adverbs and nouns.

"No, by George! while I sit in this house we'll commit
    Every Radical that laughs at our thunder;
If we can't print a libel, there's an end to the Bible,
    And virtue to vice must knock under."

The bait quickly took; the insidious hook
    Was swallow'd by men of all classes;
Jack laugh'd in his sleeve, for he didn't believe
    They'd be such consummate jack-asses.

Then to it they went, on vengeance intent,
    And order'd the Sergeant-at-Arms
To collar all those who dared to oppose,
    Nor shrunk from their awful alarms.

Poor Stockdale and Howard they tempted to bow hard,
    But in vain, for their necks were too stiff;
So the former they nail'd, and the Sheriff assail'd,
    And clapp'd 'em in *quod* in a whiff.

But still, nothing daunted, the said Howard wanted
    That *the House* and its threat she defy'd;
And young Mr. Gossett was sent from his posset,
    To tear him from home and fire-side.

Next his son, a mere lad, and his clerk, t'was too bad,
    Were seized this oppression to crown;—
Things might have been worse *but the baby and nurse*
    Had escap'd, *with mamma*, out of town.

When little Jack R-ss-ll had finished this bustle,
    They set up a *tillabulloo;*
And, like a game cock, jack look'd at the clock,
    And crow'd "Cock a doodle doo-doo!"

Then away from the house, he ran like a mouse
    From a cat in a full pan-*try;*—

But, before he could rest, he went to his chest,
  And locked up his sal-a-*ry.*

City, 20 February

The Northern Star and Leeds General Advertiser, 29 February 1840

S.J.

PRESENTATION OF THE NATIONAL PETITION

Monday, May 2nd, 1842
SONG—*"THE CHARTIST GAY DAY"*

It was Nature's gay day,
Bright smiling May day,
Each heart was yearning our country to free;
  Thy banners were bringing,
  The people were singing
Of the days of their fathers and sweet liberty.
  Merrily bounding,
  Banners surrounding,
Each slave clash'd his chains on that happy day;
  To meet thus delighted
  By all invited,
To join the brave throng 'neath freedom's bright ray.

Thousands were marshall'd,
The throng forward marched;
The burden of millions was borne and onward too,
  From the field to the Strand,[1]
  With banners and band,
The mighty assemblage of Chartist doth go,
  Their foes fill with wonder,
  As proudly they thunder
Their shouts for their Charter, their hearts with hope fill'd.

To St. Stephen's they bear it,
By the table they rear it,—
A monument to testify their woes and their will.

The evening descended,
Their freedom was ended,
The lads and the lasses walked thoughtfully away.
Still the hope brooding
Of freedom foreboding,
The enfranchised, their promises, yet would repay.
The day is passed over,
And now they discover
The Whigs and the Tories just answer them so—
Oh, slavies, believe ye,
We will not deceive ye;
Ye shall not be heard your grievance to show.[2]

Bristol

The Northern Star and Leeds General Advertiser, 4 June 1842

SONG OF FREEDOM
NINE CHEERS FOR THE CHARTER

Bright are the beams of the morning sky
    And sweet dew the free goddess sips;
How bright are the glances of cheer from her eye,
    And sweet are the truths from her lips;
Her mouth is the fountain of virtue,
    The source from whence equity flows;
Ah! who would not dwell 'neath its influence,
    As the honey bee sips of the rose.

Then we pledge, then we pledge, to bright freedom,
    Let each soul himself worthy prove;
Now we cheer, now we cheer, sons of Freedom,
    Nine cheers for the souls that we love.
        Hip, hip, hurrah, hip, hip, hurrah, hurrah, hurrah,
    hurrah,
        Nine cheers for the Charter,
        Nine cheers for the cause that we love.

Come raise, raise the banner to heaven high,
   The goddess of liberty approves,
The offering thus hallowed by ardour's true sigh,
   Is blessed with the smile-cheer of Jove.
Then ring ye the welkin with transport,
   The spell of life's great joys impart;

Our Cause, the most sacred to mortals,
   Yields the noblest of joys to the heart.
Then we pledge, then we pledge, to the Charter,
   Let each heart that loves freedom approve;
And we'll shout still we'll shout, for the Charter,
   With nine cheers for the cause that we love.
      Hip, hip, hurrah, hip, hip, hurrah, hurrah,
   Nine cheers for the Charter,
   Nine cheers for the cause that we love.

Bristol

The Northern Star and Leeds General Advertiser, 29 October 1842

T. Z. Y.

THE CONTRAST

   "The people," Lord Johnny[1] declared at l' pool,
   "Might meet, if they liked, their wrongs to unfold;
      For by meeting they'll find O'Connor's[2] a fool,
And so Stephens'[3] speeches they'll quickly grow cold."

They meet in their strength and they meet in their might;
      Confined all the day, they met in the night:
      Deprived of the sun, they raised the torch-light,
   And O'Connor and Stephens they cheered left and right.

   When a little Lord John found this was the case,
      A new light came over his noodle; and all

In a hurry he sends, for preserving the "pace,"
Lots of men, machines, bayonets, powder, and ball.

But let little Lord John and his minions beware,
Nor to play with edged tools let them hastily dare.
IF THEY DARE break the peace, let the people prepare.
To teach them good manners, by CURLING THEIR HAIR.

The Northern Star and Leeds General Advertiser, 5 January 1839

W.A.K.

THE LION AND THE GNAT[a]

"Out upon thee, thou base born!"
Exclaimed a lion to a gnat in scorn,
"Thou art an intrusive paltry creature,
"Formed from the very dregs of nature,
"Out upon thee!—out!—away!
"Nor longer in my presence stay."
To which the little gnat replied,
"Sire, I much despise thy pride,
"Think not the title of a king,
"Alarms me,—it does not such thing,—
"Nor do I feel thy mandate, law;
"So little do I think it so,
"That from this instant know,
"On thee I'll make eternal war,
"The ox is quite as strong as *thee,*
"Yet I can lead him at my fantasy."

As he thus spoke, he upwards flew,
Then darting on his neck below,
'Twas not an instant ere he had
Rendered his *majesty* half mad.

The lion foamed with deadly ire,
His eyeballs seemed emitting fire,

He ran and rolled, and roar'd so loud,
That all the beasts affrighted fled,
Breathless with dismay and dread,
Into the recesses of the wood.

And all this universal consternation,
Caused by an insect of such *low creation!*
Again the gnat renew'd the attack;
He stung the lips, and spine, and back,
And eyes, and every joint, and nose,
Without a moment of repose.

The lion's rage to madness raised,
His enemy delighted gazed,
To see how useless were his teeth and claws,
In such a very hopeless cause;
For in his rage he only tore
In deepest wounds himself, all o'er,
Which ran in copious crimson tides,
Whilst with his tail he lashed his sides,
And beat the incumambient air,
In torment and in wild despair.

At length exhausted with fatigue and pain,
He fell all bleeding on the plain.
The gnat with glory and ambition fired
To tell the story, from the fight retired;
And the *monarch* for the *time to come,*
On his own consequence was dumb.

McDouall's Chartist and Republican Journal, 14 August 1841

[a] A king amongst men is as open to the vengeance of an oppressed and injured citizen, as the king amongst the brute creation was open to the vengeance of the little gnat in the fable.

W. B.

TO THE POETS OF AMERICA

Bards of Freedom's boasted land!
  Brothers!—foremost of the free!
Ye, who with impassioned hand
  Sweep the cords of Liberty!—
Ye, to whom the boon is given
  To win the ear and melt the heart !—
Awake! and, waking earth and heaven,
  Perform the minstrel's noblest part.

Why stand ye mute? when on the ear
  A thunder-peal from sea to sea—
A peal earth's darkest haunts shall hear—
  Proclaims—*The slave shall now be free.*
Long has he drain'd the bitter cup!
  Long borne the scourge, and dragged the chain,
But now the strength of Europe's up—
  A strength that ne'er shall sleep again!

Your Garrison[1] has fann'd the flame!
  Child,[2] Chapman,[3] Pierrepont,[4] catch the fire!
And, roused at Freedom's hallow'd name,
  Hark Bryant[5]—Whittier[6]—strike the lyre!
While *here*—hearts, voices trumpet-toned—
  Montgomery[7]—Cowper[8]—Campbell[9]—Moore[10]—
The Freedom's glorious cause respond,
  In sounds that thrill to every core!

Their voice has conjured up a power
  No foes can daunt—no force arrest!
That gathers strength with every hour
  And strikes a chord in every breast!—
A power that soon, on Afric's sand,
  On Cuba's shore, on ocean's flood,

112

Shall crush the oppressor's iron hand,
   And blast the traffickers in blood!

O! *where* should freedom's hope abide,
   Save in the bosom of the *free?*
Where should the wretched negro hide,
   Save in the shade of Freedom's tree?
And *where* should minstrel wake the strain
   That cheers Columbia's forests wild?
Oh! *not* where captives clank their chain!
   For Poetry is Freedom's child!

The minstrel cannot, must not sing,
   Where fetter'd slaves in bondage pine!
Man has no voice, the muse no wing,
   Save in the light of Freedom's shrine!
O! by those songs your children sing—
   The lays that soothe your winter fires—
The hopes—the hearts—to which you cling;
   The sacred ashes of your sires!

By all the joys that crown the *free*
   Love—Honour—Fame—the hopes of Heaven!
Wake in your might! that earth may see
   God's gifts have not been vainly given!
Bards of Freedom's favoured strand!
   Strike at last your loftiest key!
Peal the watchword through the land!
   Shout till every slave is free!—

Long has he drained the bitter cup—
   Long borne the lash, and clanked the chain!
But *now* the strength of Europe's up—
   A strength that ne'er shall sleep again!

The Northern Star and Leeds General Advertiser, 9 March 1844

W. H. C.

THE VOICE OF THE PEOPLE

'Tis the voice of the people I hear it on high,
It peals o'er the mountains—it soars to the sky;
Through wide fields of heather, it wings its swift flight,
Like thunders of heaven arrayed in their might.
It rushes still on, like the torrent's loud roar;
And bears on its surges the wrongs of the poor.
It's shock like the earthquake shall fill with dismay,
The hearts of the tyrants and sweep them away.

The Northern Star and Leeds General Advertiser, 4 December 1841

John Arnott[1]

A SONG ADDRESSED TO THE FRATERNAL DEMOCRATS

AIR—"AULD LANG SYNE"

All hail, Fraternal Democrats,
  Ye friends of Freedom hail,
Whose noble object is—that base
  Despotic power shall fail.
    That mitres, thrones, misrule and wrong,
      Shall from this earth be hurled,
    And peace, goodwill, and brotherhood,
      Extend throughout the world.

Associated to proclaim
  The equal rights of man.

114

Progression's army! firm, resolved,
 On! forward lead the van.
  Till mitres, thrones, misrule and wrong,
   Shall from this earth be hurled.
  And peace, goodwill, and brotherhood,
   Extend throughout the world.

To aid this cause we here behold,
 British and French agree,
Spaniard and German, Swiss and Pole,
 With joy the day would see.
  When mitres, thrones, misrule, and wrong,
   Will from this earth be hurled,
  And peace, goodwill, and brotherhood,
   Extend throughout the world.

We now are met to celebrate
 The deeds of spirits brave,
Who struggled, fought, and bled, and died,
 Their misrul'd land to save.
  For mitres, thrones, misrule and wrong,
   From France they nobly hurled,
  And would have spread Democracy
   Throughout this sea-girt world.

Though kings and priests might then combine
 To crush sweet liberty,
We tell them *now* that they must bow,
 That man shall yet be free.
  That mitres, thrones, misrule and wrong,
   Shall from this earth be hurled,
  And peace, goodwill, and brotherhood,
   Extend throughout the world.

Oh! may that period soon arrive,
 When kings will cease to be,
And freedom and equality
 Extend from sea to sea.
  Then mitres, thrones, misrule and wrong,
   Will from this earth be hurled,
  And peace, goodwill, and brotherhood,
   Shall reign throughout the world.

Somers Town, September 1846

The Northern Star and National Trades Journal, 19 September 1846

On the occasion of their First Annual Festival to celebrate the Anniversary of the French Republic, at the white Conduit Tavern, April 21st, 1846.

Bandiera

A CALL TO THE PEOPLE

People of England! rouse ye from this dreaming—
　Sinew your souls for Freedom's glorious leap!
Look to the Future! lo! our dayspring's gleaming,
　And a pulse stirs that never more shall sleep
In the world's heart. Men's eyes like stars are throbbing!
　The traitor-kings turn pale in Pleasure's bower!
And at the sound that comes like thunder sobbing,
　The leaves from Royalty's tree fall hour by hour,—
　Earthquakes leap in our temples, crumbling throne and
　power!

Vampires have lapped the human heart's best blood;
　Kings robbed, and Priests have cursed us in God's name!
Out in the midnight of the Past we've stood,
　While fiends of darkness plied their hellish game;
We have been worshipping a gilded crown,
　Which drew Heaven's lightning—laughter on our head!
Chains fell on us as we were bending down:
　We deemed our gods divine, but lo! instead
　They are but painted clay!—with morn the charm hath fled!

Call ye this "Merrie England!" this the place—
　The cradle of great souls of self-defied—
Where smiles once revelled in the Peasant's face,
　Ere hearts were masked by gold, lips steeped in pride?
Where Toil, with open brow, went on light-hearted?
　Where twain in love, law never thrust apart?
Then is the glory of our life departed—

From us who sit and nurse this bleeding smart,
And slink afraid to break the laws that break the heart?

Hushed be yon herald on the walls of Fame,
   Trumping this people as their country's pride!
Weep rather with your souls on fire with shame:
   See ye not how the pallaced knaves deride—
Us easily-flattered fools?—how priestcraft stealthy
   Stabs at our freedom thro' its veil of night,
Plundering the poor to flush its coffers wealthy?
   Hear how the land groans in the grip of Might,
   Then quaff your cup of Wrongs, and laud a "Briton's Right!"

There's not a spot in all this flowery land
   Where Tyranny's scatheful footmark has not been:
Oh! were it not for its all-blasting brand,
   Dear God! what a sweet heaven this might have been!
Has it not hunted forth our spirits brave—
   Killed the red rose that crowned our vaunted daughters,
Wedded our living throughts to the dark grave,
   Filled happy homes with strife, the world with slaughters?
   And turned our thoughts to blood,—to gall the heart's sweet
   waters!

Go forth when night is hushed, and Heaven is clothed
   With smiling stars that in God's presence roll:
Feel the proud spirit leap to them betrothed,
   As angel-wings were fanning in the soul:
Feel the hot tears flood in the eyes up-turning,
   The tide of goodness heave its brightest waves;—
Then it is not hard to clash the godward yearning
   With the mad thought that ye are still earth's slaves?
   Oh! how long will ye make your hearts its living graves?

Is the love dead that nerved our ancient sires,
   Who, bleeding, wrung their rights from tyrants olden?
God-spirits have been here for Freedom's fires,
   From out their ashes to earth's heart enfolden,
The mighty dead lie slumbering around!
   Their names come as if God's soul shook the air;
Life leaps from where their dust makes holy-ground:
   Their deeds spring forth in glory! live all where!
   And are we traitors to th' eternal trust we bear?

O, but to give ye, slaves! this heart of mine,
  Twere sweet to kiss the scaffold-block to-morrow!
To proudly leap death's darkness, to let shine
  The Future's hope thro' your soul-binding sorrow!
There is a chasm in the coming years
  Agape for Strife's Niagara of blood!
Or to be filled with our slow ceaseless tears,
  Ere it be bridged by bond of Brotherhood!
  We've yet to stand in fight, true as the Spartan stood!

Immortal Liberty, I see thee stand
  Like morn just stept from Heaven, fresh on a mountain;
With rosy feet, and blessing-laden hand;
  Thy brow star-crowned! thy heart love's living fountain!
O when wilt thou string on the People's lyre
  Joy's broken chord? and on the People's brow
Place Empire's crown? light up thy beacon-tire
  Within their hearts with an undying glow,
Nor give us blood for milk, as men are drunk with now?

Old poets tell us of a golden age
  When earth was sinless—gods the guests of men—
Ere guilt had dimmed the heart's illumined page;
  And Sinai-voices say 'twill come again!
Oh! happy age, when love reigns in each heart,
  And time to live shall be the poor man's dower;
When martyrs bleed no more, nor poets smart;
  Mind be the only diadem of power!
  People! it ripens now! awake and strike the hour!

Hearts high and mighty gather in our cause;
  Bless! bless, O god! and crown their earnest labour!
Who dauntless go to win us equal laws,
  With brain-wrought armour, and with spirit-sabre.
Bless! bless, O God! the proud Intelligence
  That, like a sun, dawns on the People's forehead!
Humanity springs from them like incense!
  The Future burets upon them, boundless, starried!
  They weep repenting tears that they so long have tarried!

The Red Republican, 29 June 1850

George Binns

TO THE MAGISTRATES WHO COMMITTED ME TO PRISON UNDER THE DARLINGTON CATTLE ACT FOR ADDRESSING A CHARTIST MEETING

Oh! bind your fetters fast as hell
   Can forge them for your master,
I smile to think they ring your knell,
   I'LL WEAR THEM FOR THE CHARTER!

And 'ope' your dismal dungeons jaws
   To those who will not barter
For tinsel rank, a noble cause,
   I'LL ENTER FOR THE CHARTER!

And herd me with the base and bad,
   Because I'll not surrender
The rights of England to your nod,
   I STILL WILL LOVE THE CHARTER!

Then bind my limbs and lash THE DUST,
   My soul you cannot fetter;
Its chainless wing flies with the just,
   Round England and her Charter!

The Switzer's Tell—the Tyrol's pride,
   The noblest blood of Sparta;
The men who've nobly liv'd and died,
   CRY ONWARD WITH THE CHARTER!

Bishop Auckland

The Northern Star and Leeds General Advertiser, 9 May 1840

FLOWERS AND SLAVES

I saw the bonny flowers of May
  In beauty bloom before me,
And verdant fields were spangled gay
  With Summer's tints of glory.

The varied songsters of the grove
  Were tuning notes of gladness,
And azure skies were clear above
  Of hazy clouds of sadness.

The god of love seem'd joying o'er
  His wondrous works before us,
And Nature seem'd to own his power
  In universal chorus.

But midst the beauty and the light
  Of Summer's bright creation,
There burst upon my pallid sight
  A nation's lamentation.

A starving tiller of the soil,
  His bread—*a Whig oration*—
A starving host of sons of toil—
  A bleeding, captive nation!

The demon groan of ghastly want,
  Like Etna's muffled thunder,
Was rumbling in its hollow vault
  To tear restraints asunder.

I ask'd the daisy on the lea
  The cowslip gently kneeling,
The skylark, with its nature glee,
  The cloudless sky of evening—

I ask'd them why they bloom'd so fair,
  And smil'd so sweetly round us;
And man, the sweetest flower there
  Was wither'd, sad, and homeless.

Alas! they could not answer why
  The hearth should e'er be blasted;
Or hopes, descending from on high,
  Should vainly there have rested.

I turned away from fields so gay,
  From man, so lorn and blighted,
And lonely knelt me down to pray
  That England's wrongs be righted.

Before the zephyr's gentle breeze
  My raven locks disparted;
And midst the solitary trees
  I wept for FRIENDS DEPARTED!

To see the plunder'd son of toil
  Forsake his ruin'd cot,
And tearing from the thief his spoil,
  Leave palace worms to rot—

To see the mother in her pride
  Hurl lightning on the foe,
And blush to think her baby died
  A famish'd child of woe—

To hear the rolling battle drum
  Exulting beat to arms,
And see the flash of freedom's gun,
  Dispel a world's alarms—

My very heart would bound again!
  To God I'd bend the knee,
For "peace on earth—good will to men"
  Would beam upon the free.

To free my land, my ardent soul,
  My very *arm* would try—
And down my burning cheek would roll
  A rebel tear of joy!

Bishop Auckland

The Northern Star and Leeds General Advertiser, 16 May 1810

THE CHARTIST MOTHER'S SONG

TUNE—"THE ROSE OF ALLENDALE"

Yon starry light, that rules the night,
    In yonder distant sky;
It sheds its bright and bonnie light
    On thee, my Chartist Boy.
In silent flight o'er hills at night
    It never ask'd who wander'd past
But *lit* my Chartist Boy.

        Chorus.

For all yon king—a gilded thing,
    Robs poverty of joy,
It shines as free and bright on thee
    My honest Chartist Boy.
Then, on! away! be blithe and gay,
    And climb the mountain high;
And take the vow of freemen now,
    My gallant Chartist Boy.

        Chorus.

Away! away! no longer stay;
    For freedom live or die!
The heart that's true shall have its due—
    Away, my Chartist Boy.
Away, my brave, forsake thy grave,
    Forget each slavish tie,
And raise a light on England's night;
    Be free, my Chartist Boy.

        Chorus.

Be free—be free! and let them see
    Who Heaven's law defy;
Their Baal shrine shall ne'er be thine,
    My own, my Chartist Boy.
Thy father's gone; then, on, my son!
    My heart will beat with joy,

To see the foe in death laid low
   By *thee*, my Chartist Boy.

      Chorus.

Sunderland

The Northern Liberator, 29 February 1840

"GIVE US THIS DAY OUR DAILY BREAD"

When He, the wise, the great, the good,
   Threw empty thrones away;
And sought the desert solitude,
   For prostrate man to pray,

He asked not for a longer lease
   To breed usurping *things,*
But breathed a holy prayer of peace,
   To God—the King of Kings.

He asked for Judah's sons of toil,
   For England's drooping slaves,
The golden harvest of our soil,
   That summer's light wind waves.

"Give us this day our daily bread,"
   Our Great Redeemer cried;
Yet thousands moulder with the dead,
   Because that bread's denied.

Denied!—Yon living Sun that rolls
   In splendour through the sky,
Proclaims in tones that reach the poles,
   That *God* does not deny.

But *men,* with rude and demon hand,
   By sceptres and by chains,
Have dealt damnation round the land,
   To pander to their gains.

Then, Britons, be no more misled,
  But peal the heavenly notes—
"Give us this day our daily bread"—
  Give England back her votes.

The Northern Liberator, 11 April 1840

John Henry Bramwich

A HYMN

Britannia's sons, though slaves ye be,
God your Creator made you free;
He, life to all, and being, gave—
But never, never made a slave!

His works are wonderful to see—
All, all proclaim the Deity;—
He made the earth, and formed the wave—
But never, never made a slave!

He made the sky, with spangles bright—
The moon to shine by silent night—
The sun,—and spread the vast concave—
But never, never made a slave!

The verdant earth on which we tread
Was, by His hand, all carpeted;
Enough for all He freely gave—
But never, never made the slave!

All men are equal in His sight,—
The bond, the free, the black, the white;—
He made them all,—them freedom gave—
He made the man,—*Man made the Slave!*

The Northern Star and National Trades Journal, 4 April 1846

SOME MEN THAT I LIKE

I like a man whose virtuous mind
Is such that he dare tell it;
But who, if worlds were gold refined,
For worlds would never sell it.

I like a man who scorns to be
A slave to fellows mortal;
Whose spirit pants for liberty,
While passing through death's portal.

I like a man whose buoyant heart
Can float in sea of sorrow;
Who, though he feels his timbers start,
Hopes for a calm to-morrow.

I like a man that will not run
To meet, half-way, his troubles;
But boldly meets them, when they come,
As fickle fortune's bubbles.

I like a man of noble mind
And independent spirit;
Who willing is to raise mankind
But by exalted merit.

I like a man whose generous soul
Can pity feel for others,
Who looks around, surveys the whole,
And calls mankind his brothers.

I like a man whose thankful heart
Can feel a favour given,
Who, ere the crystal tear drops start,
Report the same to heaven!

The Northern Star and National Trades Journal, 18 April 1846

Sheldon Chadwick

LABOUR'S ANTHEM

Shall Labour's children perish
   Beneath the hoof of Wrong,
Still plodding on, heart-weary,
   How long, O God! how long?
Men, like common grass are sold;
Blood is alchymised to gold,
   And power is with the strong!
Souls, like stars, in dust are are rolled,
   How long, O God! how long?

Shall man scorn still his brother,
   Who groans beneath the thong,
Which crime inflicts upon him,
   How long, O God! how long?
Shall Labour's sons and daughters,
As fair as singing waters,
   Be carrion for the strong!
Food for the warrior's slaughters,
   How long, O God! how long?

Shall Freedom's dawn be never
   On Labour's heaving sea;
Shall Love, and Truth, and Beauty,
   In toiling hearts ne'er be?
Shall god-like Action veil its eyes
Before Wealth's idle mockeries,
   The weak bow to the strong?
O, when shall slaves like gods arise,
   How long, O God! how long?

Shall virtue live in sorrow,
   A world of joys among;

126

Shall genius eat blood-sodden bread,
    How long, O God! how long?
Thy world is far as heaven can be,
Make it happy, made it free.
    And peaceful as a song!
Father; make it worthy thee,
    How long, O God! how long?

They wait to see thy power,
    To crush the proud and strong;
They toil and starve in madness,
    How long, O God! how long?
Lightnings smite the iron crown!
Thunders strike the guilty throne,
    Based on fraud and wrong!
Lay the tyrant stiff as stone!
    How long, O God? how long?

The Red Republican, 28 September 1850

NOW COMETH THE STORM

Now cometh the storm, can you hear its loud rattle
Leap 'mong the crags, in delirious darkness?
Like a lion it springeth and fronteth the battle,
And shakes from its sinews the fetters of starkness!
The trembling hill-tops hear the roar of the thunder,
It rolls round the world in its splendor and might;
Hear it, ye thrones! it will drag ye asunder,
'Tis the voice of the people—the voice of the right!

From the turrets of Heaven the lightning streameth,
Like a lasso it bindeth the world in its arms;
Like a fire-blazoned banner above us it beameth,
And tyrants are mad in the flash of its charms.
From the lowest cloud, fire-shod, earthward it leapeth,
Brand-tongued, majestic, with terrible glee;
It illumines the graves were the martyr-band sleepeth,
'Tis the thought of the people—the mind of the free!

Joy! joy! to the slave-land, its slumber is broken,
Lion hearts bound to the stars in their cage!
The voice of the many for freedom hath spoken,
And crowns will be crushed in the tramp of their rage!
A Strong One is up in Time's star-crowned steeple,
Ringing a knell with its skeleton hand;
'Tis the proud, the erect, the invincible people,
Bringing to judgment the crimes of our land!

With fire, like a thunder-cloud, great hearts are throbbing,
O'er wrongs which oppression upon us hath rolled;
O'er outraged humanity seraphs are sobbing,
Mammon embraces its idol of gold.
'Mid the roar of the surf, and the thunder of breakers,
Awakes a loud cry like a hungry sea;
It comes from the hearts of "the million" truth seekers;
'Tis the voice of the people—the cry of the free!

Who can withstand it? who dares it shall perish!
We are cubs of the lions who battled of yore;
The fires that we kindle—the hopes that we cherish,
Are not to be crushed, or extinguished in gore.
Hope on, ye proud toilers, your sweat may be bloody,
Though lowly the flower, it will bloom in its time;
With Freedom your motto, and Virtue your study,
Your brows will be crowned with glory subline!

The Red Republican, 19 October 1850

L. T. Clancy

IMPROMPTU

Two Quakers once in Conference[1] elate
   One wore his hat the other sat without it
To prove the hypocrite, sham friend, complete—;
   What two could go a better way about it?

One loved his spotless tile, and would not doff
  The emblem of his creed; he feigned no barter;
The other less politely scampered off—;
  Lest his broad brim should cradle up the Charter!

                   The Northern Star and Leeds General Advertiser, 25 March 1843

Charles Cole

THE STRENGTH OF TYRANNY

The tyrants chains are only strong
  While slaves submit to wear them;
And, who could bind them on the throng
  Determin'd not to bear them?
Then clank your chains! e'en though the links
  Were light as fashion's feather,
The heart, which rightly feels and thinks,
  Would cast them altogether.

The lords of earth are only great
  While others clothe and feed them!
But, what were all their pride and state
  Should labour cease to heed them?
The swain is higher than a king:
  Before the Laws of Nature
The monarch were a worthless thing,
  The swain—a useful creature.

We toil, we spin, we delve the mine,
  Sustaining each his neighbour:
And, who can show a right divine
  To rob us of our labour?
We rush to battle—bear the lot
  In every ill and danger—
And, who shall make the peaceful cot
  To homely joy a stranger?

Perish all tyrants, far and near
  Beneath the chains that bind us:
And perish, too, that *servile fear*
  Which makes the slaves they find us,
One grand—one universal claim—
  One peal of moral thunder—
One glorious burst, in freedom's name,
  And rend our bonds asunder!

The Northern Star and National Trades Journal, 9 May 1846

THE POET'S LOVE OF LIBERTY

A boy—I dream'd of liberty;
A youth—I said, "But I am free?"
A man—I felt that slavery
  Had bound me in her chain;—
But yet the dream which, when a boy,
Was wont my musings to employ,
Fast rolling years could not destroy,
  With all their grief and pain.

No! still the thought that mocks control,
Whose only-rest is freedom's gaol,
Would mantling rise within my soul,
  Till every vein ran fire!
My spirit in a spell was bound—
The spell of an enchanting sound,
Which bade me wake, and breathe around,
  The murmurs of the lyre!

That spell is on my spirit still;
Yes, lovely freedom! yes, I will
The task by Heavens assigned fulfill.
  And wake the lyre for thee!
The dream of boyhood still is bright,
And bursting through oppressions night,
I see a radiant form of light—
  "Celestial Liberty!"

The Friend of the People, 12 April 1851

WHO MADE THE POOR?

Who made the poor?
Not He whose throne is heaven,
God: by whom earth was given,
And all that therein is, seed, herb, and tree;
And fowl that cleave the air, and fish that swim the sea;
And beast that range the field to man for food;
Not God the great and good,
Whose bounty's scattered o'er
The earth like grain on garner'd floor—
He did not make the poor!

But God made man,
Who bade the planets roll,
And formed the woundrous plan
That girds the eternal pole
Of Heaven, with world's illuming space;
He who to each assigned a place,
Gave man a reasoning soul,
And bade him stand on this terrestrial ball.
Sublime in his own form—erect, and lord of all.

Some traitors to their kind,
Whose tongues almost persuade
That night were day—have bent their mind
God gave them, to degrade
Their equals lower than the brute,
And threaten those who dare dispute
Their power, with dungeon gloom;
Yet, like a spirit from the tomb,
The voice of Nature rises still,
And while *one* good man lingers here,
Yet as it hath, it ever will;
And they who dread it shall revere
The sound of its eternal truth,
As in the earliness of youth
Ere Avarice lured the soul astray,
Or mad Ambition led the way
Through paths, whose ruggedness increase
To domes that never sheltered Peace.

Yes, yes, it shall be so;
　　The tyrant and the slave
In mutual hate, shall cease to go
　　On grappling to the grave.
　　Mind, wakening o'er the world,
　　　Uplifts the mental dart
Which, sudden as the lightning hurled,
　　Strikes to the trembling heart
Of pale oppression—deeper far
Than all the brands and bolts of war.
　　Let Reason give the word,
　　　Be that my millions spoken;
What, though the soldier grasp his sword
　　But as a weapon broken?
'Twould idle in his hand remain—
Pure bloodless battles Mind must gain.

　　Man hath been taught to bow
　　　To Cunning's traitorous sway;
But 'tis not as it hath been. Now
Behold the sturdy toiler's brow—
　　　There beams a calmer ray
Of purer intellectual fire,
Than lit the aspect of his sire;
A prouder glance that seems to say,
　　"The worse, our mental bounds are riven,
And soon shall dawn the glorious day,
　　We shall resume the gifts of Heaven."
For well he knows a sceptered King,
　　Or coronetted Lord
To be a rain, unwanted thing,
　　　Less worshipped than abhorred—
To be the enemy of toil,
All locost, like a thing of spoil;
And passing by the guarded door,
　　Where stalks the well-lashed sentinel,
Need not be told "Who made the Poor;"
　　　The fears of those within who dwell,
　　　If 'twere not known, the tale would tell.

The day will come, it must advance;
But not at point of sword or lance,
'Mid pealing shot nor spreading flame

And deeds of dread too dark to name—
Intelligence shall in its might,
And not in vain assert the right
Of labour by its toil to live,
Enjoying more than tyrants give.
Labour creates the wealth it craves,
Enweaves the cradles, shapes the graves;
Erects the palace, rears the tomb
Where despots live or lie in gloom.
God's handmaid Labour yet shall learn,
All power usurped by Pride to spurn;
To wish and have, to *will* and make
Oppression yield for Justice sake;
She asks but that: her ceaseless cry,
  In hut or hall, on heath or moor,
Is Justice—ere her children die
  Through want—from those who made the Poor.

The Northern Star and National Trades Journal, 4 January 1851

Thomas Cooper

THE LION OF FREEDOM

The lion of freedom comes from his den,
We'll rally around him again and again,
We'll crown him with laurels our champion to be,
O'Connor, the patriot of sweet liberty.

The pride of the nation, he's noble and brave
He's the terror of tyrants, the friend of the slave,
The bright star of freedom, the noblest of men,
We'll rally around him again and again.

Though proud daring tyrants his body confined,
They never could alter his generous mind;
We'll hail our caged lion, now free from his den,
And we'll rally around him again and again.

Who strove for the patriots? was up night and day?
And saved them from falling to tyrants a prey?
It was Feargus O'Connor was diligent then!
We'll rally around him again and again

The Northern Star and Leeds General Advertiser, 11 September 1841

SONNETS ON THE DEATH OF ALLEN DAVENPORT

By a Brother Bard and Shoemaker

Glory! O glory to the truly great,
  Who when death comes, can die as all should die;
  A conscience pure—their crowning victory!
And none who knew bestowing blame or hate;
  These are they who deserve our homage high,
Heroes—how low so e'er have been their state—
On whom the best encomiums should await,
  So noble 'tis to die right manfully!
And like a MAN has Davenport not died?
  Some kind friends min'string to his last few needs,
And he so calm—so inwardly fortified—
His last thread drawn—his labour gone through quite—
  While the finish all the past exceeds,
For nothing yet appears to cause the least affright.

Yes, he of whom I speak, my humble friend,
  A poet, too, philosopher—and more;
  Thus to the last courageously him bore,
And made the honest always be his end.
What he had thought, and taught of, heretofore,
  Was now his turn to practise—to commend
By's own example. "See! if you'll attend."
  So might he say, "I go the road before!"
And now they'll take him where he wishes to be—[a]
  Even by to-morrow's mid-day, where the flowers
Will grow, as comes the Spring time, lovingly,
  And charming all, who wandering near, may know

The dust imprisoned there, had once the power—
Must as it is—the boldest truths to show.

The Northern Star and National Trades Journal, 5 December 1846

ᵃThe reader will remember some verses of the now departed Davenport, which were printed in the *Star* a few weeks ago, expressive of his wish to be buried in the Kensal Green Cemetery; in which he speaks (as descriptive of the scene) of
"The groups of flowers that sweet, yet gaudy, wave,
And breathing rich perfume from every grave."
Perhaps it is needless to say, that the allusion here made is to this circumstance.

DEDICATORY SONNET

TO THOMAS CARLYLE

Right noble age-fellow, whose speech and thought
  Proclaim thee other than the supple throng
  Who glide Life's custom-smoothëd path along,—
Prescription's easy slaves,—strangers to doubt,
Because they never think!—a lay untaught
  I offer thee. Receive the humble song,—
  A tribute of the feeble to the strong
Of inward ken,—for that the theme is fraught
With dreams of Reason's high enfranchisement.
  Illustrious Schiller's limner, unto thee
Mind's freedom must be precious,—or what lent
  His toil its light, and what fires thine? The free
Of soul with quenchless zeal must ever glow
To spread the freedom which their own minds know.

Stafford Gaol, 3 May 1845

THOMAS COOPER

THE PURGATORY OF SUICIDES

BOOK THE FIRST

I.

Slaves, toil no more! Why delve, and moil, and pine,
To glut the tyrant-forgers of your chain?
Slaves, toil no more! Up, from the midnight mine,
Summon your swarthy thousands to the plain;
Beneath the bright sun marshalled, swell the strain
Of liberty; and, while the lordings view
Your banded hosts, with sticken heart and brain,
Shout, as one man,—'Toil we no more renew,
Until the Many cease their slavery to the Few!'

II.

'We'll crouch, and toil, and weave, no more—to weep!'
Exclaim your brothers from the weary loom:
Yes, now, they swear, with one resolve, dread, deep,
'We'll toil no more—to win a pauper's doom!'
And, while the millions swear, fell Famine's gloom
Spreads from their haggard faces like a cloud
Big with the fear and darkness of the tomb.
How, 'neath its terrors, are the tyrants bowed!
Slaves, toil no more—to starve! Go forth and tame the Proud!

III.

And why not tame them all? Of more than clay
Do your high lords proclaim themselves? Of blood
Illustrious boast they? or, that reason's ray
Beams from the brows of Rollo's robber-brood[1]
More brightly than from yours? Let them make good
Their vaunt of nobleness—or now confess
The majesty of ALL! Raise *ye* the feud—
Not, like their sires, to murder and possess;
But for unbounded power to gladden and to bless.

IV.

What say ye,—that the priests proclaim content?
So taught their Master, who the hungry fed
As well as taught; who wept with men, and bent,
In gentleness and love, o'er bier and bed
Where wretchedness was found, until it fled?

Rebuked he not the false ones, till his zeal
Drew down their hellish rage upon his head?
And who, that yearns for world-spread human weal,
Doth not, ere long, the weight of priestly vengeance feel?

V.

Away!—the howl of wolves in sheep's disguise
Why suffer ye to fill your ears?—their pride
Why suffer ye to stalk before your eyes?
Behold, in pomp, the purple prelate ride,
And, on the beggar by his chariot's side
Frown sullenly, although in rags and shame
His brother cries for food! Up, swell the tide
Of retribution, till ye end the game
Long practised by sleek priests in old Religion's name.

VI.

Slaves, toil no more! Despite their boast, ev'n kings
Must cease to sit in pride,—without your toil:
Spite of their sanctity,—the surpliced things
Who through all time, have thirsted to embroil
Man with his neighbour, and pollute the soil
Of holiest mother Earth with brother's gore,—
Join but to fold your hands, and ye will foil
To utter helplessness,—yea, to the core
Strike their pale craft with paler death! Slaves, toil no more!—

VII.

For that these words of truth I boldly spake
To Labour's children in their agony
Of want and insult; and, like men awake
After drugg'd slumbers, they did wildly flee
To do they knew not what,—until, with glee,
The cellar of a Christian priest they found,
And with its poison fired their misery
To mad revenge,—swift hurling to the ground
And flames—bed, cassock, wine-cups of the tipler gowned;

VIII.

For that I boldly spake these words of truth;
And the starved multitude,—to fury wrought
By sense of injury, and void of ruth,—
Rushed forth to deeds of recklessness, but nought

Achieved of freedom, since, nor plan, nor thought
Their might directed; for this treason foul
'Gainst evil tyrants, I was hither brought
A captive,—'mid the vain derisive howl
Of some who thought the iron now should pierce my soul.

The Purgatory of Suicides: A Prison Rhyme in Ten Books, 3rd ed. (London:
Chapman and Hall, 1853)

Allen Davenport

THE POET'S HOPE

The savage who can dig and plant his field,
And reap the fruits that his own labours yield;
With liberty to wander where he wills,
To trudge the valleys, or to climb the hills.
No law of trespass—no notices—"Beware!"
No steel traps, nor spring guns are planted there.
And though obscure, and to the world unknown,
The mountain goddess claims him for her own.
Nor steward, nor proctor, rent, nor tithes demand,
No TYRANT LANDLORD drives him from his land.
He feels more happy in his mountain cave,
And breathes more free than the poor white-skinned slave,
Who like the brute is doomed to bear his load,
Nor dares to wander from the common road;
His law and master claims a right divine,
And writes up everywhere—*"These fields are mine?"*

    And yet, I see, or fancy that I see,
Through the dark vista of futurity,
A glimmering light, a sort of "milky way,"
A shadowy twilight of a brighter day—
A day when every working man shall know,
Who is his truest friend and who his foe—
A day of *union* and of moral might—
A day of justice, truth, and human right—

A day when working men of every state,
Shall feel as brothers in their common fate—
A day when nations shall join heart and hand,
To drive the proud usurpers from the land—
A day when Poland shall again be free,
And plant her fields with trees of liberty!

30 March 1846

The Northern Star and National Trade Journal, 11 April 1846

IRELAND IN CHAINS

AIR—"MARSEILLAISE HYMN"

Rise, Britons, rise! with indignation,—
Hark, hark!! I hear the clanking chains,
That bind a brave and generous nation,
Where martial law and terror reign;
Her gallant sons demand assistance
Can British hearts refuse the call?
Behold them struggling for existence,
Shall Ireland, or her tyrants fall?
    See! see! the fiends of war
    Have seized on Liberty;
    Then rise, as one man declare,
    That Ireland shall be free!

Arise; and with a voice of thunder
Proclaim amidst the clashing storm,
That you to burst her chains asunder
Will meet the foe in every form.
What though the cannon point before ye,
And dungeons gape on every hand;
Unite! and put down Whig and Tory,
'Tis time the people should command.
    Dishonour'd be the grave
    Of him who quits the field;
    But crowns of glory to the brave,
    Who nobly scorns to yield.

Will you desert the Irish nation,
And see her wear her chains again,
Because her *Chief* spurns all relation
with *England* and with *Englishmen?*
No! Britons, no! do not desert her,
Return, for every evil, good,
You who hold dear the People's Charter,
And who would seal it with your blood!
    Then raise your voice, ye brave!
    She is your sister still—
    And if you have not power to save,
    Show that you have the will.

The Northern Star and National Trades Journal, 25 April 1846

THE IRON GOD

Hail! Glorious offspring of the human mind,
Thou great regenerator of mankind;
With thee the march of intellect began,
To thee we owe the moral power of man,
Which like the current of the mighty Thames,
Swells as it rolls fed by a thousand streams;
That moral power, which tyrants now must feel,
Cannot be bound by chains or crushed with steel!
What greater gift to man could genius give?
What greater favour could mankind receive?
From thee all languages the live and dead,
Receive the stamp which makes them read;
From thee the mental treasures of the soul,
Receive their wings and fly from pole to pole;
What are *the powers that be,* who hold the rod,
Compared with thee, thou mighty *Iron God!*
'Tis thou, omnipotent! must set us free,
What miracles have not been wrought by thee?
All eyes are on, all hopes are in the press;
Let that be free—and who can doubt success?
Armed with the scales of justice, and the rod,
It lashes folly, tyranny, and fraud;
Repels oppression with the might of Jove,
And causes human systems to improve;

Stamps immortality on honest fame,
And brands the villain with eternal shame!
The genius of the press shall yet prevail,
And conquer where the boldest armies fail;
For despots, though *united*, feel distress,
And tremble when the thunder of the press,
Rolls through their kingdoms in the civil storm,
Proclaiming justice, freedom, and reform.

June 1846

The Northern Star and National Trades Journal, 4 July 1846

Ebenezer Elliott

CORN-LAW RHYMES

SONG

TUNE—*"The Land o' the Leal."*

Where the poor cease to pay,
   Go, loved one, and rest!
Thou art wearing away
   To the land of the blest.
Our father is gone
   Where the wrong'd are forgiven,
And that dearest one,
   Thy husband, in heaven.

No toil in despair,
   No tyrant, no slave,
No bread-tax is there,
   With a maw like the grave.

But the poacher, thy pride,
   Whelm'd in ocean afar;
And his brother, who died
   Land-butcher'd in war;

And their mother, who sank
   Broken-hearted to rest;
And the baby, that drank
   'Till it froze on her breast;
With tears, and with smiles,
   Are waiting for thee,
In the beautiful isles
   Where the wrong'd are the free.

Go, loved one, and rest
   Where the poor cease to pay!
To the land of the blest
   Thou art wearing away;
But the son of thy pain
   Will yet stay with me,
And poor little Jane
   Look sadly like thee.

SONG

TUNE—*"Robin Adair."*

Child, is thy father dead?
   Father is gone!
Why did they tax his bread?
   God's will be done!
Mother has sold her bed;
Better to die than wed!
Where shall she lay her head?
   Home we have none!

Father clamm'd thrice a week—
God's will be done!
Long for work did he seek,
   Work he found none.
Tears on his hollow cheek
Told what no tongue could speak:
Why did his master break?
   God's will be done!

Doctor said air was best—
   Food we had none;
Father, with panting breast,

Groan'd to be gone:
Now he is with the blest—
Mother says death is best!
We have no place of rest—
    Yes, ye have one!

To all who revere the Memory of Jeremy Bentham, our second Locke, and
wish to promote the greatest happiness of the greatest number for the greatest
length of time, I inscribe these "Corn-Law Rhymes."

REFORM

Too long endured, a power and will,
That would be nought, or first in ill,
Had wasted wealth, and palsied skill,
    And fed on toil-worn poverty.

They call'd the poor a rope of sand;
And, lo! no rich man's voice or hand
Was raised, throughout the suffering land
    Against their long iniquity.

They taught the self-robb'd sons of pride
To turn from toil and want aside,
And coin their hearts, guilt-petrified,
    To buy a smile from infamy.

The philter'd lion yawn'd in vain,
While o'er his eyes, and o'er his mane,
They hung a picklock, mask, and chain—
    True emblems of his dignity.

They murder'd Hope, they fetter'd Trade;
The clouds to blood, the sun to shade,
And every good that God had made
    They turned to bane and mockery.

Love, plant of Heaven, and sent to show
One bliss divine to earth below,
Changed by their frown, bore crime and woe,
    And breathed, for fragrance, pestilence.

With Freedom's plume, and Honour's gem,
They deck'd Abaddon's[1] diadem,
And call'd on hell to shout for them,
      The holiest name of holiness.

They knew no interest but their own;
They shook the State, they shook the Throne,
They shook the world; and God alone
      Seem'd safe in his omnipotence.

Did then his thunder rend the skies,
To bid the dead in soul arise?—
The dreadful glare of sullen eyes
      Alone warn'd cruel tyranny!

A murmur from a trampled worm,
A whisper in the cloudless storm—
Yet these, even these, announced Reform;
      And Famine's scowl was prophecy!

Nor then remorse, nor tardy shame,
Nor love of praise, nor dread of blame,
But tongues of fire, and words of flame,
      Roused Mammon[2] from his apathy.

At length, a MAN to Mercia[3] spoke!
From smitten hearts the lightning broke;
The slow invincible awoke;
      And England's frown was victory!

O years of crime! The great and true—
The nobly wise—are still the few,
Who bid Truth grow where Falsehood grew,
      And plant it for eternity!

LINES

WRITTEN IN AN EDITION OF COLLINS, WITH ETCHINGS BY PLATT.

Struck blind in youth, Platt ask'd the proud for bread;
He ask'd in vain, and sternly join'd the dead.
I saw him weep—"Hail, holy light!" he cried;

But living darkness heard him, and he died.
Oh, by the light that left too soon his eyes,
And bade him starve on ice-cold charities;
Doom'd is the wealth that cold no pittance spare,
To save benighted genius from despair!

These etchings, Platt, alone remain of thee!
How soon, alas! e'en these will cease to be!
But poesy hath flowers that ever bloom;
And music, though she seal'd thy cruel doom,[a]
Shall sing a ballad o'er her pupil's tomb.

[a]The unfortunate artist, having lost his sight, attempted to learn music for subsistence. A concert, which he advertised, failed, and the cup ran over.

BATTLE SONG

Day, like our souls, is fiercely dark;
   What then? 'Tis day!
We sleep no more; the cock crows—hark!
   To arms! away!
They come! they come! the knell is rung
   Of us or them;
Wide o'er their march the pomp is flung
   Of gold and gem.
What collar'd hound of lawless sway,
   To famine dear—
What pension'd slave of Attila,
   Leads in the rear?
Come they from Scythian wilds afar,
   Our blood to spill?
Wear they the livery of the Czar?
   They do his will.
Nor tassell'd silk, nor epaulette,
   Nor plume, nor torse—
No splendour gilds, all sternly met,
   Our foot and horse.
But, dark and still, we inly glow,
   Condensed in ire!
Strike, tawdry slaves, and ye shall know
   Our gloom is fire.

In vain your pomp, ye evil powers,
   Insults the land;
Wrongs, vengeance, and *the cause* are ours,
   And God's right hand!
Madmen! they trample into snakes
   The wormy clod!
Like fire, beneath their feet awakes
   The sword of God!
Behind, before, above, below,
   They rouse the brave;
Where'er they go, they make a foe,
   Or find a grave.

THE REVOLUTION OF 1832

See, the slow Angel writhes in dreams of pain!
   His check indignant glows!
Like Stanedge, shaking thunder from his mane,
   He starts from his repose.
Wide, wide, his earthquake-voice is felt and heard;
   "Arise, ye brave and just!"
The living sea is to its centre stirr'd—
   And, lo! our foes are dust!
The earth beneath the feet of millions quakes;
   The whirlwind-cloud is riv'n;
As midnight, smitten into lightning, wakes,
   So waked the sword of Heav'n.
The angel drew not from its sheath that sword:
   He spake, and all was done!
Night fled away before the Almighty word,
   And, lo!—the sun! the sun!

The Poetical Works of Ebenezer Elliott, ed. Edwin Elliott (London: Henry S. King and Co., 1876), vol. 1.

EXTRACT FROM A PREFACE TO A FORMER EDITION

I thank the readers of my two first volumes. They are, I believe, mostly poor people, who would have bought more of my books, if they had not wanted bread; and the sale, I have no doubt, will keep pace exactly with their progress in knowledge, virtue, and freedom. I know not whether my publisher is satisfied—I trust he is; but for myself, I am sufficiently rewarded, if my poetry has led one poor despairing victim of misrule from the ale-house to the fields; if I have been chosen of God to show his desolated heart, that, though his wrongs have been heavy and his fall deep, and though the spoiler is yet abroad, still in the green lanes of England the primrose is blowing, and on the mountain top the lonely fir pointing with her many fingers to our Father in heaven—to Him, whose wisdom is at once inscrutable and indubitable, and to whom ages are as a moment—to Him who has created another and a better world for all who act nobly or suffer unjustly here; a world of river-feeding mountains, to which the oak will come in his strength, and the ash in her beauty—of chiming streams, and elmy vales, where the wild flowers of our country, and, among them, the little daisy, will not refuse to bloom.

HYMN

WRITTEN FOR THE PRINTERS OF SHEFFIELD

Lord! taught by Thee, when Caxton[1] bade
  His silent words for ever speak;
A grave for tyrants then was made,
  Then crack'd the chain which yet shall break.

For bread, for bread, the all-scorn'd man,
  With study worn, his press prepared;
And knew not, Lord, thy wondrous plan,
  Nor what he did, nor what he dared.

When first the might of deathless thought
  Impress'd his all-instructing page,
Unconscious giant! how he smote
  The fraud and force of many an age!

Pale wax'd the harlot, fear'd of thrones,
  And they who bought her harlotry:
He shook the throned on dead men's bones,
  He shakes—all evil yet to be!

The pow'r He grasp'd let none disdain;
  It conquer'd once, and conquers still;
By fraud and force assail'd in vain,
  It conquer'd erst, and ever will.

It conquers here! the fight is won!
  We thank thee, Lord, with many a tear!
For many a not unworthy son
  Of Caxton does thy bidding here.

We help ourselves, thy cause we aid;
  We build for Heav'n, beneath the skies:
And bless Thee, Lord, that Thou hast made
  Our daily bread of tyrants' sighs.

THE PRIMROSE

Surely that man is pure in thought and deed,
Whom spirits teach in breeze-borne melodies;
For he finds tongue in every flower and weed,
And admonition in mute harmonies;
Erect he moves, by truth and beauty led,
And climbs his throne, for such a monarch meet,
To gaze on valleys, that, around him spread,
Carpet the hall of heav'n beneath his feet.
How like a trumpet, under all the skies
Blown, to convene all forms that love his beams,
Light speaks in splendour to the poet's eyes,
O'er dizzy rocks and woods, and headlong streams!
How like the voice of woman, when he sings.

To her beloved, of love and constancy,
The vernal odours, o'er the murmurings
Of distant waters, pour their melody
Into his soul, mix'd with the throstle's song
And the wren's twitter? Welcome then, again,
Love-glistening primrose; though not parted long,
We meet, the lovers, after years of pain.
Oh, thou bring'st blissful childhood back to me!
Thou still art loveliest in the lonest place;
Still, as of old, day glows with love for thee,

And reads our heav'nly Father in thy face.
Surely thy thoughts are humble and devout,
Flower of the pensive gold! for why should heav'n
Deny to thee his noblest boon of thoughts,
If to earth's demigods 'tis vainly given?
Answer me, sinless sister! Thou hast speech
Though silent. Fragrance is thy eloquence,
Beauty thy language; and thy smile might teach
Ungrateful man to pardon Providence.

Alone, beneath the sky,
    I stood the storm before:
No! God, the Storm, and I—
    We trode the desert floor;
High on the mountain sod,
    The whirlwind's dwellingplace,
The Worm, the Storm, and God
    Were present, face to face.
From earth a shadow brake,
    E'en where my feet had trode;
The shadow laugh'd and spake
    And shook his hand at God.
Then up it rear'd its head;
    Beneath the lightning's blaze;
"Omnipotent!"   it said,
    "Bring back my yesterdays."
God smiled the gloom away;
    Wide earth and heav'n were bright;
In light my shadow lay,
    I stood with God in light;
With Him who wings the storm,
    Or bids the storm be still,
The shadow of a worm
    I Ield converse on the hill.

ANTICIPATION

Hail, Realm of gloom! whose clouds are ice! whose air
    Is made of thought-sick sighs!
Whose fields are dead men's dust, from which despair
    Shrinks as he dies!

Though on thee, and within (sad Infinite!)
   Are darkness, death, and doom;
Beyond thee shines the sun of mind and might,
The Power that made thee, God—hail, Holy Light!
   I come, I come.

PRESTON MILLS

The day was fair, the cannon roar'd,
   Cold blew the bracing north,
And Preston's Mills, by thousands, pour'd
   Their little captives forth.

All in their best they paced the street,
   All glad that they were free;
And sung a song with voices sweet—
   They sung of Liberty!

But from their lips the rose had fled,
   Like "death-in-life" they smiled;
And still, as each pass'd by, I said,
   Alas! is that a child?

Flags waved, and men—ghastly crew—
   March'd with them, side by side:
While, hand in hand, and two by two,
   They moved—a living tide.

Thousands and thousands—all so white!—
   With eyes so glazed and dull!
O God! it was indeed a sight
   Too sadly beautiful!

And, oh, the pang their voices gave
   Refuses to depart!
This is a wailing for the grave!
   I whisper'd to my heart.

It was as if, where roses blush'd,
   A sudden blasting gale,

O'er fields of bloom had rudely rush'd,
  And turn'd the roses pale.

It was as if, in glen and grove,
  The wild birds sadly sung;
And every linnet mourn'd its love.
  And every thrush its young.

It was as if, in dungeon gloom,
  Where chain'd despair reclined,
A sound came from the living tomb,
And hymn'd the passing wind.

And while they sang, and though they smiled,
  My soul groan'd heavily—
O who would be or have a child?
  A mother who would be?

FAMINE IN A SLAVE SHIP

They stood on the deck of the slave-freighted barque,
All hopeless, all dying, while waited the shark;
Sons, Fathers, and Mothers, who shriek'd as they press'd
The infants that pined till they died on the breast—
A crowd of sad mourners, who sigh'd to the gale,
While on all their dark faces the darkness grew pale.

White demons beheld them, with curse and with frown,
And cursed them, from morn till the darkness came down;

And knew not compassion, but laugh'd at their pray'r,
When they called on their God, or wept loud in despair;
Till again rose the morn, and all hush'd was the wail,
And on cheeks stark and cold the grim darkness was pale.

Then the white heartless demons, with curse and with frown,
Gave the dead to the deep, till the darkness came down:
But the angel who blasteth, unheard and unseen,
Bade the tyrants lie low where their victims had been:
And down dropp'd the waves, and stone-still hung the sail,
And black sank the dead, while more pale grew the pale.

Stern angel, how calmly his chosen he slew!
And soon the survivors were fearfully few;
For, wall'd o'er their heads the red firmament stood,
And the sun saw his face in a mirror of blood;
Till they fed on each other, and drank of the sea,
And wildly cursed God in their madness of glee!

What hand sweeps the stars from the cheek of the night?
Who lifts up the sea in the wrath of his might?
Why, down from his glance, shrinks in horror the shark?
Why stumbles o'er mountains the blind foodless barque?
Lo, his lightning speaks out, from the growl of the gale!
And shrieking she sinks—while the darkness turns pale!

THE DYING BOY TO THE SLOE BLOSSOM

Before thy leaves thou com'st once more,
    White blossom of the sloe!
Thy leaves will come as heretofore;
But this poor heart, is troubles o'er,
    Will then lie low.

A month at least before thy time
    Thou com'st, pale flower, to me;
For well thou know'st the frosty rime
Will blast me ere my vernal prime,
    No more to be.

The Poetical Works of Ebenezer Elliott, vol. 2

Alfred Fennel

THE RED FLAG

air—"dark loch na gar"

'Tis in the Red Flag true Republicans glory;
   Red is the emblem of Justice and Right—
By martyrs blood dyed, whose names live in story;
   The victors, though fallen, in Liberty's fight.
Fast flow our tears for the fetter'd and slaughter'd;
   And exiles who wander o'er valley and crag.
Too long has the earth by tyrants been tortured;
   They shall crouch yet, and cower, before our Red Flag!

Away to the winds with the cant "moderation!"
   Mercy is not with king, tiger, or snake,
Crush to the dust as they've crush'd each nation
   In the day of our triumph, kings tremble and quake.
"Mercy!" yes, *Mercy* such as *they* gave us
   Such we'll return, and throneless we'll drag
From their high places those who enslave us,
   To bow—mean and abject—before our Red Flag!

"Mercy!" whilst Haynau[1] riots in murder,
   And tiger-like, gloats o'er the blood of mankind;
While the serfs of the Czar[2] poor Poland engirder—
   The betrayers of France Rome's chains[3] again bind—
Sicily crush'd 'neath the Bourbon lies bleeding—
   And Hungary curses the Austrian rag,
The nations oppress'd pray the time may be speeding
   When in triumph and glory shall fly our Red Flag!

That glad time shall come, kings; though patriots you slaughter,
   Fresh legions shall rise for the martyrs who fall.
Through tempests and sunshine the nations have fought for
   Fair Freedom, benignant, who yet shall bless all;

Then we'll remember wrongs despots have wrought us.
  Of their "Right divine" power no more shall they brag.
"Moderation" is madness, (experience hath taught us,)
  When at Freedom's next summons we hoist the Red Flag!

The Democratic Review of British and Foreign Politics, History and Literature,
April 1850

Edwin Gill

THE CHARTER FOR EVER SHALL WEATHER THE STORM

AIR—"OLD ENGLAND FOR EVER SHALL WEATHER THE STORM"

O Freedom! thy absence has long been lamented,
  And thy sons now have set all their hopes on the sea,
In a bark called the Charter—for liberty bound,
  The port where the millions are happy and free.

Though the darkness of night may at present surround us,
  The clouds shall disperse—and appear the bright morn;
And thou, blessed freedom, shall tell the glad story—
  The Charter for ever shall weather the storm.

Our captain, O'Connor, was ever true to us,
  And our bark has the stars for her compass and guide,
Whilst our crew are a set of sterling brave fellows,
  Who laugh at the storm, and its fury deride.

Then hurrah for the Charter, the good ship we sail in,
  'Till the waves shall engulf us, no fears shall deform;
But like a sea-bird, her whole voyage shall be glorious—
  The Charter for ever shall weather the storm.

Though the quicksands of "Humbug"[1] are laid in our way,
  And "Tyrannical rocks"[2] oppose us in our course;
Though "Treacherous blasts"[3] our tight bark are assailing,
  Triumphant she sails, nor shrink we from their force.

Oh! no! for each heart is with pure freedom burning,
   "No surrender"[4] our cry, while we treat foes with scorn;
And hark! the high heavens re-echo the cry—
   The Charter for ever shall weather the storm!

Sheffield

The Northern Star and Leeds General Advertiser, 29 October 1842

AN ODE

Oh, shame to the land of the free,
   Whose children submit to be slaves,
Who basely to tyranny bend the vile knee,
   Or sink to their ignoble graves.
The scorn of the just and the good,
   Shall for ever cling to the isle;
The cry of the widow and orphan for food
   Shall greet thee, instead of their smile;
And thy glory and greatness descend to the tomb,
   Unmourn'd and forgot in futurity's gloom.

Ah! where is the spirit of old,
   That burnt in the breasts of your sires,
When, with giant might, and with freedom bold,
   They cherish'd pure liberty's fires?
When freedom's flag floated on high,
   And justice and truth were unfurl'd.
Liberty or death was their battle cry,
   'Midst the cheers and praise of the world;
And their falchions flash'd fire, and the steel clank'd loud,
And the crimson-tide stain'd the false foeman's shroud.

Awake! arouse from thy slumbers,
   Throw aside delusions's dark veil,
Join the ranks of the brave in your numbers,
   And the "good old cause" shall prevail.
Hurl tyranny down from its throne,
   Raise Liberty up in its stead;
And your sons with pride will their fathers own,
   And their mem'ries bless when dead.

Then hail the bright banner of sweet Liberty!
All hail to the Charter, the right of the Free!

Sheffield

The Northern Star and Leeds General Advertiser, 22 April 1843

George Julian Harney

"ALL MEN ARE BRETHREN"

A Song for the Fraternal Democrats

Hail to the flag of Fraternity flying,
  "Nail'd to the mast" our bright banner waves,
Kingly and lordly brigands defying,
  Breaking our fetters, we scorn to be slaves.
      From the north to the southward,
      The east to the westward,
  The union rally-cry ring near and far;
      Till all the nations, round,
      Till the whole earth resound,
  "All Men are Brethren! hip! hip! Hurrah!"

By the scourge of oppressors long we've been driven,
  Long have we bent 'neath the yoke and the chain;
Our labour, our blood, our lives have been given
  To pamper the tyrants who scoff at our pain.
      The earth they have plunder'd,
      Mankind they have sunder'd,
Nation 'gainst nation excited to war.
      But no more disunited,
      Our wrongs shall be righted,
  "All Men are Brethren! hip! hip! Hurrah!"

Tremble, ye purple-clad, princely oppressors;
  Woe to ye, haughty and gold-grasping lords;
Curs'd be your false-hearted priestly abettors—
  More fatal their frauds than your blood-reeking swords.

Like the cataract dashing,
The avalanche crashing,
The on-rushing millions shall scatter you far.
Like the hurricane roaring,
Their voices are soaring:
"All Men are Brethren! hip! hip! Hurrah!"

As Bright as the sky when the tempest is ended,
As fair as the earth when the winter is o'er—
Shall glory and freedom for ever be blended,
When the dark freezing reign of oppression's no more,
The happy communion,
Of nations in union,
The serpent of selfishness never shall mar.
Then sing, brothers, sing,
Let the chorus loud ring,
"All Men are Brethren! hip! hip! Hurrah!"

The Northern Star and National Trades Journal, 19 September 1846

William Hick

THE PRESENTATION OF THE NATIONAL PETITION, AND THE MOTION OF MR. DUNCOMBE

Hark to the cause of liberty!
The "dead" are awaken'd again!
The voice of the people is heard to be free
O'er mountain, and valley, and plain.
Full nobly, they stir them to save
The exil'd, and prisoners dear;
Once more, their petition has gone for the brave,
And liberty gives them a cheer;
For the "fustians"[1] have sworn, in the power of their might,
To win them their freedom or die in the fight.

Full boldly they enter the hall,
Their escort all gallant and gay,
With the shout of that people whom Whigs would enthral:

'Tis the voice they are call'd to obey!
Each senator rush'd to the spot,
   Impell'd by a magical fear,
The "prayer" of the people whose claims are forgot,
   To behold in its grandeur appear.
Then Duncombe[1] obedient directed its way,
And bravely our "fustians" the summons obey.

In the House[2] the "petition" 's unfurl'd,
   And there is it treated with scorn;
The hopes of the millions—the pride of the world—
   Again are insulted and torn.
The logic of fools is display'd,
   Their multiplied follies to screen;
The baseness of faction, of justice afraid,
   All "mercy" ascribe to the Queen.
With malice and subterfuge bolting secure
The dungeons our patriot-hearts must endure.

Oh, where is the justice of old?
   The spirit of Alfred the great?[3]
Ere the throne was debas'd by corruption and gold,
   When the people were one with the state?
'Tis gone with our freedom to vote;
   'Tis under each despot's control;
And now, e'en the right to petition is naught;
   A farce and a mock'ry the whole,
O shade of the honour'd and patriot king,
Thy mantle o'er modern royalty fling!

But joy' to the "fustians" who sign'd!
   And joy to the glorious "eighteen"!
And joy be to him in whose heart we're enshrin'd,
   Though a barrier of bolts is between;
For time on its quick-paced wing,
   The might of the future shall tell;
When down to the dust the base factions we'll bring,
   And destroy the corruptions of hell.
For the law of each country our Charter must be,
Till all ends of the earth shall be happy and free.

Leeds, June 1841

The Northern Star and Leeds General Advertiser, 5 June 1841

"It was borne to the House on the shoulders of eighteen "fustian jackets,"[4] who performed their duty well-preceded by a procession of the members of the Convention, and other leading Chartists, amidst the deafening shouts of congregated thousands."

The Northern Star n.d.

Thomas Hood

THE SONG OF THE SHIRT

With fingers weary and worn,
  With eyelids heavy and red,
A Woman sat, in unwomanly rags,
  Plying her neddle and thread—
    Stitch! stitch! stitch!
In poverty, hunger and dirt,
  And still with a voice of dolorous pitch
She sang the 'Song of the Shirt!'

'Work! work! work!
While the cock is crowing aloof!
  And work—work—work
Till the stars shine through the roof!
It's O! to be a slave
  Along with the barbarous Turk,
Where woman has never a soul to save,
  If this is Christian work!

'Work—work—work
Till the brain begins to swim;
  Work—work—work
Till the eyes are heavy and dim!
Seam, and gusset, and band,
  Band, and gusset, and seam,
    Till over the buttons I fall asleep,
  And sew them on in a dream!

'O! Men, with Sisters dear!
  O! Men! with Mothers and Wives!

It is not linen you're wearing out,
 But human creatures' lives!
  Stitch—stitch—stitch,
 In poverty, hunger, and dirt,
Sewing at once, with a double thread,
 A Shroud as well as a Shirt.

'But why do I talk of Death?
 That Phantom of grisly bone,
I hardly fear his terrible shape,
 It seems so like my own—
 It seems so like my own,
 Because of the fasts I keep,
Oh! God! that bread should be so dear,
 And flesh and blood so cheap!

'Work—work—work!
 My labour never flags;
And what are its wages? A bed of straw,
 A crust of bread—and rags.
That shatter'd roof—and this naked floor—
 A table—a broken chair—
And a wall so blank, my shadow I thank
 For sometimes falling there!

'Work—work—work!
From weary chime to chime,
 Work—work—work—
As prisoners work for crime!
 Band, and gusset, and seam,
 Seam, and gusset, and band,
Till the heart is sick, and the brain benumb'd,
 As well as the weary hand.

 'Work—work—work,
In the dull December light,
 And work—work—work,
When the weather is warm and bright—
 While underneath the eaves
 The brooding swallows cling
As if to show me their sunny backs
 And twit me with the spring.

'Oh! but to breathe the breath
Of the cowslip and primrose sweet—
    With the sky above my head,
And the grass beneath my feet,
For only one short hour
    To feel as I used to feel,
Before I knew the woes of want
    And the walk that costs a meal!

'Oh, but for one short hour!
    A respite however brief!
No blessed leisure for Love or Hope,
    But only time for Grief!
A little weeping would ease my heart,
    But in their briny bed
My tears must stop, for every drop
    Hinders needle and thread!'

With fingers weary and worn,
    With eyelids heavy and red,
A Woman sate in unwomanly rags,
    Plying her needle and thread—
        Stitch! stitch! stitch!
    In poverty, hunger, and dirt,
And still with a voice of dolorous pitch,
Would that its tone could reach the Rich!
    She sang this 'Song of the Shirt!'

The Penguin Book of Socialist Verse, ed. Alan Bold (Middlesex, 1970)

Alexander Huish

THE RADICAL'S LITANY

From nobles that at court do sit,
to rule our land as they see fit,
Whom many a beggar could outwit,
    Good Lord deliver us.

From independent gentry, who
Consume our grain as locusts do,
And rob the labourer of his due,
      Good Lord deliver us.

From honours being conferred, all
Upon the rich, both great and small,
Though with skulls thick as China's wall,
      Good Lord deliver us.

From Church established by the law,
And tithes enforced to glut the maw
Of every idle strutting daw,
      Good Lord deliver us.

From bishops and all procurations,
Synodals and confirmations,
And every such like botheration,
      Good Lord deliver us.

From foul hypocrisy and cant,
And selfish minds of virtue scant,
And juggling Methodistic rant,
      Good Lord deliver us.

From that cursed thing the New Poor Act,
Which Tories sanction, Whigs exact,
Of hellish deeds the most compact,
      Good Lord deliver us.

From bullies, beadle, with their crew
Of hellish miscreants, Whig and Blue,
Whose greatest joy's the poor to screw,
      Good Lord deliver us.

From lawyers, policemen, and spies,
That deal in fraud, deceit, and lies,
Whose devilry the world outvies,
      Good Lord deliver us.

From suffrages of brick and mortar,
Likewise elective bribe and barter,

With all that's hostile to the Charter,
  Good Lord deliver us.

The Northern Star and Leeds General Advertiser, 20 February 1841

Iota

SONNETS DEVOTED TO CHARTISM

I

Once more I visit thee, sweet rural walk,
  'Tis long since last I came this pleasant way,
  And many a sad event hath had its day
In yonder little town since then. The talk
  Of all the empire it hath been. The gay
Have laughed—the sober heaved a heart-felt sigh
When Newport[1] hath been named. The tearful eye
Hath been its tribute o'er the grave to pay,
Where mothers, widows, sisters, brothers wept
O'er those who there in death untimely slept,
  The fallen brave!—fall'n in a glorious cause,
Howe'er mistaken in their way;—to gain
Their country's liberty they strove; though slain,
  Not fruitless was their fight, but worthy our applause.

Newport, Monmouthshire, May 1840

The Northern Star and Leeds General Advertiser, 9 May 1840

II

Even yet thou shalt not be unknown to fame—
  Some future bard shall sing thy triumph, SHELL![2]
  And all thy virtues, all thy worth shall tell.
Thy countrymen shall glory in thy name,
Thy fall reflects upon thy foes a shame
  Which ages shall not wipe away. The yell

That tyranny raised o'er thy ruined frame
   Hath sunk no more o'er murdered worth to swell.
Thy patriot spirit hovering o'er the land
   That gave thee birth, and far too soon a grave,
   In spite of all the tyrant's power shall have
The joy, e'er long, to see the glorious stand
   Which Walia—Scotia—England's slaves *can* make
   For Labour—Virtue—Honour—Freedom's sake!

The Northern Star and Leeds General Advertiser, 27 June 1840

III

Along this favorite walk was wont to wend,
   One of the noblest patriots of the age;
Each step I take reminds me of that friend
   Of man—and victim of the tyrant's rage.
   But late he wandered o'er this pleasant way,
   With heart-felt ardour for his country's weal,
And fond anticipations of the day
   When England's glory—*Freedom,* should be real.
When worth and virtuous labour should obtain
   Their rights untrammelled by oppression's law;
When men no more should be the slaves of gain,
   Nor infants die to fill the Moloch maw
Of despot lordlings—tyrants of the loom,
Who yearly hurt their thousands to th' untimely tomb.

Gold-tops, May 1840

The Northern Star and Leeds General Advertiser, 27 June 1840

VIII

Peace, plenty and content in peasant's cot,
   And closely-huddled houses of the poor,
   As well as in the palace, through whose door
It is the prince, the peer, the priest's proud lot
To tread. Strife, wrath, and rage being all forgot,
   And lost in love and concord evermore.
   Laws administered impartially o'er
All the land; being themselves without spot,
Or shadow of injustice. Magistrates

Extensively informed in all the laws,
    And men of soundest sense, free from the fear
Of man, which brings a "snare;" whom not applause
    Nor scorn would move from Virtue's stern career:
Such and superior good the patriot contemplates.

Newport, Monmouthshire

The Northern Star and Leeds General Advertiser, 15 August 1840

Ebenezer Jones

A COMING CRY

The few to whom the law hath given the earth God gives to all
Do tell us that for them alone its fruits increase and fall:
They tell us that by labour we may earn our daily bread,
But they take the labour for their engines that work on unfed.
And so we starve; and now the few have publish'd a decree—
Starve on, or eat in workhouses the crumbs of charity;
Perhaps it's better than starvation,—once we'll pray and then
We'll all go building workhouses, million, million men!

We'll all go building workhouses,—million, million hands,
So jointed wondrously by God, to work love's wise commands;
We'll all go building workhouses,—million, million minds,
By great God charter'd to condemn whatever harms or binds;
The God-given mind shall image, the God-given hand shall
    build
The prisons for God's children, by the earth-lords will'd;
Perhaps it's better than starvation, once we'll pray, and then
We'll all go building workhouses,—million, million men.

What'll we do with the workhouses? million, million men!
Shall we all lie down and madden, each in his lonely den?
What! we whose sires made Cressy! we, men of Nelson's mould!
We, of the Russells' country,—God's Englishmen the bold!
Will we, at earth's lord's bidding, build ourselves dishonour'd
    graves?

Will we who've made this England, endure to be its slaves?
Thrones totter before the answer!—once we'll pray, and then
We'll all go building workhouses, million, million men.

Kovalev, Y. V., ed. *An Anthology of Chartist Literature*

SONG OF THE KINGS OF GOLD

Ours all are marble halls,
Amid untrodden groves,
Where music ever calls,
Where faintest perfume roves;
And thousand toiling moan,
That gorgeous robes may fold
The haughty forms alone
Of us—the Kings of Gold.

CHORUS—We cannot count our slaves,
Nothing bounds our sway,
Our will destroys and saves,
We let, we create, we slay.
Ha! ha! who are Gods?

Purple, and crimson, and blue,
Jewels, and silk, and pearl,
All splendours of form and hue,
Our charm'd existence furl;
When dared shadow dim
The glow in our wine-cups roll'd?
When droop'd the banquet-hymn
Raised for the Kings of Gold?

The earth, the earth is ours!
Its corn, its fruits, its wine,
Its sun, its rain, its flowers,
Ours, all, all!—cannot shine
One sunlight ray but where
Our mighty titles hold;
Wherever life is, there
Possess the Kings of Gold.

And all on earth that lives,
Woman, and man, and child,
Us trembling homage gives;
Aye trampled, sport-defiled,
None dareth raise one frown,
Or slightest questioning hold;
Our scorn but strikes them down
To adore the Kings of Gold.

On beds of azure down,
In halls of torturing light,
Our poison'd harlots moan,
And burning toss in sight;
They are ours—for us they burn;
They are ours, to reject, to hold;
We taste—we exalt—we spurn—
For we are the Kings of Gold.

The father writhes a smile,
As we seize his red-lipp'd girl,
His white-loin'd wife; ay, while
Fierce millions burn, to hurl
Rocks on our regal brows,
Knives in our hearts to hold—
They pale, prepare them bows
At the step of the Kings of Gold.

In a glorious sea of hate,
Eternal rocks we stand;
Our joy is our lonely state,
And our trust our own right hand;
We frown, and nations shrink;
They curse, but our swords are old;
And the wine of their rage deep drink
The dauntless Kings of Gold.

CHORUS—We cannot count our slaves,
Nothing bounds our sway,
Our will destroys and saves,
We let, we create, we slay.
Ha! ha! who are Gods?

Kovalev, Y. V., ed. *An Anthology of Chartist Literature*

Ernest Jones

OUR SUMMONS

Men of the honest heart,
  Men of the stalwart hand,
Men, willing to obey,
  Thence able to command:

Men of the rights withheld,
  Slaves of the power abused,
Machines cast to neglect,
  When your freshness has been used.

Ye labourers in the vineyard,
  We call you to your toil!
Though bleak may be the furrows,
  The seed is in the soil.

'Tis not to raise a palace,
  Where Royalty may dwell,
Nor build for broken hearts
  The petty parish hell;

'Tis not to turn the engine,
  'Tis not the field to till,
That, for the meed *you* gain,
  Might be a desert still!

'Tis not to dig the grave,
  Where the dying miner delves;
'Tis *not* to toil for *others*
  But to labour for *yourselves*.

And nobler coin will pay you,
  Than Kings did e'er award

To the men, they hired to murder,
  The brothers they should guard.

No glittering stars of knighthood,
  Shall soil your simple vest—
But the better star of honour
  Brave heart in honest breast.

No changing Norman titles,
  To hide your English name—
But the better one of *freemen*,
  With its blazoning of fame.

Up! Labourers in the vineyard!
  Prepare ye for your toill
For the sun shines on the furrows,
  And the seed is in the soil.

Mount Vernon, Hampstead

The Northern Star and National Trades Journal, 16 May 1846

A CHARTIST CHORUS

Go! cotton lords and corn lords, go!
  Go! Ye live on loom and acre,
But let be seen—some law between
  The giver and the taker.

Go! treasure well your miser's store
  With crown, and cross, and sabre!
Despite you all—we'll break your thrall,
  And have our land and labour.

You forge no more—you fold no more
  Your cankering chains about us;
We heed you not—we need you not,
  But you can't do without us.

You've lagged too long, the tide has turned,
  Your helmsmen all were knavish;

And now we'll be—as bold and free,
  As we've been tame and slavish.

Our lives are not your sheaves to glean—
  Our rights your bales to barter:
Give all their own—from cot to throne,
  But ours shall be THE CHARTER!

Hampstead, 26 May 1846

The Northern Star and National Trades Journal, 6 June 1846

OUR DESTINY

Labour! labour! labour! toil! toil! toil!
  With the wearing of the bone and the drowning of the mind;
Sink like shrivelled parchment in the flesh-devouring soil;
  And die, when ye have shouted it till centuries shall hear!
  Pass away unheeded like the waving of the wind!

Build the marble palace! sound the hollow fame!
  Be the trodden pathway for a conqueror's career!
Exhale your million breathings to elevate one name!
  And die, when ye have shouted it till centuries shall hear!

"By right divine we rule ye. God made ye but for us!"
  Thus cry the lords of nations to the slaves whom they subdue.
Unclasp God's book of nature—its writings read not thus!
  Hear! tramplers of the millions!—Hear! benders to the few!

God gave us hearts of ardour—God gave us noble forms—
  And God has poured around us his paradise of light!
Has he bade us sow the sunshine, and only reap the storms?
  Created us in glory, to pass away in night?

No! say the sunny heavens, that smile on all alike;
  The waves, that upbear navies, yet hold them in their thrall;
No! shouts the dreadful thunder, that teaches us to strike
  The proud, for *one* usurping, what the Godhead meant for *all*.

No! no! we cry united by our suffering's mighty length:
  Ye—ye have ruled for ages—now we will rule as well!

No! no! we cry triumphant in our right's resistless strength;
  We—we will share your heaven—or ye shall share our hell!

Hampstead, 15 June 1846

The Northern Star and National Trades Journal, 11 July 1846

OUR WARNING

Ye lords of golden argosies!
  And Prelate, prince, and peer;
And members all of Parliament,
  In rich St. Stephens, hear!

We are gathering up through England,
  All the bravest and the best;
From the heather—hills of Scotland,
  To the green Isle of the West.

From the corn field and the factory,
  To the coal-belt's hollow zone;
From the cellars of the city,
  To the mountain's quarried stone.

We want no courtiers golden
  and *ye* no bayonets need;
If tales of ages olden
  Arightly ye will read.

'Tis justice that ensureth
  To statutes, they shall last;
And liberty endureth
  When tyrannies have passed.

We seek to injure no man;
  We ask but for our right;
We hold out to the foreman
  The hand that he would smite!

And, if ye mean it truly,
  The storm may yet be laid,
And we will aid you duly,
  As brothers brothers aid;—

But, *if ye falsely play us,*
   And if ye but possess
The poor daring to betray us,
   Not the courage to redress;
Then your armies shall be scattered,—
   If at us their steel be thrust,—
And your fortresses be battered,
   Like atoms in the dust!

And the anger of the nation
   Across the land shall sweep,
Like a mighty Devastation
   Of the winds upon the deep!

Hampstead, July 1846

The Northern Star and National Trades Journal, 1 August 1846

OUR CHEER

My countrymen! why languish
   Like outcasts of the earth,
And drown in tears of anguish
   The glory of your birth?
Ye were a free-born people
   And heroes were your race:
The dead, they are our freemen,
   The living—our disgrace!

You bend beneath your fetters,
   You fear your foes to spurn:
March! when you meet your betters,
   'Tis time enough to turn!
Undam the tide of Freedom!
   Your hearts its godlike source,
Faith, honour, right and glory,
   The currents of its course.

And were it death awaits ye:
   Oh! Death is liberty!
Then quails the power, that hates ye,
   When freemen dare to die.

He shall not be a Briton
  Who dares to be a slave!
An alien to our country!
  And a mockery to the brave!

Down with the cup untasted!
  Its draught is not for thee.
Its generous strength were wasted
  On all, but on the free!

Turn from the altar, bondsman!
  Nor touch a British bride!
What? Woulds! thou bear her blushing
  For thee at thine own side?

Back from the church door, craven!
  The great dead sleep beneath,
And liberty is graven
  On every sculptured wreath.
For whom shall lips of beauty,
  And history's glories be?
For whom the pledge of friendship?
  For the free! the free! the free!

Hampstead, July 1846

The Northern Star and National Trades Journal, 8 August 1846

THE BLACKSTONE-EDGE GATHERING

On the 2nd of August, 1846

AIR—*"THE BATTLE OF HOHENLINDEN"*

O'er plains and cities far away,
All lorn and lost the morning lay,
When sunk the sun at break of day,
  In smoke of mill and factory.

But waved the wind on Blackstone height
A standard of the broad sunlight,

And sung, that morn, with trumpet might,
 A sounding song of Liberty.

And grew the glorious music higher,
When pouring with his heart on fire,
Old *Yorkshire* came, with *Lancashire*,
 And all its noblest chivalry.

The men, who give,—not those, who take;
The hands, that bless,—yet hearts that break;
Those toilers for their foemen's sake;
 Our England's true nobility!

So brave a host hath never met,
For truth shall be their bayonet,
Whose bloodless thrusts shall scatter yet
 The force of false finality!

Though hunger stamped each forehead spare,
And eyes were dim with factory glare,
Loud swelled the nation's battle prayer,
 Of—death to class monopoly!

Then every eye grew keen and bright,
And every pulse was dancing light,
For every heart had felt its might
 The might of labour's chivalry.

And up to Heaven the descant ran,
With no cold roof 'twixt God and man,
To dash back from its frowning span,
 A church prayer's listless blasphemy.

How distant cities quaked to hear,
When rolled from that high hill the cheer,
Of—Hope to slaves! to tyrants fear!
 And God and man for liberty!

Kirkstall Abbey, Yorkshire, August 1846

The Northern and National Trades Journal, 22 August 1846

THE FACTORY TOWN

The night had sunk along the city,
   It was a bleak and cheerless hour;
The wild-winds sung their solemn ditty
   To cold, grey wall and blackened tower.

The factories gave forth lurid fires
   From pent-up hells within their breast;
E'en Ætna's burning wrath expires,
   But *man's* volcanoes never rest.

Women, children, men were toiling,
   Locked in dungeons close and black,
Life's fast-failing thread uncoiling
   Round the wheel, the *modern rack!*

E'en the very stars seemed troubled
   With the mingled fume and roar;
The city like a cauldron bubbled,
   With its poison boiling o'er.

For the reeking walls environ
   Mingled groups of death and life
Fellow-workmen, flesh and iron,
   Side by side in deadly strife.

There, amid the wheel's dull droning
   And the heavy, choking air,
Strength's repining, labour's groaning,
   And the throttling of despair,—

With the dust around them whirling,
   And the white, cracked, fevered lips,
And the shuttle's ceaseless twirling,
   And the short life's toil-eclipse:

Stood half-naked infants shivering
   With heart-frost amid the heat;
Manhood's shrunken sinews quivering
   To the engine's horrid beat!

Woman's aching heart was throbbing
  With her wasting children's pain,
While red Mammon's hand was robbing
  God's thought-treasure from their brain!

Yet the master proudly shows
  To foreign strangers factory scenes:
  "These are men—and engines those—"
  "I see nothing but—*machines!*"

Hark! amid the bloodless slaughter
  Comes the wailing of despair:
"Oh! for but one drop of water!
"Oh! for but one breath of air!

"One fresh touch of dewy grasses,
  "Just to cool this shrivelled hand!
"Just to catch one breeze that passes
  "From our blessed *promised* LAND!"

No! though 'twas night of summer
  With a scent of new mown hay
From where the moon, the fairies' mummer,
  On distant fields enchanted lay!

On the lealands slept the cattle,
  Slumber through the forest ran,
While, in Mammon's mighty battle
  Man was immolating man!

While the great, with power unstable,
  Crushed the pauper's heart of pain,
As though the rich were heirs of *Abel*
  And the poor the sons of *Cain*.

While the priest, from drowsy riot,
  Staggered past his church unknown,
Where his God in the great quiet,
  Preached the livelong night alone!

Still the bloated trader passes,
Lord of loom and lord of mill;

On his pathway rush the masses,
    Crushed beneath his stubborn will.

Eager slaves, a willing heriot,
    O'er their brethren's living road
Drive him in his golden chariot,
    Quickened by his golden goad.

Young forms—with their pulses stifled,
    Young heads—with eldered brain,
Young hearts—of their spirit rifled,
    Young lives—sacrificed in vain:

There they lie—the withered corses,
    With not one regretful thought,
Trampled by thy fierce steam-horses,
    England's mighty *Juggernaut!*

Over all the solemn heaven
    Arches, like a God's reproof
At the offerings man has driven
    To Hell's altars, loom and woof!

And the winds with anthems ringing,
    Cleaving clouds, and splitting seas,
Seem unto the People singing:
    "Break your chains as we do these!"

And human voices too resound:
    Gallant hearts! take better cheer!
The strongest chains by which you're bound,
    Are but the chains of your own fear!

Weavers! 'Tis your shrouds you're weaving,
    Labourers! 'Tis your graves you ope;
Leave tyrants toil-deceiving!
    Rise to freedom! Wake to hope!

Still, the reign of guilt to further,
    Lord and slave the crime divide:
For the master's sin is *murder,*
    And the workman's—*suicide!*

Up in factory! Up in mill!
  Freedom's mighty phalanx swell!
You have God and Nature still.
  What have they, but Gold and Hell.

Fear ye not your masters' power;
  Men are strong when men unite;
Fear ye not one stormy hour:
  Banded millions need not fight.

Then, how many a happy village
  Shall be smiling o'er the plain,
Amid the corn-field's pleasant tillage,
  And the orchard's rich domain!

While, with rotting roof and rafter,
  Drops the factory, stone by stone,
Echoing loud with childhood's laughter,
  Where it rung with manhood's groan!

And flowers will grow in blooming-time,
  Where prison-doors their jarring cease:
For liberty will banish crime—
  Contentment is the best *Police.*

Then the palaces will moulder,
  With their labour-draining joys;
For the nations, growing older,
  Are too wise for *royal toys.*

And nobility will fleet,
  With robe, and spur, and scutcheon vain;
For Coronets were but a cheat,
  To *hide* the brand upon a *Cain!*

And cannon, bayonet, sword and shield,
  The implements of murder's trade,
Shall furrow deep the fertile field,
  Converted into hoe and spade!

While art may still its votaries call;
  Commerce claim and give its due;

Supplying still the wants of all,
  But not the wastings of the few.

Gathering fleets may still resort,
  With snowy canvass proudly bent,
For bearing wealth from port to port
  But not for war or banishment!

Then, up, in one united band,
  Both farming slave and factory-martyr!
Remember, that, *to keep the* LAND,
  The best way is—*to gain the* CHARTER!

The Labourer: A Monthly Magazine of Politics, Literature, and Poetry, 1847, vol. I, p. 49

A SONG FOR MAY

Spring is come, and shades depart
Lighter beats each human heart;
Ghost-like snow—is fleeting slow,
And the green spring-grasses grow.

Streams, that long have crept like slaves,
Dash along their gallant waves:
Man, that wanderest by the brink,
Pause upon thy way, and—*think!*

Every bud is filled to bursting
  With its future fruit and flower:
Hearts of men! are ye not thirsting
  For the fruit of Freedom's hour?

See! the fields are turning fairer,
  And the skies are more divine:
Oh! what glorious growth shall ripen!
  Oh! what glorious light will shine!

And shall man in slavish darkness,
  Moulder downward to the Sod?
God made earth an earth for freemen:
  Thou! be worthy of thy God!

All that beauty of creation,
  On the hills, and winds, and waves,
All its endless animation
  Was not—was not meant for slaves!

See the sower freely striding
  With the seed-sheets round him wound,
And the gold grain-corn abiding
  In the treasure-clasping ground.

See the furrows open kindly
  Where the earth with generous sap,
Like a mother, nurseth blindly
  Fairy-growth on dark-brown lap.

Think! of all the treasure teeming
  In that earth, and sea, and air,—
Labour's toil to Mammon's scheming—
  What shall fall to Labour's share!

Think upon the hour of harvest—
  Little mouths shall ask for bread—
But the wain goes past thy cottage,
  To the farmer's rich home-stead.

Dies away the children's laughter—
  Hungry hearts are tame and still—
And the autumn's on the forest,
  And the winter's on the hill.

Then, amid the desolation,
  Stand—a helpless human thing;
Cry: 'We are a glorious nation!
  Love the church! and serve the king!'

Then toil on with brow of anguish,
  From the cradle to thy grave:
Oh, if that be God's intention,
  Man is but a wretched slave!

But they tell us of a guerdon,
  Won by Labour's thrifty toil,

And how he who folds the furrow,
   Should be owner of the soil.

How the means for man's redemption,
   In his own possession rest,
How the country can be happy,
   And the people can be blest.

And how some have chosen wisely,
   And how some have acted right:
How the taverns grow more empty,
   And the cottages more bright.

And how these are proud as monarchs,
   Living gaily on their own,
With their freehold for their empire,
   And their fireside for their throne.

Where the corn-lands' pleasant tillage,
   Over-waves the graceful hill,
And a wood-embosomed village,
   Rise at O'CONNORVILLE.

And they beckon to their brothers,
   Who are still in slavery's wake,
To be striving and be stirring,
   For their own—their children's sake.

People, rise! and arm thee well!
Hope, that care cannot dispel,
Self-reliance, firmly wrought,
Wisdom by Experience taught,
Thrift and order, courage true,
These are arms to lead us through!
Wield them now—as you would thrive!—
Onward! 'tis the time to strive!

The Labourer: A Monthly Magazine of Politics, Literature, and Poetry,
1874, vol. I, p. 193

THE ROYAL BOUNTY

A Legend of Windsor

A song for the Queen! our gracious Queen,
  Who giveth her subjects bread!
Paupers! throw up your caps in the air;
Little for the Poor laws ye need care,
  For the Queen will see you fed.

In Windsor Palace, 'neath plate and chalice,
  The many tables groan:
The Queen has eaten and drunk her fill;
And she thinks (thought cometh, do what you will)
  How the children of Famine moan.

The thought it was one too wo-begone
  For a Queen's digestive powers:
She had never a wink of sleep that night;
She had time to think, by the morning light,
  Of the world a "State" devours.

The very next day, scarce the Dean could pray
  For a blessing on the meat,
When the Queen stood up with a pleasant face;
Thought she, it would be a much better grace
  To give the Poor folk to eat.

So her Grace spoke out, not round about
  But straightway to the point:
Quoth she—"Lord Steward! methinks you carve
Too recklessly, while our subjects starve!
  Good Lord! how you hack the joint!

"Is there never a hound in the royal ground
  Would be glad of these dainty scraps?
Who knows but some unfed human thing,
Worn, and naked and perishing,
  Might care for them—perhaps!"

"There is never a hound upon royal ground
  But is sleekly overfed;
To be sure there are poor in Windsor town,

Paupers with misery overgrown;"
   Says the Queen—"Give them the bread!—

"The dogs love meat; it would be no treat
   To dish for them the crumbs:
There's a race, I think, call'd the Skilly-fed;
Suppose you give them the broken bread,
   To any one that comes?"

At the Queen's command, now every hand
   Is grabbling on the floor:
The fat dogs sleep while the courtly rout
Sweep up the crumbs, and fling them out
   To the paupers round the door.

And day by day—newspapers say—
   The Royal bounties pour:
Our gracious Queen so giveth a zest
To pauper meals, and thankful breast
   To—thirty slaves or more.

Yet some will doubt, if a hearty shout
   From Windsor flies to Heaven
For the Royal Lady, whose bounteous heart
Daily returneth SO SMALL A PART
   Of all from the pauper riven.

A story is told of a traveller bold
   Who, being in want of food,
Cut off and ate the tail of his hound,
Returned him the bone, and strangely found
   The brute had no gratitude!

The Labourer:A Monthly Magazine of Politics, Literature, and Poetry,
1847 vol. I, p. 234

From a recent number of the *Court Journal* we learn that the Queen, in consideration of the sufferings of her starving subjects, has been "graciously pleased" that the crumbs of bread from the Royal tables should be given to the Poor, instead of being thrown into the dust-bin.

ONWARD

Who bids us backward—laggards, stay!
As soon wave back the light of day!
We have not marched so long a way
To yield at last, like craven things,
To worn-out nobles, priests, and kings.

Go bid the eagle clip its wing!
Go bid the tempest cease to sing,
And streams to burst, and tides to spring;
And, should they listen to your call,
We'll onward still, and face you all!

Oh! we have battled long and true;
While you were many, we were few,
And stronger chains we've broken through:
Think not *your* paltry silken bands
Can bind Progression's giant hands.

Go stay the earthquake in the rock,
Go quench the hot volcano's shock,
And fast the foaming cataract lock:
Ye cannot build the walls to hold
A daring heart and spirit bold.

Forbid the flowery mould to bloom,
Where years have scathed a tyrant's tomb,
And tell us slavery is our doom:
E'en as the peaceful march of time
Moulders the rampart's stony prime,
So calm Progression's steady sway
Shall sap and sweep your power away.

The Labourer: A Monthly Magazine of Politics, Literature, and Poetry,
1847, vol. II, p. 1

A SONG FOR THE PEOPLE

AIR—"THE BRAVE OLD OAK"

A song to the men—the working men,
    Who long in their chains have sighed,
'Neath the usurer's frown—and lord and Crown,
    And the Churchman's greedy pride.

There's strength in our bands—and our fate's in our hands;
    If we knew but to use our power,
The foul-class rule—of the knave and fool,
    Needn't last for a single hour.

Then down to the dust—with titled lust,
    And down with the gold king vile,
For the world shall see—that we will be free,
    And free be the sister-isle.[1]

In the days of old—when hearts beat bold,
    To the flap of Freedom's wing,
The dust at our feet—was the winding sheet,
    That wrapt a headless king.

Are we happier now?—No! the millions bow,
    'Neath a yoke ten times more black:
Ten times more strong—we'll march along,
    And drive the vermin back.

Then down to the dust—with titled lust,
    And down with the gold king vile,
For the world shall see—that we will be free,
    And free be the sister-isle.

Do they think we'll stand—with an idle hand,
    And starve, while they gorge their fill?
They yet may wake—to their grand mistake,
    And find there are men here still.

We seek not strife—and we value life,
    But only when life is free;
And we'll ne'er be slaves—to idle knaves,
    Whatever the cost may be.

Then down to the dust—with titled lust,
   And down with the fold king vile,
For the world shall see—that we will be free,
   And free be the sister-isle.

The Northern Star and National Trades Journal, 4 March 1848

THE MARCH OF FREEDOM

The nations are all calling
   To and fro, from strand to strand;
Uniting in one army
   The slaves of every land.

Lopsided thrones are creaking,
   For 'loyalty' is dead;
And commonsense is speaking
   Of honesty instead.

And coming Freedom whispers,
   'Mid the rushing of her wings,
Of loyalty to nature,
   Not loyalty to kings.
   The gold along the counters,
   Rings no longer pure and clear;
For 'tis coined with blood of childhood,
And 'tis stamped with manhood's tear.

And the bank-notes of the usurer,
   That 'justice' buy and sell,
Are the title-deeds ensuring
   His heritage in hell.

The church doors are worm-eaten,
   Where the well-paid parson drones;
And the loud bells in the steeples.
   Have learned unwonted tones:

In Padua and Pavia,
   'Tis not to prayers they call;

But they summon all the citizens,
   To conquer or to fall.

Well may the bell-tower tremble,
   And the parson shake betimes;
For the sanctuary shall cease to be
   A sanctuary for crimes.

From mountains old and hoary,
   First Liberty came down;
Like the avalanche her footfall,
   Like the thunder-cloud her frown.

On Friburg's towers she lighted,
   And the Lawine rushed below;
And the blackness of long bigotry,
   Was swept as white as snow.

And far among the glaciers
   Were answering voices found,
As the thunder-blast of Freedom
   Reverberated round.

And she gazed from her Lake-Palace,
   From Lucerne's mimic sea,
And smiling she beheld
   That Switzerland was free.

Then from her southward mountains
   Looked downward where, below,
The Arno wind and Lido,
   And the Brenla and the Po.

She saw the Austrian Tiger,
   In Lombardy the fair,
Preparing for a bound
   As he crouched within his lair.

But downward still she wandered
   To monarchy's own home;
And the dust of empires trembled
   As she passed the gate of Rome.

And: 'I will make ye battle,
   Ye conquerors of mankind:
The tyranny of force
   With the tyranny of mind!'

Then she brought the twain together
   In the gorgeous Vatican:
The pontiff and the emperor,
   The monarch and the man.

And who think ye won the battle?
   Thus the rapid changes fled—
'Twas the man of mind who conquered,
   And the man of swords who fled!

Then Freedom rose immortal,
   As Freedom ever must,
Though Cæsar's tombs are ruins,
   And Mammon's temples dust.

And southward still she wandered
   To Naples' fairy bay,
Where 'neath its grand volcano,
   The town-volcano lay.

Vesuvius unto Ætna
   Then waved its wild alarms,
Till news were brought to Naples
   That Trinacria was in arms.

On the mole the people gathered,
   As they saw the troops return,
From their death-bed at Palermo,
   To Napoli their urn.

And a heart-quake heaved around—
   And the city poured its might:
A tyrant reigned at morn,
   And a people reigned at night.

Then threatened loud the Austrian,
   And said he'd march his men

And loudly answered Italy:
  'We'll hurl them back again!'

Why stays the Austrian bloodhound,
  Tho' he scents each noble prey—?
He's strong and armed and mighty—
  And he fears—*for so are they!*

And the bayonet's insufficient
  To do the work of war,
So he arms his gallant soldiers
  With—what, think you?—*a cigar!*[1]

Ah! nations! take the omen,
  That tyranny is broke—
And all its powers and greatness
  Are passing hence—*in smoke!*

Then northward wandered Freedom,
  Where Elbe and Danube flow,
And Ferdinand and Frederick[2] have
  Their people for their foe!

Like unbound Roman fasces,
  Lie the states with dukes and kings:—
She'll bind them in one rod
  To scourge the sceptred things.

By Hungary she's passing,
  And blunt grows Szela's knife;
And the famished of Silesia
  Are thinking of their life.

Bohemia's mountains echo
  Tones of Ziska's[3] drum,
And the nobles see in thought
  The modern Hussites[4] come.

E'en Russia's frozen north
  Is dawning on our ken,
And sends Bakounine[5] forth
  To tell us it has *men!*

She breathed on Poland's plains
   And her tears fell thick and fast:
Conqueror of the future,
   And martyr of the past!

But prouder grew her glance
   And sterner grew her mien,
As westward still she wandered
   To Rhone and Loire and Seine.

She frowned in high defiance,
   Where the Bastille once had frowned
And she spoke no word of wonder,
   But she pointed all around.

Then Paris rose impatient,—
   So impatient at delay,
It could not bide to wait
   A dying tyrant's day.

And 'neath its hundred Bastilles
   The cry heaved to and fro:
The victory's the completer,
   The stronger is the foe.

Blow, breezes of La Vendée,
   Mistuned by brave Charette!
Ring, thunders of Napoleon,
   To nobler music set!

March, old imperial soldiers,
   But march in better cause,
And bare the blade of tyrants
   To fight in Freedom's wars.

This time the people's power
   The people's cause shall own;
Then up with the Republic,
   And downward with the throne!

Still onward Freedom wandered,
   Till she touched the British soil;

Elysium of money
  And *Tartarus of toil!*

And loudly here she chided;
  'My chosen people, ye!
I gave ye many chances:
  Why so long in growing free?

'Ye bend in resignation,
  A tame and patient herd!
Union be the motto,
  And *onward!* be the word!

'Why weeps your sorrowing sister,[6]
  Still bleeding unredressed,
'Neath *Russell*, England's *Nicholas*,
  The Poland of the west?

'Cry: "Liberty to Erin!"[7]
  It is a debt ye owe:
Had *ye* not armed his hand,
  He ne'er had struck a blow.

'Cry: "Liberty to Erin!"
  With iron in the tone,
For while ye slight *her* rights,
  Ye scarce deserve your own.'

The Briton and the Celt
  Are gathering side by side;
What ocean cannot part,
  That man shall not divide.

Athwart that famous 'gulf,'
  Though swift its current hies,
We soon can build a bridge
  With dead monopolies.

For hark! to Freedom's call
  The fatal spell is broke;
Repeal means—*Union* of the *slaves*,
  And *reverence* of the *yoke*.

Then, Hurrah for the Charter,
  On Shannon, Thames, and Tweed;
Now, scythemen! to the harvest!
  Reap! you who sowed the seed.

The Northern Star and National Trades Journal, 18 March 1848

THE MARSEILLAISE

Sons of freedom! break your slumbers
The day of glory's drawing nigh,
Against us tyranny's red numbers
Rear their bloody banner high.
  Rear their bloody banner high.
Hark! hirelings fierce for brutal strife,
Far and near sound war's alarms,
And outrage in your very arms,
The hopes—the partners of your life.

To arms! brave citizens! Array each gallant band!

March on! march on! your tyrants' blood
Shall drench the thirsty land!!!!
We'll march! we'll march! our tyrants' blood
Shall drench the thirsty land!!!!!

What demand their banded minions?
What dares each despicable king?
Amid the flap of Freedom's pinions,
Hear their rusty fellers ring.
  Hear their rusty fetters ring.
For us? 'Tis but an insult vain
That shall arouse our hearts the more,
We broke their manacles before,
We'll dash them into dust again.

  To arms! brave citizens, etc.

Shall an alien crew conspiring,
Make laws to blight a freeman's hearth?
Shall the mercenary hireling
Tread all our manly pride to earth?

Tread all our manly pride to earth.
Great God! shall mighty millions cower
And 'neath a yoke so paltry yield,
Shall petty despots basely wield
A nation's strength—a people's power?

    To arms! brave citizens, etc.

Tremble, tyrants! traitors! tremble,
Plague spots of the factious few!
Plot, conspire, betray, dissemble.
You shall not escape your due!
    You shall not escape your due!
For we'll be soldiers one and all—
If hundreds die—fresh thousands stand—
Every death recruits a band
Vowed to crush you or to fall.
    To arms! brave citizens, etc.

And now, like warriors, gallant-hearted,
Learn by turns to strike and spare—
Pity those, whom faction parted,
And would be with us, did they dare!
    They would be with us, did they dare!
But for those despotic knaves,
Who make them play the minion's part
And tear their bleeding country's heart,
Onward—onward o'er their graves!
    To arms! brave citizens! etc.

Children of each hallowed martyr!
Kindle fresh the kindred strife—
'Mid their ashes Freedom's Charter
Shall set the seal upon their life.
    Shall set the seal upon their life.
Less eager to survive the brave
Than to partake their honoured rest,
Now dare the worst—and hope the best,
But never—never die a slave.
    To arms! brave citizens! etc.

Our country's sacred love inspires—
Freedom!—those who fight with thee!

For the land—for the land of our sires,
The home and birthright of the free!
  The home and birthright of the free!
Fight with us Freedom—at thy voice
Victory hails our strong career
Till stricken tyrants dying hear,
The liberated world rejoice!
To arms! brave citizens! Array each gallant band!
  March on! march on! your tyrants' blood
  Shall drench the thirsty land.
  We'll march! we'll march! our tyrants' blood
  Shall drench the thirsty land.

The Labourer: A Monthly Magazine of Politics, Literature, and Poetry,
1848, vol. III, p. 153

THE SONG OF THE GAGGERS

    Gag—gag—gag!
Is the cry of the traitor band,
  While they try, with a printed rag,
  To ride like a midnight hag
On the breast of a sleeping land.

Come—knave and villain, informer and spy,
To the government mint, where you coin a lie!
    Gold—gold—gold!
  Is the pay for the ready slave,
Whose word at a breath can destroy the bold,
In the halls where justice is bought and sold,
And the whithering glance falls keen and cold
  On the heart of the true and brave.

    Gag—gag—gag!
Is the cry of the traitor band
  While they try, with a printed rag,
  To ride like a midnight hag
On the breast of a sleeping land.

We'll stay the stream in its fullest force,
We'll stop the world in its onward course—

Gag—gag—gag!
The voice of six thousand years
Shall begin at our bidding to fail and flag
Not a lip shall breathe, not a tongue shall wag
And history's page be an idle brag,
　　Compared to Russell's fears.

Gag—gag—gag!
Is the cry of the traitor band,
　　While they seek with a printed rag,
　　To ride like a midnight hag,
On the breast of a sleeping land.

In vain shall the blood of an Emmett have flowed,
In vain shall the breast of a miser have glowed!
　　Gag—Gag—Gag!
The thought in the teeming brain!
The pulse in the heart of the world shall lag,
And nations the burden of misery drag,
And Lilliput[2] trample on Brobdingnag.[2]
　　As long as a Russell shall reign.

Gag—gag—gag!
Is the cry of the traitor band,
　　While they seek, with a printed rag,
　　To ride like a midnight hag
On the breast of a sleeping land.

The Labourer: A Monthly Magazine of Politics, Literature, and Poetry,
1848, vol. III, p. 199

BONNIVARD

To Chillon's donjon damp and deep,
　Where wild waves mount eternal guard,
Freedom's vigil long to keep,
　They dragged our faithful Bonnivard.

Within their rocky fortress held,
　They thought to crush that captive lone!
That captive left their rock, unquelled,
　Altho' his foot had worn the stone.[1]

They hoped his gallant heart to slay,
    And o'er it bound their chain accurst.
'Twas not his gallant heart gave way—
    It was the chain that broke the first.

O'er Chillon's donjon damp and deep,
    Where wild waves mount eternal guard,
Oblivion's ivied fingers creep,—
    But all the world loves Bonnivard.

July 1848

Notes to the People, 1851, vol. I, p. 63

PRISON BARS

Ye scowling prison bars
    That compass me about,
I'll forge ye into armour
    To face the world without.

Bold Aspiration's furnace
    Shall fuse ye with its heat,
And stern Resolve shall fashion
    With steady iron beat.

Experience' solid anvil
    The burning mass shall hold;
And Patience' bony fingers
    Each grove exactly mould.

Then with my modern armourer
    Above my ancient scars,
I'll march upon my foemen
    And strike with prison bars.

November 1848

Notes to the People, 1851, vol. I, p. 64

PRISON FANCIES

Troublesome fancies beset me
    Sometimes as I sit in my cell,
That comrades and friends may forget me,
    And foes may remember too well.

That plans which I thought well digested
    May prove to be bubbles of air;
And hopes when they come to be tested,
    May turn to the seed of despair.

But tho' I may doubt all beside me,
    And anchor and cable my part,
Whatever—whatever betide me,
    Forbid me to doubt my own heart!

For sickness may wreck a brave spirit,
    And time wear the brain to a shade;
And dastardly age disinherit
    Creations that manhood has made.

But, God! let me ne'er cease to cherish
    The truths I so fondly have held!
Far sooner, at once let me perish,
    Ere firmness and courage are quelled.

Tho' my head in the dust may be lying,
    And bad men exult o'er my fall,
I shall smile at them—smile at them, dying,
    The Right is the Right, after all!

Notes to the People, 1851, vol. I, p. 64

Composed when confined to a solitary cell, on bread and water, without books or writing materials, May 1849

THE SILENT CELL

They told me 'twas a fearful thing
    To pine in prison lone:
The brain became a shrivelled scroll,
    The heart a living stone.

Nor solitude, nor silent cell
    The teeming mind can tame:
No tribute needs the granite-well;
    No food the planet-flame.

Denied the fruit of others' thought,
    To write my own denied,
Sweet sisters, Hope and Memory, brought
    Bright volumes to my side.

And oft we trace, with airy pen
    Full many a word of worth;
For Time will pass, and Freedom then
    Shall flash them on the earth.

They told me that my veins would flag,
    My ardour would decay;
And heavily their fetters drag
    My blood's young strength away.

Like conquerors bounding to the goal,
    Where cold, white marble gleams,
Magnificient red rivers! roll!—
    Roll! all you thousand streams!

Oft, to passion's stormy gale,
    When sleep I seek in vain,
Fleets of Fancy up them sail,
    And anchor in my brain.

But never a wish for base retreat,
    Or thought of a recreant part,
While yet a single pulse shall beat
    Proud marches in my heart.

They'll find me still unchanged and strong,
    When breaks their puny thrall;
With hate—for not one living soul—
    And pity—for them all.

Notes to the People, 1851, vol. I, p. 66

Composed, during illness, on the sixth day of my incarceration, in a solitary cell, on bread and water, and without books,—August 1849

HYMN FOR LAMMAS-DAY

Sharpen the sickle, the fields are white;
  'Tis the time of the harvest at last.
Reapers, be up with the Morning light,
  Ere the blush of its youth be past.
Why stand on the highway and lounge at the gate,
  With a summer day's work to perform?
If you wait for the hiring 'tis long you may wait—
  Till the hour of the night and the storm.

Shapen the sickle; how proud they stand,
  In the pomp of their golden grain!

But, I'm thinking, ere noon 'neath the sweep of my hand
  How many will lie on the plain.
Though the ditch be wide, the fence be high,
  There's a spirit to carry us over;
For God never meant his people to die,
  In sight of so rich a store.

Sharpen the sickle; how full the ears!
  While our children are crying for bread;
And the field has been watered with orphans' tears,
  And enriched with their fathers dead.
And hopes that are buried, and hearts that broke,
  Lie deep in the treasuring sod:
Then sweep down the grain with a thunderstroke,
  In the name of humanity's God!

July 1850

Notes to the People, 1851, vol. I, p. 70

WE ARE SILENT

We are dead, and we are buried!
Revolution's soul is tame!
They are merry o'er our ashes,
And our tyrants rule the same!
But the Resurrection's coming
As the Resurrection came.

All in silence glides the larva
Thro' its veins of red-hot ore;
All in silence lightnings gather
Round the mountain's glacier hoar;
Weight on weight, and all in silence
Swells the avalanche's snow,
Till a scarce-heard whisper hurls it
Crushing on the world below;

Drop by drop, and all in silence,
At their mound the waters grow,
Till the last wave proves too heavy,
And away the barriers go!

In the depth of toiling masses
Feeds the fire and spreads the flame,
And the foot of freedom passes
O'er the doubtings of the tame.
God-like Freedom! Glorious Freedom!
Kindling spirits into flame.

Times will set the coldest burning,
Times that come with great events,
Like the deluge-tides returning
On decaying continents,
Sweeping worn-out wrongs before them,
Wrecks, and wrongs, and discontents.

Silent as the snowflake sinking,
Truth on truth keeps gathering strong,
Till the nations turn to thinking,
Thinking of their right and wrong:
Then some sudden thaw of feeling,
Then some unomened whisper stealing,
Hurls the mighty mass along.

"We are dead and we are buried!"
Not so! life is in us yet.
There's too much of good to hope for—
Too much evil to forget!
Rich man! mark! the tide is turning!
See! the ripples backward roll!

Brains are thinking, hearts are burning
Nations tending to their goal.

Yes! there is a few among you!
Fear of freedom's coming day;
Like ghosts amid your palaces
Thoughts of poor men force their way.
Light your glittering chandeliers:
They must die when dawn appears,
Dawn of freedom's glorious day.

Notes to the People, 1851, vol. I, p. 92

FAREWELL OF THE NEW RHEINISH GAZETTE

(19th May, 1849)

By Ferdinand Freiligrath[1]

No open blow in an open fight—
But with quips and with quirks they arraign me,
By creeping treachery's secret blight
The western Calmucks have slain me.
The fatal shaft in the dark did fly;
I was struck by an ambushed knave;
And here in the pride of my strength I lie,
Like the corse of a rebel brave.

With a deathless scorn in my dying breath;
In my hand the sword still cherished;
"REBELLION!" still for my shout of death,
In my manhood untainted I perished.
Oh! gladly, full gladly the Pruss and the Czar,
The grass from my grave would clear;
But Germany sends me, with Hungary far,
Three salvoes to honour my bier.

And the tattered poor man takes his stand
On my head the cold sods heaving!
He casts them down with a diligent hand,

Where the glory of toil is cleaving.
And a garland of flowers and May be brought
On my burning wounds to cast;
His wife and his daughters the wreath had wrought,
When the work of the day was past.

Fareewell! farewell! thou turbulent life!
Farewell to ye! armies engaging!
Farewell! cloud canopied fields of strife!
Where the greatness of war is raging!
Farwell! but not for ever farewell!
They can *not* kill the spirit, my brother!
In thunder I'll rise on the field where I fell,
More boldly to fight out another.

When the last of crowns like glass shall break.
On the scene our sorrows have haunted,
And the peoples the last dread "guilty" speak,
By your side ye shall find me undaunted.
On Rhine, or on Danube, in word and deed,

You shall witness, true to his vow,
On the wrecks of thrones, in the midst of the free,
The rebel who greets you now!

Notes to the People, 1851, vol. I, p. 186

It is proposed to make the English people acquainted with the works of this great poet and patriot of Germany, now in England—a compulsory exile from his country. In his life and in his writings he stands alike before us, the pure democrat—and while too many other poets have sought the sunshine of an easy celebrity or the gain of a wide circulation, by a mean pliancy to existing powers, or, at least, by pandering to the prejudices and ignorance of a rich middle-class, this great man has scorned so to degrade his talents and violate his mission—and has ever consistently proved the poet and the champion of the working-man.

The paper alluded to was the polar star of German insurrection, it raised the revolutionary spirit—it brought it to its height,—it survived its power alone and undaunted, and with still increasing boldness, despite every persecution, maintained the field till May, 1849, and then, hurling its last thunder at its triumphant enemies, disappeared with the following proud farewell from the pen of Freiligrath:—

LIBERTY

Thy birth-place, where, young Liberty?
   In graves, 'mid heroes' ashes.
Thy dwelling, where, sweet Liberty?
   In hearts, where free blood dashes.

Thy best hope, where, dear Liberty?
   In fast upwinging time.
Thy first strength, where, proud Liberty?
   In thy oppressor's crime.

Thy safety, where, stray Liberty?
   In lands, where discords cease.
Thy glory, where, bright Liberty?
   In universal peace.

Notes to the People, 1851, vol. I, p. 295

BREAD

(*FROM THE FRENCH OF PIERRE DUPONT*)[1]

When on the stream's deserted bank
   No busy mill shall fan the air,
And, idling on the pasture dank,
   The lazy mules no burden bear,—

Then, as a wolf at noontide roams,
   While gathering tempests load the sky,
Hunger shall break into men's homes,
   And deeply roll the rising cry:

Ye tyrants! ye shall hush in vain
   A hungering people's clamour dread;
For nature bids us cry amain—
   Bread! bread! we must—we will have bread!

Grim hunger from the village comes—
   He enters through the city arch:
Go meet him with your pikes and drums!

Repel him with your iron march!
Despite your cannon's hottest shower,
  He mocks you with his eagle flight,
And, on your rampart's highest tower,
  His sable banner clouds the light,

Ye despots! Ye shall hush in vain
  A hungering people's clamour dread;
For nature bids us cry amain—
  Bread! bread! we must—we will have bread!

Array your hireling legions all,
  With equal pace, and arm, and boast—
But from our rustic arsenal
  We too have armed grim hunger's post.
  From forth the sod we've torn the spade;
The sickle from the waiting corn,
  Nay, e'en the soft breast of the maid
Against the sword beats full and warm.

Ye despots! ye shall hush in vain
  A hungering people's clamour dread;
For nature bids us cry amain—
  Bread! bread! we must—we will have bread!
Up! swell the people's fearless flood,
  Whoever bears a scythe or pike!
Let thirsty tyrants threaten blood!
  Let scaffolds rise and axes strike!
But when the axe has flickered fast
  Above the gloomy circling crowd,
And life's last throb of pride has passed,
  Our blood itself shall cry aloud—

Ye despots! ye shall hush in vain
  A hungering people's clamour dread;
For nature bids us cry amain—
  Bread! bread! we must—we will have bread!

Bread! bread's our right!—Bread! Bread's our need!
  Like air and water,—(ours as yet!)
We are the ravens God must feed—
He *owed* us bread—his mighty debt!
But lo! he *paid* the debt he owed;

He gave the land to grow the corn,
And suns have o'er his harvests glowed,
  For all that live of woman born!

Ye despots! ye shall hush in vain
  A hungering people's clamour dread:
For nature bids us cry amain—
  Bread! bread! we *must*—we will have bread!

Notes to the People, 1851, vol. I, p. 307

CHRISTIAN LOVE

Oh! Christian Love is a thing divine,
  And Charity saveth ten fold;—
But a Christian HATE is a thing as sublime—
  The hatred of sin and the idol's shrine,
  Where Mammon is worshipped in gold.

The hatred of murder, and craft, and deceit,—
  The upholdeth the money-lord's sway:
Oh, if British hearts had a manful beat,
Tho' the tyrants stood thick as the stones in the street,
I'd trample them down like the dust at my feet,
  In the light of a single day!

Oh! War, they say, is a sinful thing,
  And a blessing is peace, they say—
And obedience and patience their guerdon shall bring:
But well they may preach to the suffering—
  When none are the gainers but they!

They may shrink in horror from bloodshed and fight,
  And the words that they speak may be true:
But there is such a thing as the Wrong and the Right,
And there is such a thing as tyrannical might;
And the tears of the many are worse in my sight,
  Aye! e'en than the blood of the few.

Llanidloes, 18 August 1851

Notes to the People, 1851, vol. I, p. 337

THE PRISONER TO THE SLAVES

From my cell,[1] I look back on the world—from my cell,
    And think I am not the less free
Than the serf and the slave who in misery dwell
    In the street and the lane and the lea.

What fetters have I that ye have not as well,
    Though your dungeon be larger than mine?
For England's a prison fresh modelled from hell,
    And the jailors are weakness and crime.

In my cell, in my cell!—Yet I should not repine
    Tho' lying in Solitude's lap;
These walls will all crumble, far sooner than time
    Can raze them by siege and by sap.

They may shut out the sky—they may shut out the light
    With the barriers and ramparts they raise:
But the glory of knowledge shall pierce in despite,
    With the sun of its shadowless days.
They may stifle the tongue with their silencing rules,
    They may crush us with cord and with block;
But oppression and force are the folly of fools,
    That breaks upon constancy's rock.

They shall hear us again on the moorland and hill,
    Again in street, valley and plain:
They may beat us once more—but we'll rush at them still—
    Again—and again——and again!

Notes to the People, 1851, vol. I, p. 339

THE FISHERMEN

Three fishermen sat by the side
  Of the many toned popular stream
That rolled with its heavy proud tide,
  In the shade of its own dark dream.

Now sullen, and quiet, and deep,—
  Now fretful, and foaming, wild;

Now like a giant asleep,
   And now like a petulant child.

First sat there the fisher of France,[1]
   And he smiled as the waters came,
For he kindled their light with a glance
   At the bait of a popular name.

Next the fisher of Russia[2] was there,
   Fishing for German States,
And throwing his lines with care,
   He made his own daughters the baits.

Next the Austrian fisher[3] dwarf set
   His snares in the broad river's way—
But so widely he stretched his net
   It half broke with the weight of his prey.

And next on an Island I saw
   Many fishermen catching with glee,
On the baits of peace, freedom, and law,
   Slave-fish, while they christened them "free."

And still as they hooked the prize,
   They cried with a keen delight,
And held up the spoil to their eyes:
   "The gudgeons! they bite! they bite!"

But the hooks with time grow dull,
   And the lines grow weak with age,
And the thaw makes the rivers full,
   And the wind makes the waters rage.

And spoilt is the fishermen's trade.
   And the zest of their bait is passed,
And those on the fish who prey'd,
   Are the prey of the fish at last.

Notes to the People, 1851, vol. I, p. 360

EXTRACT FROM THE NEW WORLD

In sunny clime behold an Empire rise,
Fair as its ocean, glorious as its skies!
'Mid seas serene of mild Pacific smiles—
Republic vast of federated isles
Sleepy Tradition, lingering, loves to rest,
Confiding child! on calm Tahiti's breast.
But Science gathers, with gigantic arms,
In one embrace, the South's diffusive charms.
Nor there alone she rears the bright domain—
Throughout the world expands her hallowing reign.
Then, bold aspiring as immortal thought,
Launched in the boundless, mounts the aeronaut;
While o'er the earth they drive the cloudy team,
Electric messenger, and car of steam;
And guide and govern on innocuous course,
The explosive mineral's propelling force;
Or, mocking distance, send, on rays of light,
Love's homeborn smiles to cheer the wanderer's sight
Mechanic power then ministers to health,
And lengthening leisure gladdens greatening wealth;
Brave alchemy, the baffled hope of old,
Then forms the diamond and concretes the gold;
No fevered lands with burning plagues expire,
But draw the rain as Franklin[1] drew the fire;
Or far to mountains guide the floating hail,
And whirl on barren rocks its harmless flail.
Then the weird magnet, bowed by mightier spell,
Robbed of its secret, yields its power as well;
With steely fingers on twin dials placed,
The thoughts of farthest friends are instant traced;
And those fine sympathies that like a flame,
Fibre to fibre draw, and frame to frame,
That superstition, in its glamour-pride,
At once misunderstood, and misapplied,
As virtue ripens, shall be all revealed,
When man deserves the trust—such arms to wield.
Then shall be known, what fairy love mistaught
When Fancy troubled Truth's instinctive thought,
Then He who filled with life each rolling wave,
And denizens to every dewdrop gave,
Left not his hollow globe's caverned space

The only void, unpeopled dwelling place.
Then shall the eye, with wide extended sight,
Translate the starry gospel of the night;
And not as now, when narrower bounds are set,
See, but not read, the shinning alphabet.
Unhooded knowledge then shall freely scan
That mighty world of breathing wonders—man!
How act and will are one, shall stand defined;
How heart is feeling, and how brain is mind.
Then each disease shall quit the lightened breast;
By pain tormented while by vice oppressed;
And Life's faint step to Death's cool threshold seem
The gentle passing of a pleasant dream.

John Saville, *Ernest Jones: Chartist. Selections from the Writings and Speeches of Ernest Jones* (London: Lawrence and Wishart Ltd., 1952)

The New World: a democratic poem. Written while Jones was in prison—July 1848 to July 1850. The extract follows a description of the rise and fall of feudal and bourgeois societies, and is a vision of a classless society.

THE SONG OF THE LOW

We're low—we're low—we're very, very low,
    As low as low can be;
The rich are high—for we make them so—
    And a miserable lot are we!
    And a miserable lot are we! are we!
      A miserable lot are we!

We plough and sow—we're so very, very low,
    That we delve in the dirty clay,
Till we bless the plain with the golden grain,
    And the vale with the fragrant hay.
Our place we know—we're so very low,
    'Tis down at the landlord's feet:
We're not too low—the bread to grow
    But too low the bread to eat.
      We're low, we're low, etc.

Down, down we go—we're so very, very low,
    To the hell of the deep sunk mines.

But we gather the proudest gems that glow,
    When the crown of a despot shines;
And whenever he lacks—upon our backs
    Fresh loads he deigns to lay.
We're far too low to vote the tax
    But we're not too low to pay.
      We're low, we're low, etc.

We're low, we're low—mere rabble, we now,
    But at our plastic power,
The mould at the lordling's feet will grow
    Into palace and church and tower—
Then prostrate fall—in the rich man's hall,
    And cringe at the rich man's door,
We're not too low to build the wall,
    But too low to tread the floor.
      We're low, we're low, etc.

We're low, we're low—we're very, very low
    Yet from our fingers glide
The silken flow—and the robes that glow,
    Round the limbs of the sons of pride.
And what we get—and what we give,
    We know—and we know our share.
We're not too low the cloth to weave—
    But too low the cloth to wear.
      We're low, we're low, etc.

We're low, we're low—we're very, very low,
    And yet when the trumpets ring,
The thrust of a poor man's arm will go
    Through the heart of the proudest king!
We're low, we're low—our place we know,
    We're only the rank and file,
We're not too low—to kill the foe,
    But too low to touch the spoil.
      We're low, we're low, etc.

Notes to the People, 1852, vol. II, p. 953

    The Song of the Low was among the most popular of Jones's poems. It was set to music by John Lowry.

THE SONG OF THE FUTURE

AIR—"THE FOUR-LEAVED SHAMROCK"[a]

1

The land it is the landlord's:
  The trader's is the sea;
The ore the usurer's coffer fills,
  But what remains for me?

The engine whirls for masters' craft
  The steel shines to defend,
With labour's arms, what labour raised,
  For labour's foe to spend.

The camp, the pulpit and the law
  For rich men's sons are free;
Theirs, theirs is learning, art, and arms
  But what remains for me?

The coming hope, the future day,
  When wrong to right shall bow,
And but a little courage, man!
  To make that future—NOW.

2

I pay for all their learning,
  I toil for all their ease;
They render back in coin for coin,
  Want, ignorance, disease.

Toil—toil—and then a cheerless home,
  Where hungry passions cross.
Eternal gain to them, that give
  To me eternal loss!

The hour of leisure happiness
  The rich alone may see;
The playful child, the smiling wife—
  But what remains for me?

The coming hope, the future day,
  When wrong to right shall bow,
And but a little courage, man!
  To make that future—now.

                3

They render back, those rich men,
  A pauper's niggard fee,
Mayhap a prison—then a grave,
  And think they are quits with me;

But not a fond wife's heart that breaks—
  A poor man's child that dies,
We score not on our hollow cheeks,
  And in our sunken eyes:

We read it there—whene'er we meet,
  And, as the sum we see,
Each asks: "The rich have got the earth,
  And what remains for me?"

The coming hope, the future day,
  When wrong to right shall bow,
And but a little courage, man!
  To make that future—now.

                4

We bear the wrong in silence.
  We store it in our brain;
They think us dull—they think us dead:
  But we shall rise again.

A trumpet thro' the lands will ring;
  A heaving thro' the mass;
A trampling thro' their palaces,
  Until they break like glass.

We'll cease to weep by cherished graves,
  From lonely homes will flee.
And still as rolls our million-march,
  Its watchword brave shall be:

The coming hope—the future day,
   When wrong to right shall bow,
And but a little courage, man!
To make that future—NOW

Notes to the People, 1852, vol. II, p. 993

   ᵃIn the Four-leaved Shamrock there are three verses in each stanza. I have written four—the third being a repetition of the melody of the word. Of course, this can occasion no difficulty in the singing.

THE POET'S DEATH

A brave old warrior of poesy,
   Grown grey-haired in the service of his lyre;
A soul like an imprisoned Liberty—
   A mind like an imprisoned fire.

Vain tyranny would chain his eagle wings,
   Vain malice would his heavenly visions tame:
Still through the prison-bars the angel sings,
   Still breaks through dungeon-walls the flashing flame.
Forth, o'er the coldness of the outer world,
   Burst from his heart deep feeling's fiery flow;
Thus from the volcano's rim unfurled,
   The lava-banner waves o'er ice and snow.

Hail to the bard, who ever sang the right!
   Hail to the river on a desert rolled!
Hail to the veteran from the Titan-fight!
   Hail to the heart that dies but grows not old!

Slow down the tide of the departing years,
   The venerable shadow flits along.
No tears for him, who ne'er gave rise to fears;
   His requiem be an echo of his song.

Jones, *The Battle-Day and Other Poems* (London: G. Routledge & Co., 1855)

THE POET'S MISSION

Who is it rivets broken bands
   And stranger-hearts together,
And builds with fast-decaying hands
   A home to last for ever?

From thunder-clouds compels the light,
   And casts the bolt away,
Upluring from the soulless night
   The soul's returning day?

Who is it calls up glories past
   From tombs of churches old?
And proudly bids the hero last,
   Tho' fades his grassy mould?

Who is it, with age-vanquished form,
   Treads death's ascending path:
Yet stronger than the fiery storm
   Of tyrants in their wrath?

Whose voice, so low to human ears,
   Has still the strength sublime
To ring thro' the advancing years—
   And history—and time?

Who is it in love's servitude,
   Devotes his generous life,
And measures by his own heart's good
   A world with evil rife?

The Bard—who walks earth's lonely length
   Till all his gifts are given;
Makes others strong with his own strength,
   And then fleets back to Heaven.

Jones, "The Poet," in The Battle-Day and Other Other Poems

WAR, LOVE AND LIBERTY

I.—THE SLAVE-SONG

Where's the slave would wear a fetter,
  Made to Mammon's modern curse?
He who yields shall fare no better;
  He who strives can fare no worse.

Where's the man of manly daring,
  Wise in word and bold in deed—
Self-unsparing—danger-sharing
  With a brother in his need?

Blind hoodwinking—dastard shrinking,
  Heaven and Earth shall curse alike;
Rise! the brain is fired with thinking,
  Rise! the arm is strong to strike.

No receding—no retreating!
  Every man must do his part,
While the march of freedom's beating
  In the blood of every heart.

By the starving infant's crying,
  By the mother's moan for bread,
By the millions of the dying,
  By the thin, unburied dead—

By the land that you inherit,
  From the Father, God, who gave—
By the Heaven you cannot merit
  If you die a willing slave:

Will you let your children perish,
  At the rich man's 'scutcheoned gate,
And the wife, you fondly cherish,
  Serve his lust and swell his state?

Tell the tyrant—tell the traitor,
  Who grows rich on your distress,
You are Man—and *who* is *greater?*
  You are Man—and *he* is *less!*

Tell the thing of lordly malice,
    Labour means to claim its due;
While for *him* there is the *palace*,
The *bastile* is not for YOU.

And if then he proudly brave you,
    Sconced within his golden might;
Use the right your Maker gave you—
    sweep him—Sweep him from my sight!

II.—THE AMERICAN MAID.

And shall I wed a slave?—she said,
    When I asked her mine to be.
My heart is for the brave—she said,
    My hand is for the free!

And what thy home, and where?—she said.
    (Oh! she was proud to see!)
The Mill-lord's lustful lair—she said,
    Is never a home for me!

I'd gladly share thy lot—she said,
    Come wealth or poverty,
And toil and falter not—she said,
    As long as I toiled for thee:

But not for landlord's spoil—she said,
    My household thrift I dree;
And my children shall not toil—she said,
    For Mammon's niggard fee.

And couldst thou take a wife—she said,
    A thing of scorn to be?
Go! better lose thy life—she said,
    Than keep thy slavery!

But when the foe is cast—she said,
    A suppliant at thy knee,
And the great Atlantic blast—she said,
    Brings gladness o'er the sea—

Then come back from thy home—she said,
    And cry: I've made it free,

And lightly o'er the foam—she said,
  Thy wife shall follow thee!

The Laborer: A Monthly Magazine of Politics, Literature, and Poetry, 1847, Vol. II

THE AGE OF PEACE

Men! exult with one another,
  See how wrong and bloodshed cease!
Man in man beholds a brother—
  'Tis—oh! 'tis the age of peace!

Peace! ha! ha! be wind and vapour,
  Foolish thought of feeble soul,
Keep alight thy twinkling taper,
  While the whirlwind seeks its goal!

Hark! from distant eastern waters,
  To the farthest western wave,
Comes the voice of many slaughters,
  O'er the earth's unclosing grave.

Hark! in seas of China booming,
  How the loud artillery roars;
And a thousand masts are looming
  On La Plata's battered shores.

Hark! the Caffir groans unheeded,
Scourged by strong invader's hand;
And the Indian lance is needed
  To defend the Affghan's land.

Hark! along the wide Zahara,
  Rings the volley—flames the steel;
From Morocco to Boccara,
  Columns march and squadrons wheel.

Hark! by Otaheite's garden,
  Threats and flames the French corvette;
And the blackened bodies harden,
  Where the west its wigwam set.

Hark! to slaughter's ruddy riot,
  Where New Zealand's mountains soar;
And the gathering storm's unquiet,
  Over Madagascar's shore.

Hark! between the Grecian islands,
  Speeds the fleet with captive crowds;
Hark! along Albanian highlands,
  Lie the dead in bloody shrouds.

Hark! beneath Circassia's mountains,
  Moloch sports with human right,
Veins are torrents, hearts are fountains,
  For the streams of freedom's fight.

Then! exult with one another.
  See, how wrong and bloodshed cease!
Man in man beholds a brother—
  'Tis—oh! 'tis the age of Peace!

Peace! The lightning-shaft must shatter
  Chains, the sunshine cannot part.
Peace with all your canting clatter!
  Sword in band! and hope in heart!

"Oh! but this is all the ravage
  Of untamed barbarian life!"
Not so—European savage!
  It is you who brought the strife.

Go to each enlightened nation!
  Little need afar to roam—
Bid your mild civilisation
  Look at home—ay! look at home!

Hark! In plains of Poland blighted,
  Murdered men in myriads fall;
And the fires of faith are lighted
  In the Minsk confessional.

Hark! the Austrians in Ferrara,
  And the Goth has passed the Po,

And the Pontiff's peace-tiara
   Is a helm to fight the foe!

Hark! there's murder in Messina;
   Treachery rules in Naples' bay,
Where Sicilia's crowned hyaena
   Reigns to trample, lives to slay.

Hark! In Spain the armies gather,
   Myriads fell where myriads fall!
In the Asturias stormy weather,
   Treason in the capital.

Hark! Oporto's lines are tinted
   Red with sally and assault;
And the fields of fight are stinted
   But to fill the prison-vault.

Hark! the Swiss to battle sounding!
   Clans on clans defying call;
'Mid the bayonets all-surrounding
   Of the Austrian and the Gaul.

Hark! the mason's horrid clangour
   Piles the fort round Paris' streets,
To defy a nation's anger
   At a crowned impostor's cheats.

All thy cannon will be wanted
   When thy withered pulses cease,
For thy death-bed will be haunted,
   Thou Napoleon of Peace!

Hark! 'mid Mexico's surrender,
   Comes a challenge ill repressed.
Where's thy honour? poor pretender!
   Shame! Republic of the West.

Talk no more of freedom's glory,
   Manhood's truth and people's right
Thy *"stripes"* on slavery's back are gory,
   Thy "stars" shine truly, but in night.

Mourn to mark thy institutions,
  Vice's kingly semblance take!
Mighty child of revolutions,
  Young America, awake!

Hark to bleeding Ireland's sorrow!
  Tyrants, take your fill to-night;
'Tis the people's turn to-morrow—
  Wait awhile. 'Twill soon be light!

Hark to England's voice of wailing!
  Not alone the People rue;
Commerce tarries—banks are failing,
  And the smiter's smitten too.

Baffled League and palsied faction,
  Lords of land and lords of trade,
Stagger 'neath the vast reaction
  Of the ruin they have made.

Hark! the poor are starving daily;
  Gold is jingling, bayonets clank;
Hark! the great are living gaily,
  And corruption's smelling rank.

But the sands of time are running;
  Ever hope, and never fear!
Oh! the people's hour is coming!
  Oh! the people's hour is near!

Then! exult with one another,
  Then shall wrong and bloodshed cease;
Man in man respect a brother,
  And the world be won for peace!

The Labourer: A Monthly Magazine of Politics, Literature, and Poetry, 1847, vol. II

THE BETTER HOPE

A child of the hard-hearted world was I,
  And a worldling callous of heart,
And eager to play with the thoughtless and gay,
  As the lightest and gayest, a part.

With a rich old name and a passionate thought,
   The brightest or darkest to span:
But a struggle to fight for my natural right,
   Of a place in the homes of man.

My father's house in the lordly square
   Was cold in its solemn state,
And the sculptures rare that the old walls bear,
   Looked down with a quiet hate.

My father's hall was a dark old spot,
   With a dark old wood around,
And large quiet streams, like watery dreams,
   On the verge of a haunted ground.

And the dwellers were filled in that solemn place,
   With the trance of a sullen pride;
For the scutcheoned grace of a titled race
   Is the armour the heart to hide!

Oh! the eye sees but half through a blazoned glass
   The smile of the sunshiny earth,
And a laugh cannot pass through a marbly mass,
   But it loses the pulse of its mirth.

And I thought: there beyond, in the broad, laughing world,
   Men are happy in life's holiday!
And I passed one and all, through each old-fashioned hall,
   And wandered away and away!

The trees, they shrunk back on my venturous track,
   Old trees that my childhood had seen;
And the mansion looked dun in the light of the sun,
   Like a grave its long grasses between.

But alas! for the change of what might have been fair,
   And the gloom of what should have been bright!
The wind weltered by like one great swelling sigh,
   And the noonday was darker than night.

For a giant had risen, all grisly and grim,
   With his huge limbs loud-clattering and vast!

And he breathed his steam-breath through long channels of
     death,
Till the soul itself died on the blast.

And fibre and flesh he bound down on a rack,
     Flame-girt on a factory-floor;
And the ghastly steel-corse plied its horrible force,
     Still tearing the hearts of the poor.

Like a wine-press for mammon to form a gold-draught,
     It squeezed their best blood through its fangs;
And he quaffed at a breath the quick vintage of death,
     While it foamed with humanity's pangs.

Oh! then I looked back for my cold, quiet home,
     As the hell-bound looks back for the grave:
But I heard my soul cry, Who but cowards can fly,
     While a tyrant yet tramples a slave?

Then I bound on my armour to face the rough world,
     And I'm going to march with the rest,
Against tyrants to fight—for the sake of the right,
     And, if baffled, to fall with the best.

                              Jones, *The Battle Day and Other Poems*

LABOUR'S HISTORY

Beneath the leaf-screened vault of heaven
Lay a child in careless sleep,
Amid the fair land, God had given
As his own to till and reap.

From afar three Outlaws came;
Each seemed to each of kindred guise,
For each one thought—felt—hoped the same:
Upon the fall of man to rise!

The first one wore a golden crown:
The second raised a mystic sign,

And darkened, with a priestly frown,
The faith that might have been—divine!

The third flashed forth his flaming blade,
And reeked of blood and sulphury strife;
He gloried in his horrid tra-d—
A hireling, taking human life!

They bound the child in slumber's hour,
With chains of force, and fraud, and craft,—
And, round the victim of their power,
King,—*Priest,*—and *Soldier* stood and laughed.

Then centuries raised from time's dark womb
A bloated form, in cunning bold:
The gold-king of the mine and loom, Who tramples all that bows
    to gold.

On feudal power denouncing hate,
He challenged it the strife to bide.—
For money bought the church and state,
And money deadened martial pride.

Before their battle they arrayed
Each sought the slave and promised fair—
And those, who conquered through his aid,
Tightened his chains and—left him there!

But now the child has grown a man.
Thinking, reasoning, strong and bold,—
And they, who that false game began,
Are withered, feeble, failing, old!

And, lo! those chains of Priests and kings
As grows the frame, expanding under,
Those cankered, miserable things!
Burst like rotten threads asunder.

Rise then, strong self-liberator!
Hurl to earth the weak oppressor!
Scorn the aid of faction's traitor!
Be thyself thy wrong's redressor!

Kings have cheated—Priests have lied—
Break the sword on Slavery's knee,
And become, in manhood's pride,
That which God intended—FREE!

Jones, *Chartist Poems* (London: n.p., 1846)

ENGLAND GREATNESS

On foreign hordes impose a conqueror's yoke,
And tell your victims, that their chains are broke,
Bind arts of Europe round the Tatar's throne,
And, while you wreck his realm, destroy your own.

Are nations great, because like hordes they roam,
And foreign capitals become their homes!
Are nations great, whose power is only planed
On Millions' suffering for the few's command?
Are nations great, because o'er Afric's wave
They free the slave, themselves remaining slaves?

That the many should die to enrich the few
Labor makes England great.

The Northern Star and National Trades Journal, 4 July 1846

Eugene La Mont

THE LAND OF THE BRAVE AND THE FREE!

Hail, Britain! Ocean's noblest born,
Hail! mistress of the waves!
Whose sons are like the native oak,
Whose daughters own no slaves.

Surrounding nations turn to thee,
Where plenty seems to smile;

And wish their fate was like to thine,
Sons of the sea-girl isle.

But hark! what sound is this that's borne
On every passing breeze,
Like the distant tramp of armed men,
Or the moan of swelling seas?

It is! it is a people's groan,
Beneath the tyrant's rod;
It is a people's burning prayer
To peace and freedom's God.

Ah! see them raise their shackled hands
To the bright and beauteous sky;
But its very splendour seems to make
More dark their misery.

They turn their eyes in agony
On their fathers' honoured graves;
Can they be children of such sires
Yet bear the brand of slaves?

Despair is in their blood-shot eye,
Shame on their burning brow;
Ah! Britain, where's thy boasted strength?
And where thy "glory" *now?*

The Northern Star and Leeds General Advertiser, 15 August 1840

UNIVERSAL LIBERTY—THE CHARTIST REACTION

See the banner of 'reedom, now proudly unfurl'd—
Hear the glad voice of liberty sound through the world;
And it calls on the sons of oppression to rise;
Hark! it rings through the earth, and it enters the skies;
And it bears on its mighty breath on high
The resolve of a people to conquer or die!
Then up! for behold, on the wings of the blast,
The spirit of vengeance is hurrying fast;
And the cloud that now darkens our once happy isle,
Shall burst on the foes of the children of toil.

Too long hath the sting of your power been felt;
And our land has been drenched with the blood ye have spilt,
While the scaffold, the block, or a foreign grave,
Hath been, and is still, your reward to the brave.

Too long have we languished 'neath tyranny's chain,
While they laughed at our cries, and they mock'd at our pain:
But our prayers have arisen to the Father of light,
And HIS mighty arm only lingers to smite.

Then rouse thee! then rouse thee! the signal is given,
And our glorious CAUSE has the sanction of Heaven!!

O! come, like the shock of the waves on our shore,
Win freedom or death! and be slaves no more!

The Northern Star and Leeds General Advertiser, 26 September 1840

Jonathan Lefevre

THE ENSLAVED

Up, Britons, up! ye trampled slaves, be free!
Your banner, hope—your watchword, Liberty:
Determination be your motto now,
Stern be each eye, unflinching be each brow.
Plant firm the standard—let it wave on high;
To crouch in servile fear is infamy,
        Britannia's slaves!

Up, Britons, up!—what! fettered are ye now?
Rouse, every arm! glance, every burning brow!
Flash from each thigh a weapon, Multitude!
Forward! ye trampled on—yet unsubdued—
The badge of Freedom wear on every breast;
For yet with plenty shall your homes be blest,
        Britannia's slaves!

Oh Liberty! abused, deformed, disgraced,
By tyrants mocked, by knaves and fools misplaced;
Rouse from thy slumber—from thy shackles bound,
A million at thy voice will start around.
Unfurl thy banner. Justice! glance thine eye;
Nerve the weak arm with strength! ye glorious free,
      Help us to conquer!

I heard a sigh beneath the banian tree.
I looked, and lo! the heir of misery!
His fettered hands he clasped, in anguish groaned,
Then looked to heaven! The waving forest moaned;
The pale moon gazed. Just like some giant oak
By lightnings scathed, he lay, and thus he spoke—
      "Oh England, hear!

"I groan in bondage, while in Freedom's land,
Beneath the caress of her guardian hand,
Ye know not slav'ry—wear no galling yoke,
Nor toil for others' wealth." As thus he spoke,
Another voice creid—"Hold! your eyelids steep
With bitter tears, and bear the tearing whip
      Both undisguised.

"With you 'tis open, avowed slavery;
With us, 'tis masked—a damned treachery.
Toil not for others' wealth! What meaneth then
That thousand squalid cheeks—those sighs of pain?
One in his chariot drives amid the throng,
The thousands round him scarce can creep along,
      By famine crushed."

Ye who are left, last of the garrison
Which right defended, quit yourselves likc men.
The dwelling fired, and murder, and not yours:
The steady eye, the unflinching hand, insures
The fall of despotism—the tyrants' flight;
Then sheathed the sword, and ended thus the fight,
      Britain is free!

Bristol, 11 March 1840

The Northern Star and Leeds General Advertiser, 28 March 1840

William James Linton

RHYMES FOR THE LANDLORDED

II.
PROPERTY.

The black cock on the pathless moor,
   The red deer in the fern,
Yon cloud of rooks the plough'd field o'er,
The river-watching hern,
The pheasant in the lofty wood,—
   Aud all God's creatures free
To roam through earth, and air, and flood,—
   These are not Property.

But earth, its mines, its thousand streams,—
   And air's uncounted waves,
Freighted with gold and silver beams
   To brighten lowliest graves—
The mountain-cleaving waterfall,—
   The ever-restless sea,—
God gave, not to a few, but all,
   As common Property.

What thou hast grown, or nurtured,—that
   Thou well may'st call thine own:
Thy horse, thy kine, thy household cat,—
   The harvest thou hast sown.
But earth belongeth to the whole,—
   God gave it not to thee;
Nor made the meanest human soul
   Another's Property.

Spartacus

The Friend of the People, 21 December 1850

RHYMES FOR THE LANDLORDED

IV—THE CONSECRATED LAND.

The consecrated Land!—
Our fathers' and, alas! our children's grave:
Growing from out their hearts the wild flowers wave
O'er that dear earth, and on it yet doth stand
    The poor man's shrine.
What prince dare lay his hand
    On this, and say—"Tis mine!"

Is not our martyrs' earth
Held sacred too? not merely the low ditch,
Where kings can fling them, but the wide land which
Should be more than the grave stone of their worth.
    Where Hampden and Fitzgerald trod,—
What "peer" can own that earth?
    None—none but God.

The "consecrated" soil!
Is not the round earth God's—his sacred field,
Where man may learn celestial arms to wield,
And grow divine through sanctity of toil!—
    What landlord dare
To dispossess God's seed! what power shall spoil
    Those whom God planted there!

Spartacus

The Friend of the People, 4 January 1851

LABOUR AND PROFIT

Labour "lives" from hand to mouth,
    Labour starveth daily;
Trade-per-cent, has rankest growth,
    Mammon's heirs live gaily.
Richard Arkwright's[1] patent heir
    Hath a doom too splendid;

Hargreaves[2] dwelleth with Despair,
    And Crompton[3] dies untended.

Mammon Arkwright rolls in wealth,
    Hath too much to squander:
Mammon Arkwright, child of Stealth!
    Radcliffe[4] starveth yonder.
Manchester homes cotton lords—.
    Peels[5] and Cobdens[6] many:
William Radcliffe 'mid their hoards,
    Dies unhelp'd of any.

Corn-law League can cheapen bread:
    Cannot Toil be cheaper?
Are your Paupers over-Fed?
    Can't you starve the reaper?
Trade-per-cent, hath rankest growth,
    Free-Trade liveth gaily,
Saves its millions, nothing loath,
    Starveth Labour daily.

The Labourer: A Monthly Magazine of Politics, Literature, and Poetry,
1847, vol. II, p. 82

Sir Richard Arkwright, more than suspected of stealing his "inventions," left an immense fortune to his son, while Hargreaves and Crompton, the real inventors of the spinning-jenny and the mule-lrame, died neglected and destitute. The late Richard Arkwright (son of Sir Richard) is said to have been the wealthiest commoner in England. Of his vast fortune, he had not the heart to spend more than £3000 a year; and Wm. Radcliffe, of Stockport, the inventor of dressing-machines, the veritable father of the power-loom system, died at the age of 80 years, in the most abject poverty, unaided by any of those excellent and liberal profit-mongers, whose wealth was owed to his genius. Through some indirect channel a grant of £150 was procured from government, and reached *him* in time to prevent a parish funeral.

THE DIRGE OF THE NATIONS

1.

Yet the gory-headed Vulture
    Teareth the Promethean heart;
Yet dead Hope, denied sepulture,
    Roams a weary ghost apart,—

On this side of Charon's river
Wandering for ever, ever.
O to be graved with Hope, to see
The shore of our eternity!

2

Agonistes, as I lean'd
On my rock, whose edge was green'd
   With my sorrow's ceaseless falling,—
While the fierce winds, curse-like, drove
Full in my face that could not move
For its weight of snowy hair
And the chain of my despair,—
   Even then I heard thy calling,
Music's Loved Disciple! thou
Stir'dst the Etna of my brow,
As thy presence fill'd the den
Of my torture, Beethoven!
Thy sublimest words were driven
   Down my thought precipitous,
With the force by which are riven
   Rock-grown walls acclivitous;
Through my spirit's winter chasms
Burst thy song in mighty spasms,
With a shout like cannon-thunder
And the tramp of Nations under;
   As an army through an arch
Tempest-span'd, thy Funeral March[a]
Rush'd along, Time's feeble wings
Outspeeding with its imagings.

3

   Vision of the fearful New,
Glaring through the cloven snow
Whence my lava thoughts are pour'd,
   Echoing thee, as word by word
Falls the fire-shower of my verse,
Underneath the smoky hearse
Hurrying the Present on
   To the tomb of the Unknown!
   Yet dost thou my sense control;

Through the ruins of my soul
  Is thy sad procession pouring,
  And between the cannons' roaring
Yet I hear the heavy tread
Of the Nations with their Dead,
  And their voices call to me
  Through the midst of agony.

7

Yet is peace in England, peace
In Ireland: O most beautiful Peace,
Lying on Famine's knees! the nurse
  Rocketh her gentle babe to sleep:
Sweet Peace, with thy grave-universe
  Wherein the starved worms scarcely creep!
Yet is peace in England, peace
In the vile coward hearts that cease
Even to feel their slavery:
  The peace of hounds in their kennel, awed
And scourged: such peace remains to thee
  Shop-keeping England! who hast flaw'd
Thy honour for the price of shame
  That buys not even thy children's food,—
And sold thy once respected name,
  Thine own and Europe's future good,—
That thy fat, insolent lords may be
At peace to murder Liberty.

8

O Tyrant-trampled! Synonym
Of baffled Hope! thine eyes are dim
With ceaseless tears. O weary Earth,
Moveless in thy straiten'd girth!
Though thy heart no more upheave,
  Even though human freedom hath
No echo, though thou cease to grieve
  For wrong,—yet I will wake thy wrath,
Though I rend thee with the cries
Of thine offspring's agonies.
Yet the Nation's woes shall pierce
  Through thy darkest lids, thou Tomb!

As the flame-swords of my verse
  Fire the horizon of thy doom.
Thou shalt hear me, though thou be
Dull as English Infamy,
Though thou diest hearing me.

9

Through my brain your shrieks are ringing,
And my thoughts responsive singing
Your sad dirge, king-stricken Nations!—
  Let us strive no more, but perish
  With the hopes we may not cherish!
Let the Earth be Desolation's,
On its own pain whirl'd and wear
Our curses for an atmosphere!
Like a corse hung in the sky:
An Austrian Eternity.—
Round the dead Earth sweep the cries
Of our ghostly Agonies.

13

'O Faith! why hast thou fled
  Out of the land of Milton? O brave Spirit,
Who our forefathers led!—
  Let us curse God and die! since we inherit
Nothing of English valour, but'—The rest
Died 'mid choking sobs, the breast
  Of the pale ghost so was loaded
With vain rage and grief repress'd.
  Then again came utterance, goaded
By the furies swift and fierce,—
The wrath-winged thoughts that pierce
Ever, with relentless zeal,
In the old wounds ere they heal;
And compel without remission
Torture's fiercer repetition.

14

Wherefore die for Man's redemption,
When Defeat hath Toil's pre-emption?

Wherefore should I care to struggle,
  Slave to the false smile of Hope,
Whose best promise is a juggle?
  How may the prophetic cope
With the Absolute? We pile
Mount on mount-top: Power the while
Shakes the basement of our might,
From his inaccessible height
Laughing on us thunderously.
O ye, Titans! are not we
Mad to vex Almighty Wrong?
Though our giant Woes be strong,
What can they against God's Hate
Throned above the reach of Fate?—
Ye have answer'd—At your forges
  Ye are singing reckless hymns
To the stooping Fiend that gorges
  In your hearts. The garbage dims
The Vulture's gory eyes: but ye,
Dull'd by Pain's monotony,
Care not so he be content
Nor increase your Punishment.
  Ye have done well! so exempt
Even from honest self-contempt,
Crawl through your untroubled graves,
Loathliest of heaven's slaves!b
I, on this bare rock tear-dew'd,
With my anguish aye renew'd
By my own rebel will that ever
Seeks the eternal links to sever,—
I alone the torture bear,
I alone the red crown wear
Of my pain's eternity.
Hell's own Furies pray for me,
Seeing in my lidless eyes
The fore-looking Agonies.

16

'Not so!'—Near me, on the ground,
Lay One with a ghastly wound
In his side, through which I saw
His heart beating.—

'Yet the maw
Of Hate shall be o'ergorged; and Power,
  Powerless grown from its excess,
Lie beneath the Avenging Hour,
  As we watch now, motionless.
Let us bear, and let us toil!
Though the Future hide our spoil.
We have wrung the secret out
From the Inscrutable; our shout
  Hath o'er-ridden Fate's decree;
And the thunder of our glee
Yet shall roll through Heaven's gates
  On the western clouds of Doom:
Lo! the morrow, past the gloom
Of the midnight grief, awaits
The clear dawning of our fame!'

The Republican, 1848

ᵃBeethoven's wondrous "Sonata with the funeral march."
ᵇThe Titans were fabled to have been imprisoned by Jupiter under Mount
Etna, whose eruptions were occasioned by their rebellious heavings. We have no
volcanos here: our Titans lying quietly under any load, even of taxation.

THE LAMENT OF THE PRESENT

One by one the leaves are shaken
    From the tree;
One by one our Best are taken,
And our hopes fail, Hope-forsaken;
When, O God! wilt thou awaken,
    When, O Liberty!

Sinks the moon behind the forest,
    Lost in cloud;
Darkly thou thy way explorest:
So even when our need is sorest,
Freedom thou our trust ignorest
    In thy bloody shroud.

One by one our Best are taken:—
    Hasten we!

By our swift curse o'ertaken,
Thrones and powers again are shaken;
Yet the Avenger shall awaken
  Murder'd Liberty.

The Red Republican, 1848, p. 232

FOR ROME!

"For Rome! for Rome!" That shout hath sped
  To earth's extremest bound;
And every hope by honour led
  Repeats the glorious sound,
For Rome! for Rome! let patriots now,
  Where'er they draw their breath,
Re-echo back Mazzini's vow—
  "Free Rome or Roman death."

For Rome! for Rome! ay, for the world!
  Our quarrel is the same,
Where'er a flag may be unfurl'd,
  Or beacon-summons flame.
Beneath the gleam of Kossuth's sword,
  Or in our darken'd streets,
'Tis Freedom's sacred battle word,
  Our cry, our hope repeats.

For Rome! for Rome! for human right;
  For liberty and growth!
Our words foredoom Oppression's might:
  Our lives fulfil that oath.
"For Rome! for Rome!" Come weal or woe,
  Maintain the Roman cry;
And every heart be Roman now!—
  We will be free or die.

June 1849

The Democratic Review of British and Foreign Politics, History and Literature,
1849, p. 113

A GLEE

AIR—"WHEN ARTHUR FIRST AT COURT BEGAN"

When Royalty, for change, began
    To wear wide laughing-sleeves,—
It entertain'd three serving-men,
    And all of them were thieves.

The first, he was a Bishop proud;
    The second, a rascal Peer;
And the third, he was a Parliament-man:
    And all were rogues, I hear.

The Bishop stole for the love of God;
    The Peer for the love of plunder;
And the Parliament-man as a go between,
    His fellow vagabonds under.

The first was damn'd for his blasphemy;
    The next was hang'd for a thief;
And the People took charge of the Parliament-man:
    So that Royalty died of grief.

The Friend of the People, 8 February 1851

PEACE AND HOPE

(*CROMWELL'S CHARGING-CRY AT WAISBY-FIELD*)

For 'Peace and Hope' our Heroes bared their swords:
Our Whigs slay Peace and Hope with peaceful words.

The English Republic, 1851, p. 112.

THE GATHERING OF THE PEOPLE

A Storm-Song

Gather ye silently,
  Even as the snow
Heapeth the avalanche:
  Gather ye so!
Gather ye so,
  In the wide glare of day,
Sternly and tranquilly;
  Melt not away!
Flake by flake gather;
  Bind ye the whole
Firmly together—
  One form and one soul!
Are ye all gather'd?
  Welded in one?
Hark to the thunder-shout!
  Now roll ye on!
Roll ye on steadily;
  Steadily grow;
Swifter and swifter roll!
  Who stays you now?
Leap from your hill of right;
  Burst on the plain!
Ye were born in those valleys;
  There shall ye reign.
Roll on in thunder!
  Man's buildings are there,
Lo! they mock'd at your movement:
  Now hide their despair!
Roll, roll, world-whelmingly!—
  Calm in your path
Glory walks harvest-ward:
  God rules your wrath.

'It is accomplished:'
  Melt we away!
The phœnix To-morrow
  Is child of To-day.

Gather ye silently!
  Even as the snow

Buildeth the avalanche,
  Gather ye, NOW!

The English Republic, 1851, pp. 136–37

MODERN MONUMENTAL INSCRIPTIONS

In the Jesuits' Burial Ground

A murderer to the very bone
  A traitor to the marrow,
Cain and Iscariot both in one:
  Here lies Odillon Barrot.[1]

The English Republic, 1851, p. 210

On the Tomb of General Eugène Cavaignac

(The Brother of the Republican)[1]

Remembering Godfrey, History spares Eugene:
Branding him not as CAVAIGNAC, but CA . . . I . . . N . . .

The English Republic, 1851, p. 210

For a Small Column in Memory of the Affliction of M. Theirs

Thiers[1] has had a cancer on his tongue.
  No wonder! Would you know the reason why?
When pimples have from trivial falsehoods sprung,
  What must he have whose life is a lie?

The English Republic, 1851, p. 210

Under a Statue of Alphonse De Lamartine

(Erected by Himself)

Poet and orator[1] and statesman eke:
All Europe listen'd but to hear him speak.
O heart of froth, how eloquently weak!

The English Republic, 1851, p. 210

For an Obelisk in Printing-House Square

(Erected to the Gentlemen of Puddledock)

A page of the "Times" the Devil read,
    And he flung it down:—Ahem!
I'm father of lies, I know, he said;
    But I'm damn'd if I father them.

The English Republic, 1851, p. 249

Another for Lord John

(Michael and Satan contended for the Body of Moses)

Michael and Satan once again
    Have had a serious tustle;
For Satan would not foul his reign
    With such a corpse as Russell.

The English Republic, 1851, p. 249

RHYMES AND REASONS AGAINST LANDLORDISM

THE SLAVE OF THE SOIL

The ass is fed, they muzzle not
    The ox that treads the corn:
But they leave their human labourer
    To starve and die forlorn.
The rich man's hound hath his kennel, and
    His meat both night and morn:
'Tis only the human labourer
    Is left to die forlorn.

They tell us we are heirs of heaven,
    Like them God's children born;
But the power that makes man's law hath laugh'd
    God's holiest law to scorn.
We toil far worse than the lowest beasts;
    And the beasts when lamed or worn

Are kill'd: 'tis only the human jade
    Is left to die forlorn.

Our youth is sad, our manhood's strength
    Before its prime is shorn;
If we marry, we do but curse the day
    Or ever a child is born.
O God of the weak and sore-oppress'd,
    Look down upon where we mourn;
And let not Thy human labourers
    Be left to die forlorn!

The English Republic, 1851, p. 94

'FROM THE CENTRE UPWARDS'

If Puddledock can vomit truth,
    Or truth be venom'd lies,—
If Russell-Castlereagh[1] know ruth,
    Whig 'Statesmaniship' be wise,—
If butcher's meat grow wholesomer
    By dint of carrion flies,—
King Property owns earth and air,
    From the centre to the skies.

So pursy Athol swears he doth,—
    'Keep off the waste!' he cries;
And sky and moor, he'll fence them both
    From depredating eyes.
While Minos in a Highland kilt
    Guards Eden from surprise,
There's scarce a doubt his Grace of Tilt
    May own both earth and skies.

No urchin his red lips shall smear
    With Autumn's luscious prize;
No milkmaid stint her song to hear
    The lark that heavenward hies
'Tis theft, sir! theft; wild fruit, wild tones,
    And wild flowers' varied dyes,

Are grown on Lordling's land, who owns
   From the centre to the skies.

When starvelings tire of fattening drones—
   'Why then,' his Grace replies,
We'll clear our lands, nor let your bones
   "Manure our Paradise;
'We'll have Steam-Power for helot then.'
   But what if Labour rise,
And land you, scarecrow gentlemen,
   Somewhere 'twist earth and skies?

The English Republic, 1851, p. 120

PROPERTY

The black cock on the pathless moor,
   The red deer in the fern,
Yon cloud of rooks the plough'd field o'er,
   The river-watching hern,
The pheasant in thy lofty wood,—
   And all God's creatures free
To roam through earth, and air and flood,—
   These are not Property.

But earth, its mines, its thousand streams,—
   And air's uncounted waves,
Freighted with gold and silver beams
   To brighten lowliest graves,—
The mountain-cleaving waterfall,—
   The ever-restless sea,—
God gave, not to a few, but all,
   As common Property.

What thou hast grown, or nurtured,—that
   Thou well may'st call thine own:
Thy horse, thy kine, thy household cat,—
   The harvest thou hast sown.
But earth belongeth to the whole,—
   God gave it not to thee;

Nor made the meanest human soul
   Another's Property.

The English Republic, 1851, p. 149

FREE TRADE

But 'Free Trade—demand—supply':
   Freight your ships with human woe.
Is Free Trade then half a lie?
   Ask of Cobden, Poland's foe.[a]
Why not trade in Freedom's blood?
   Why not barter Right for gain?
Let a Nation pine for food,
   While old Mildew hoardeth grain.
Free to sell, and free to buy,—
   Free to toil for famine wage;
Free to reap,—and free to die,—
   Famish'd youth and foodless age.
'Export' should not mean *despoil;*
   'Free Trade,'—let the words be true:
Free and fair trade on the soil;
   And export grain and landlords too!

The English Republic, 1851, pp. 153–54

[a] The Statesman who in his anxiety for cheap bread forgot that Poland *was* a corn-growing country.

REVENGE

The leaves are still; not a breath is heard:
   How bright the harvest day!
'Tis the tramp of a horse, the boughs are stir'd
   The Agent[1] comes this way.
Was it an old gun-muzzle peep'd
   Behind you crimson leaf?
A shot!—and Murder's bloody sheaf
   Is reap'd.

Who sold the farm above his head?
Who drove the widow mad?
Who pull'd the dying from her bed?
Who rob'd the idiot lad?
Who sent the starv'd girl to the streets?
Who mock'd grey Sorrow's smart?
Yes! listen in thy blood. His heart
    Yet beats.

Not one has help for the dying man;
    Not one the murderer stays,
Though all might see him where he ran,
    Not even the child betrays.
  O wrong! Thou hast a fearful brood:
  What inquest can ye need,
Who know Revenge but reap't the seed
    Of blood.

The English Republic, 1851, p. 188

EMIGRANTS

We'll not forget you, Mother!
  In the land that's far away;
We'll think of you, dear! at our work,
  And bless you when we pray.
Look cheerly, that your smile may be
  Before me night and day,
On our long journey o'er the sea,
  To the land that's far away.
    Stay those sobs of woe;
      Smooth thine hair so grey:
    'Twill wring my heart to see thee so,
In the land that's far away.

You'll tend the white rose, Mother!
  On our little Nelly's grave:
I can not help these foolish tears,—
  And yet I'm very brave.
And you'll take care of Tom's dog, poor thing!
  And Nelly's skylark, too;

And think whene'er you hear him sing,
  He sings of us to you.
    Nay! look calmly, do!
      Mother, Mother, pray:
      How will I bear to dream of you
In the land that's far away?

We'll write so often, Mother!
And Father—he can read;
And you'll get some neighbour write to us,
  To say if you're in need.
And tell us how you bear the cold,
  If Father's lameness mends:
Dear life! he's not so very old;
  And God will bring you friends.
    O, this parting pain!
      Mother, darling! pray,
Let me see you smile again,
    Before I go away!

We'll save our earnings, Mother!
  To help your failing years;
And some day come back to you, love!
  And kiss away your tears.
Who knows but we may send for you?
  You'll live to see that day:
O, Mother darling! bear it through,
  While we are far away.
    Stay those sobs of woe!
      Smooth thine hair so grey!
      'Twil wring my heart to leave thee so,
    In the land that's far away.

The English Republic, 1851, p. 252

EMIGRATION

Stoops the sun behind the ocean;
  Darker shadows hide the bay;
And the last weak words are spoken
From heart-breaking to heart-broken,

As the ship gets under-weigh.
Now the yellow moon is waning
  On the dim and lessening strand;
Darkly speeds 'The Exile,' draining
  The life-blood of the land.

Reck not Youth's intense emotion,
  Weeping Love or white-brow'd Care;
Look on Manhood spirit-broken,
On the dark signs that betoken
  Progress of the Plague Despair.
Hopeless are the dim eyes straining
  Tow'rd that woe-worn pilgrim band;
Darkly speeds 'The Exile,' draining
  The life-blood of the land.

Yet the patriot's life-devotion—
  Fierce and bitter his reply:—
'Love is mindful, by the token
'That his young hopes, famine-broken,
  "in yon clouded grave-yard lie;
'Dead, as dogs die, scarce complaining:
  Let us quit the accursed strand!'
Darkly speeds 'The Exile,' draining
  The life-blood of the land.[a]

The English Republic, 1851, p. 253

[a] I do not reproach the emigrants. How many, tracked by the bloodhounds of the law for their share in endeavouring to raise their country, are compelled to leave it! How many, too, have no resource but emigration to keep them from dying of famine here! And, if those better able to help also emigrate, it is not much to be wondered at. But the fact remains the same; and the terrible revenge of consequence halts for no conscientious justifications of individuals.

THE WAY OUT

Hold together, flinch for nought!
Set thy foot by mine, my brother!
Shield of each one shade the other!
  Well resolved is bravely fought:
  Well begun is half-way wrought:
  Hold together, halt for nought!

Hold together, flinch for nought!
Let our hearts beat close together!
Love can fence the foulest weather:
    Faith o'erflies the runner Thought:
    Fairly aim'd is firmly caught:
    Hold together, halt for nought!

Hold together, flinch for nought!
Right and Will are friend and brother:
We'll take counsel of none other!
    True as steel is Captain Ought:
    Worth is won wherever sought:
    Hold together, halt for nought.

The English Republic, 1851, p. 275

SWING

'We are betray'd: what matters unto us
    'Their surer bargain? we must bear the same
'They could not see *our* miseries: light them thus!
    'Mayhap they'll read them by yon granary's flame.
'We'll trust to no one now but Captain Torch:
'Let "Too far" bargain with him, at his porch"[a]

Ay! there is water, plenty,—handy too;
    And men; if only will to help were here.
But savage crowds stand round who bandy you
    Ill words of hate, and bitter gibe and jeer.
'You'll feel, may be, for others while you scorch:
'Ha! ha! he listens now to Goodman Torch!'

House, barn, and stock consumed; and, look again!
    Yon sky is lurid too; and there; and there:
Revenge, like a volcano's fiery rain,
    Is scatter'd from the wild hands of Despair.
'We'll have no leader now but Captain Torch:
'They'll hear his smooth tongue whispering at their porch!'

'Too late!' 'Too late!'—Yet, ere the dream be true,
    Bethink you how all interests are the same:

And Love, the Just, the Pitying, captain you!
   I hear your answer: from warm hearts it came,—
No mocking fiend shall whisper at our porch—
The darkness of your deeds requires a torch!'

The English Republic, 1851, p. 276

  [a]I am neither recommending nor defending incendiarism, I only call attention
to an historic lesson of but too frequent occurrence.

TRY AGAIN

The coldest hours are close upon the morn;
  Night ever neareth day:
Up, man! and wrestle ye! again, with scorn;
Each footstep is all,—move on thy way!
      Try again!

Is baffled beaten? Will the hero fail
  Flung down beneath a wall?
Another ladder! Let our comrades scale
The top, o'er us piled stair-like as we fall!
      Try again!

O Hope forlornest, masked like Despair!
  Truth must some day succeed
Thy failure proves—What?—thy once failing there.
Fail yet again if there be martyr need!
      Try again!

The English Republic, 1851, p. 345

NEARING IT

Every minute in the night,
  Be it dark and dread,
As a step toward the light
  On the mountain head:
Till our eyelids reach the dawn,

And the fearful night is gone,
As swift as startled fawn
    From the hunter's tread.

Every blow struck in the fight
    On a foeman's shield
Is a promise for the Right,
    That the Wrong shall yield:
And each determined word,
Like some ancient hero's sword,
Returneth to its lord
    With his hest fulfill'd.

Every step into the light,
    As the dawn-mists fly
The hours increase in might,
    Till the noon rides high:
And as night's black clouds disperse
At the sun god's burning curse,
So drives Oppression's hearse
    From our conquest-cry.

The English Republic, 1851, p. 345

IRISH HARVEST SONG

This land is ours,—God gave it us;
    We will maintain our own.
This land is ours,—we will not starve
    Where corn is grown:
We will not starve in harvest-time because some alien-born
    Would speculate in corn.

Our arms are strong, our sickles keen,—
We will not idly stand
While others reap the golden grain
    On our own land:
We will not starve in the midst of bread that some few 'Noble-
borne'
    May steal the peasants' corn.

O by the strength of our despair,
    Our unrequited toil,
By God who gave us choice of death
    On our own soil,—
Reap, though our reaping-hooks be swords, and let the robber-
    born
        Glean plenteously our scorn!

Our native land,—it shall be ours:
    The land where we have sown
So many hopes—Fitzgerald's[1] land—
    We yet will own.
The Spirit of Davis singeth clear over the ruddy corn,
    Blessing our harvest-morn.

The English Republic, 1851, pp. 346–47

LANDLORDISM

Landlord Acres nothing needeth,—
    Full his purse and paunch;
On the grass the peasant feedeth,—
    Famine dogs are staunch:
Apoplectic Acres crammeth,—
    How hardwork'd is he;
Landless Labour ever clammeth:
    Who the cause can see?

'O the Irishman is lazy:
    'Other lands we know
'Have' no paupers; have no crazy
    Homes of peasant woe;
Have no toilers fever-stricken,
    Wanting bread to eat;
Do not see their young men sicken
    'Mid the shocks of wheat.

O 'the lazy Irish peasant'!
    Easily 'tis said:
Famine's smile is very pleasant,
    Reaping landlords' bread.

Is is laziness or loathing?—
   Lazy!—Yes, while he,
Who takes all and gives him nothing,
   Mocketh Industry

TENANT-RIGHT

'Idle rascal! on your lands
   'See the rank weed growing;
'While you sit with folded hands,
   'Weeds more weeds are sowing.
'Clean the ground, man! till, and sow.'
   But—'Who will have the reaping?'
Labour's hand is ever slow,
   Tyrants' granaries heaping.

Idler!—Make the land his own,—
   He'll not shirk the weeding;
Right assured,—'tis that alone,
   Not the lash he's needing,
Then he'll clean and till and sow,
   Nor need your help in reaping
Labour's hand is never slow,
   His own granaries heaping.

OUR HERITAGE

God's gift, the Land, our common heritage,—
   To Adam and his seed, and not entail'd
   Upon a few!—What 'deed' hath countervail'd
That tenure handed down from age to age?

God's only curse is labour: with the sweat
   Of honest brows to earn the fruit of toil.
   He plagued us not with landlords to despoil
The labourer of his God-acknowledged debt.

Parcel the measured ocean; fence the air;
   Claim property in clouds and spray-top'd waves;

In sun and stars; in heaven, as in our graves:
If thou art earth-lord, Tyrant! and God's heir.

Linton, *Prose and Verse Fifty Years: 1836–1886* (London, Simpkin and Marshall,
1865), vol. x.

THE POET'S MISSION

Learn higher apprehending
  Of the Poet's task!
To him are God and Nature lending
  Ore of mighty thought,
That for such use as the world's need may ask,
  Fit iron may be wrought.

The passionate impulse furnaced
  In the Poet's heart
Must weld stern word and action earnest:
  Poet word and deed
In harmony: that he may take God's part,
  And earn a true life's meed.

Clear vision ever lendeth
  Faith to his life:
Then only he his mission comprehendeth,
  When he can wield his soul
Or to creative thought or the daily strife,
  With artist-like control.

Not in the purer heaven
  Of his own thought
To dwell, enparadised, to him was given
  The poet-fire:
But that a grander, truer life be wrought,
  The world exampled higher.

Not only do God's angels
  Behold him with clear eyes:
But day and night they speed his dread evangels
  Over the world;

Their seraph-wings of act and sacrifice
  Eternally unfurl'd.

    "The Poet's mission
    Is but prophetic vision:
To him the daring heart is granted—
    Not the hand."
        From the German of Herwegh.

Ernest Jones, ed. *The People's Paper* (London, 1858).

MONSTERS

I.

Poor wretch, arrested on life's path,
  We only pity thee;
We may not hate whom nature hath
  But formed imperfectly.
So henceforth, when we look on one
  Who acts a loathly part,
We'll say—What else could he have done
  With such a reptile heart?

II.

There's yonder crowned and purpled Thing,
  That o'er the nations' heads
Crawleth in likeness of a king,
  And whereso'er he treads
Bequeaths a poisonous track of slime—
  Thou change from what thou art?
How should'st thou dare a doom sublime
  With but a reptile's heart?

III.

Yon Weakness in the place of power—
  Peel—Russell—Aberdeen—
Who dares not hope Occasion's dower,
  Whose greatest act is mean;

Yon statesman evermore afraid
  Of every petty smart—
Nay! I curse not one whom nature made
  With but a reptile's heart.

IV.

This easy patriot talks of peace,
  And that of party need;
One only giveth Wrong "a lease,"
  And one bids a Shame succeed.
What wrath at them will help our dream,
  When manliness departs?
The Reptile-hearted rule supreme,
  A race with reptile hearts.

V.

Why blame the serf creeps o'er our fields
  Where men should walk erect?
Earth's mud its utmost product yields—
  What else would you expect?
From sediment of trading lies
  What hero thought may dart?
Minerva from Jove's head must rise,
  Not from a reptile's heart.

Spartacus

The Poet's Mission, vol. VI, pp. 62–63

"Let us trace this law (of progressive development) in the production of certain classes of monstrosities. A human fœtus is often left with one of the most important parts of its frame imperfectly developed; the heart, for instance, goes no further than the three chambered form, so that it is the heart of a reptile."
                                                                    —*Vestiges of Creation.*

THE "IMPRISONED"

Whom will they imprison?—He
Who upholdeth Liberty,
Who maintaineth native right.

In old Precedent's despite,
He is first upon the list
Of the ermined Anarchist.

Whom will they imprison?—Slaves
Own unprosecuted graves;
Who his country can betray
Hath his privilege and pay;
Many ungyved lords there be,
While felons gaol Integrity.

Hear the charge of Tyranny!
Whoso pleads for Poverty,
Who would lead the poor to heaven,
Is the sinner unforgiven;
Who would set the bondman free
Well hath earned captivity.

Let the unfetter'd Slave reply!
Be the traitor and the spy,
And the absent renegade,
Of his country's hope afraid,
Dungeon'd by your laws; but ye
Have no power to hold the Free.

Ye shall never bury him:
As ye bind him, limb by limb,

Shall the iron crumble off;
And your malice be the scoff
Of the mighty soul which ye
Destine unto slavery.

Ye may trample down our lives;
Ye may give us scourge and gyves;
Ye may brand our arms, our name,
Heaping o'er us shame on shame:
From all bonds the spirit free
Leaps to glorious victory.

Spartacus

The Labourer: A Monthly Magazine of Politics, Literature and Poetry, 1848, vol. III,
pp. 139–140

'WAR!'—WAR!

Who taketh up arms in the tyrants' wars?
Who selleth his life to the infamous scars
Of Tyranny's service? who will be
Beast-like butcher'd for Tyranny?

Who bareth the steel of the Homicide,
To fatten the idiot spite or pride
Of the Thieves of Power? What beast will be
Scourged to the shambles of Tyranny?

What would the hired murderer have?
What gain ye from War? A scoundrel grave;
Shrouded in blood or infamy:
Your conquest-cry with the worm shall be.

Corpses of scourged slaves, that sell
The triumph-wheels of the royal Ghoul:
If ye must drink blood, let your foul thirst be
Quench'd in the thick blood of Tyranny!

Starvelings of Trade! whose wasted thews
Are bought and sold for the brigands' use:
What have ye done, that your bones should be
Axe staves for the hangman Tyranny?

What have the throned 'Legtimates' done
For the bread-tax'd Labourer,—if the sun
Must look on a battle-field—that he
Should bleed in the ranks of Tyranny?

Pauper! if Bastile tales are true,
What have the Throned done for you?
If your blood must flow; say! shall it be
To cement new prisons for Loyalty?

'Artisan! leave thine idle loom;
'Hie thee to glory!' My Lords want room!
If ye must perish, can not ye
Die for your homes and Liberty?

Look to it, Anarch: Sword and Fire
Turn to thy palaces for their hire.
S'bad we give thee our blood; and shall none be
Pour'd on the altar of Liberty?

Who taketh up arms in the tyrants' wars?
Whip him with curses! shames be his scars!
The murderer's spirit can never be
Absolved, except by Liberty.

Draw ye no sword! it may not be
In a less quarrel than Liberty.
If the torch of war must illumined be,
Let it light the coming of Liberty!

Spartacus

Prose and Verse, vol. III, p. 150

Robert Lowery

THE COLLIER BOY

Oh! mark yon child, with cheeks so pale,
As if they never felt the gale
That breathes of health and lights the smile;
It tells of nought but lengthened toil.
Its twisted frame and actions rude
Speak mind and form's decrepitude,
And show that boyhood's hours of joy
Were never known to the Collier Boy.

'Tis night, when youth with pleasure dreams
Of meads and woods and gurgling streams—
Soft cooling baths, in sunny hours
Whose banks are blooming with gay flowers;—
Of birds and beasts, and all the play
Fancy forms for the coming day:

The Collier's lonely calls destroy
Those dreams of bliss to the Collier Boy.

Bright morn has come, each young heart hies
To chase the gaudy butterflies,
Or to follow the flight of the humming bee
Amid the wild wood's minstrelsy;
Entomb'd in earth, far, far, away
From all the light of glorious day,
Hard toil and danger doth employ
For the dreary mine, the Collier Boy.

'Tis eve—the cattle seek their fold,
The western sky's a flood of gold;
The old men sit, and tell the tale
Of youthful deeds, and quaff their ale,
And looking round them, smile to see
The urchins playing merrily;—
He wants, yet cannot it enjoy,
So toil-worn is the Collier Boy.

Oh! curse upon that love of gold
For which the young heart now is sold,
With care and sickness withering
The sunshine of its early spring.
Oh! shame upon that barbarous state
That toil for infant years create,
Whose accursed influences destroy
The mind and form of the Collier Boy.

The Charter, 23 June 1839

Charles Mackay

THE GOOD TIME COMING

There's a good time coming, boys,
  A good time coming;
We may not live to see the day,

But earth shall glisten in the ray
   Of the good time coming.
Cannon-balls may aid the truth,
   But thought's a weapon stronger;
We'll win a battle by its aid—
   Wait a little longer.

There's a good time coming, boys,
   A good time coming;
The pen shall supersede the sword,
And right, not might, shall be the lord,
   In the good time coming.
Worth, not birth, shall rule mankind,
   And be acknowledged stronger;
The proper impulse has been given—
   Wait a little longer.

There's a good time coming, boys,
   A good time coming;
War in all men's eyes shall be
A monster of iniquity
   In the good time coming.
Nations shall not quarrel then,
   To prove which is the stronger,
Nor slaughter men for glory's sake—
   Wait a little longer.

There's a good time coming, boys,
   A good time coming.
Hateful rivalries of creed
Shall not make their martyrs bleed
   In the good time coming.
Religion shall be shorn of pride,
   And flourish all the stronger:
And Charity shall tim her lamp—
   Wait a little longer.

There's a good time coming, boys,
   A good time coming.
And a poor man's family,
Shall not be his misery
   In the good time coming;
Every child shall be a help,

To make his right arm stronger;
The happier he, the more he has—
    Wait a little longer.

There's a good time coming, boys,
    A good time coming:
Little children shall not toil,
Under, or above, the soil,
    In the good time coming.
But shall play in healthful fields
    Till limbs and mind grow stronger;
And every one shall read and write—
    Wait a little longer.

There's a good time coming, boys,
    A good time coming:
The people shall be temperate,
And shall love instead of hate,
    In the good time coming.
They shall use, and not abuse,
    And made all virtue stronger;
The reformation has begun—
    Wait a little longer.

There's a good time coming, boys,
    A good time coming:
Let us aid it all we can,
Every woman, every man,
    The good time coming.
Smallest helps, if rightly given,
    Make the impulse stronger;
'Twill be strong enough one day—
    Wait a little longer.

Patrick Scott, *Victorian Poetry 1830–1870*, (London: Longman
Group Limited, 1971)

FRANCE AND ENGLAND

We make no boast of Waterloo;
    Its name excites no pride in us;
We have no hatred of the French,

No scorn of Yankee or of Russ,
The *glory* that our fathers gained
 In bloody warfare years agone,
And which they talk of o'er their cups,
Gives us no joy to think upon.

And in this year of "forty-six,"
 We rising men in life's young prime,
Are men who think the French have done
 The world good service in their time.
And for their sakes, and for our own,
 And freedom's sake all o'er the earth,
We'd rather let old feuds expire,
 And cling to something better worth,

To be at strife, however just,
 Has no attraction to our mind:
And as for nations fond of war,
 We think them pests of humankind.
Still—if there "must" be rivalry
 Betwixt us and the French,—why then
Let earth behold us, while we show
 Which of the two are better men.

We'll try the rivalry of Arts,
 Of Science, Learning, Freedom, Fame—
We'll try who first shall light the world
 With Charity's divinest flame—
Who best shall elevate the poor,
 And teach the wealthy to be true—
We want no rivalry of arms,
 We want no boast of Waterloo.

The Northern Star and National Trades Journal, 4 July 1846

THE THREE PREACHERS

There are three preachers, ever preaching,
 Each with eloquence and power—
One is old, with locks of white,
Skinny as an anchorite;

And he preaches every hour,
With a shrill fanatic voice,
   And a bigot's fiery scorn:—
"Backwards, ye presumptuous nations!
   Man to misery is born—
Born to drudge, and sweat, and suffer—
   Born to labour, and to pray.
Priests and kings are God's viceregents;
   Man must worship and obey,
Backwards, ye presumptuous nations!
   Back! be humble, and obey!"

The second is a milder preacher;
   Soft he talks, as if he sung.
Sleek and slothful is his look;
And his words, as from a book,
   Issue glibly from his tongue.
With an air of self-content,
   High he lifts his fair, white hands—
"Stand ye still, ye restless nations;
   And be happy all ye lands!
Earth was made by one Almighty;
   And to meddle is to mar.
Change is rash, and ever was so—
   We are happy as we are.
Stand ye still, ye restless nations,
   And be happy as ye are!"

Mightier is the younger preacher;
   Genius flashes from his eyes,
And the crowds who hear his voice
Give him, while their souls rejoice,
   Throbbing bosoms for replies.
Awed they listen, yet elated,
   While his stirring accents fall:—
"Forward! ye deluded nations;
   Progress is the rule of all.
Man was made for healthful effort;
   Tyranny has crush'd him long:
He shall march from good to better,
   Nor be patient under wrong.
Forward! ye awaken'd nations,
   And do battle with the wrong.

"Standing still is childish folly—
    Going backward is a crime,
None should patiently endure
Any ill that he can cure.
    Onward! keep the march of Time—
Onward, while a wrong remains
    To be conquer'd by the right—
While Oppression lifts a finger
    To affront us by his might;
While an error clouds the reason;
    While a sorrow gnaws the heart;
While a slave awaits his freedom,
    Action is the wise man's part:
Forward; ye awaken'd nations!
    Action is the people's part.

"Onward! there are ills to conquer—
    Ills that on yourselves you've brought,
There is wisdom to discern,
There is temperance to learn,
    And enfranchisement for thought.
Hopeless poverty and toll
    May be conquer'd if you try.
Vice, and wretchedness and famine
    Give beneficence the lie,
Onward! onward! and subdue them!
    Root them out—their day has pass'd;
Goodness is alone immortal;
    Evil was not made to last
Forward! ye awaken'd people!
    And your sorrow shall not last."

And the preaching of this preacher
    Stirs the pulses of the world,
Tyranny has curb'd its pride;
Errors that were deified
    Into darkness have been hurl'd.
Slavery and liberty,
    And the wrong and right have met,
To decide their ancient quarrel.
    Onward, preacher! onward yet!
There are pens to tell your progress;
    There are eyes that pine to read;

There are hearts that burn to aid you;
  There are arms in hour of need.
Onward, preacher! onward nations!
  Will must ripen into deed.

The Northern Star and National Trades Journal, 4 July 1846

Clarence Mangan

THE SONG OF HATRED

Yes, Freedom's War!—though the deadly strife
  Makes earth one charnel bone-yard!
The last kiss now to the child and wife,
  And the first firm grasp of the poniard!
Blood soon shall run in rivers above
  The bright flowers we to-day tread;
We have all had more than enough of love,
  So now for a spell of Hatred!
We have all had more than enough of love,
  So now for a spell of Hatred!
How long shall the hideous ogre, Power,
  Rear column of skulls on column?
Oh, Justice! hasten thy judgment-hour,
  and open thy doomsday volume!
No more oiled speech!—it is time the drove
  Of despots should hear their fate read—
We have all had quite enough of love,
  Be our watchword henceforth Hatred!
We have all had quite enough of love,
  Be our watchword henceforth Hatred!

Cold steel! To that it must come at length—
  Nor quake to hear it spoken!
By the blows alone *we* strike in our strength
  Can the chains of the world be broken!
Up, then! No more in city or grove.
  Let Slavery and Dismay tread!

We have all had more than enough of love,
  Let us now fall back upon Hatred!
We have all had more than enough of love,
  Let us now fall back upon Hatred!

My friends! the tremendous time at hand
  Will show itself truly in earnest!
Do you the like!—and take your stand
  Where its aspect frowns the sternest!
Strive now as Tell and Korner strove!
  Be your sharp swords early and late red!
You have all had more than enough of love—
  Test now the talisman, Hatred!
You have all had more than enough of love,
  Test now the talisman, Hatred!

The Labourer: A Monthly Magazine of Politics, Literature, and Poetry, 1847, vol. I

Gerald Massey

SONG OF THE RED REPUBLICAN

Ay, tyrants, build your bulwarks! forge your fetters! link your
    chains!
As brims your guilt-cup fuller, our's of grief runs to the drains:
Still, as on Christ's brow, crowns of thorn for Freedom's martyrs
    twine,—
Still batten on live hearts, and madden o'er the hot blood-wine!
Murder men sleeping; or awake—torture them dumb with pain,
And tear with hands all bloody-red Mind's jewels from the brain!
Your feet are on us, tyrants: strike, and hush Earth's wail of
    sorrow!
Your sword of power, so red to-day, shall kiss the dust to-
    morrow!
Oh, but 'twill be a merry day, the world shall set apart,
When Strife's last sword is broken in the last crown'd pauper's
    heart!
And it shall come—despite of rifle, rope, and rack, and scaffold:

Once more we lift the earnest brow, and battle on unbaffled!
Alas! the hopes that have gone down, the young life vainly spilt,
Th' Eternal Murder still sits crown'd and thron'd in damning
    guilt!
Still in God's golden sun the tyrants' bloody banner burns;
And priests—Hell's midnight bravoes—desecrate Rome's patriot
    urns!
See how th' oppressors of the poor with serpents hunt our
    blood!
Hear from the dark the groan and curse go madd'ning up to
    God!
They kill and trample us poor worms till Earth is dead men's
    dust;
Death's red tooth daily drains our hearts; but end—ay, end it
    must!
The herald of our coming Christ leaps in the womb of Time;
The poor's grand army treads the Age's march with step
    sublime!
Our's is the mighty Future, and what marvel, brother men,
If the devoured of ages should turn devourers, then?
Our hopes ran mountains high,—we sung at heart,—wept tears
    of gladness.—
When France, the bravely beautiful, dash'd down her sceptred
    madness;
And Hungary her one-hearted race of mighty heroes hurled
In the death-gap of the nations, as a bulwark for the world!
Oh, Hungary—gallant Hungary—proud and glorious thou wert,
Feeding the world's soul like a river gushing from God's heart!
And Rome—where Freedom's heroes bled, to make her breast
    beat higher.
How her eyes redden'd with the flash of her ancestral fire!
Mothers of children, who shall live the Gods of future story—
Your blood shall blossom from the dust, and crown the world
    with glory!
We'll tread them down yet—curse and crown, Czar, Kaizer,
    King, and Slave;
And Mind shall lord it in the court of high-throned fool and
    knave!
Oh, brothers of the bounding heart! I look thro' tears and smile;
Our land is rife with sound of fetters snapping 'neath the file;
I lay my hand on England's heart, and in each life-throb mark
The pealing thought of freedom ring its tocsin in the dark!
I see the toiled hath become a glorious, Christ-like preacher,

And as he wins a crust shines proudly forth the great world
  teacher;
Still he toils on; but, tyrant, 'tis a mighty thing when slaves,
Who delve their lives into their work, know that they dig your
  graves!
Anarchs, your doom comes swiftly, brave and eagle spirits climb
To ring Oppression's thunder knell from the watch-towers of
  time!
A Spirit of Cromwellian might is stirring at this hour;
And thought burns eloquent in men's eyes with more than
  speechful power!
Old England, cease the mummer's part! wake starveling, serf
  and slave!
Rouse, in the majesty of wrong, great kindred of the brave!
Speak, and the world shall answer with her voices myriadfold;
And men, like gods, shall grapple with the giant wrongs of old!
Now, mothers of the people, give your babes heroic milk!
Sires, soul your sons to daring deeds: no more soft words of silk!
Great spirits of the heaven-homed Dead—take shape, and walk
  our mind!
Their glory smites our upward look! we seem no longer blind!
They tell us how they broke their bonds, and whisper "so may
  ye!"
One sharp, stern struggle, and the slaves of centuries are free!
The people's heart, with pulse like cannon, panteth for the fray!
And brothers, gallant brothers, we'll be with you in that day!

The Red Republican, 1850, no. 1

THE RED BANNER

Fling out the Red Banner! o'er mountain and valley,
  Let earth feel the tread of the Free, once again;
Now, Soldiers of Freedom, for love of God, rally—
  Old Earth yearns to know that her children are men;
We are nerved by a million wrongs burning and bleeding.
  Bold thoughts leap to birth, but, the bold deeds must come,
And, wherever humanity's yearning and pleading,
  One battle for liberty strike ye heart-home!

Fling out the Red Banner! its fiery front under,
  Come, gather ye, gather ye! Champions of Right!

And roll round the world with the voice of God's thunder
  The wrongs we've to reckon—oppressors to smite;
They deem that we strike no more like the old heroband
  Martyrdom's own battle-hearted and brave;
Blood of Christ! brothers mine, it were sweet, but to see ye stand
  Triumph or tomb! welcome! glory or grave!

Fling out the Red Banner! achievements immortal
  Have yet to be won by the hands labour-brown,
And few, few may enter the proud promise-portal,
  Yet, wear it in thought, boys! the glorious crown!
And, oh! joy of the conflict! sound trumpet! array us!
  True hearts would leap up, were all hell in our path,
Up! up! from the slave land! who stirreth to stay us
  Shall fall as of old in the Red Sea of wrath!

Fling out the Red Banner! and range ye around,
  Young spirits, abiding to burst into wings,
We stand, by the coming events, shadow-crowned,
  There's a grim hush in heaven! and the Bird of Storm sings:
"All's well!" saith the Sentry of Tyranny's tower,
  "Even Hope by their watch-fire is grey and tearblind."
Aye, all's well! Freedom's altar burns hour by hour—
  Live brands for the fire-damps with which ye are mined.

Fling out the Red Banner! the patriots perish!
  But where their bones moulder the seed taketh root—
Their heart's-life ran red the great harvest to cherish,
  Then gather ye Reapers, and garner the fruit.
Victory! victory! Tyrants are quaking,
  The Titan of Toil from the bloody thrall starts,
The Slaves are awaking! the dawnlight is breaking!
  The footfall of Freedom beats quick at our hearts!

The Red Republican, 1850 no. 1

LOVERS' FANCIES

Sweet heaven, I do love a maiden,
Radiant, rare, and beauty laden!
When she's near me heaven is round me,

Her sweet presence doth so bound me,
I could wring my heart of gladness,
Might it free her lot of sadness,
Give the world and all that's in it,
Might I press her hand a minute.
Yet she weeteth not I love her,
    Never do I tell the sweet
Dream, but to the stars above her,
    And the flowers that kiss her feet!

Might I live and linger near her,
And in tearful moments cheer her,
I would be a bird to lighten
Her dear heart, her sweet eyes brighten;
Or like fragrance from a blossom
Give my life up on her bosom!
For my love's without measure,
Even its pangs are precious pleasure.
Yet she weeteth not I love her,
    Never do I tell the sweet
Dream, but to the stars above her,
    And the flowers that kiss her feet.

The Red Republican, 1850 no. 3

THEY ARE GONE

When hope's blossoms many-numbered—
    Stirred as if to burst—
When on earthquake-edge all slumbered—
    Who have man accurst—
When our hearts like throbbing drums,
Beat for Freedom, ha! it comes
God! they stumbled among tombs.

    They are gone.
Freedom's strong ones young and hoary,
    Beautiful of faith;
And her first dawn-blush of glory—
    Gilds their camp of death.—
There they lie in shrouds of blood,

Murdered where for Right they stood!
Murdered, Christ-like, doing good.

    They are gone,
And 'tis good to die, up-giving
   Valour's vengeful breath—
To nurse heroes of the living.
   Thus divine is death!
One by one, dear hearts! they left us,
Yet Hope hath not all bereft us,
Triumph lamps the gap they cleft us.

    They are *here!*
Here! where life ran bloody rain—
   When power from God seem'd wrencht—
Here! where tears fall molten brain,
   And hands are agony-clencht!
See them! count their wounds! ha! now
There's a glory where the plough
Of Pain's fire-crown seam'd each brow.

    They are *here!*
In the Etna of each heart,
   Where Vengeance laughs hell-mirth!
In the torture-tears that start
   O'er their glorious worth!
Tears? aye, tears of fire! proud weepers!
T'avenge these soul-sepultured sleepers!
Fire! to smith Death's blood-seed reapers.

    They are *here!*
In the starry march of Time,
   Beating at our side!
Let us live their lives sublime,
   Die as they have died!
God shall wake! these martyrs come
Myriad-fold, from their heart tomb!
In the Despot's day of doom.

The Friend of the People, 14 December 1850

THE MEN OF "FORTY-EIGHT"

They rose in Freedom's rare sunrise,
    Like giants roused from wine!
And in their hearts, and in their eyes,
    The God leapt up divine!
Their souls flashed out like naked swords,
    Unsheathed for fiery fate;—
Strength went like battle with their words,
    The men of Forty-eight.
                  Hurrah!
    For the men of Forty-eight.

Dark days have fall'n! yet in the strife,
    They bate no more sublime,—
And bravely works the fiery life,—
    Their hearts' pulse thro' the time.
As grass is greenest trodden down,
    So suffering makes men great;
And this dark tide shall grandly crown
    The men of forty-eight.
                  Hurrah!
    For the men of Forty-eight.

Some, in a bloody burial sleep,
    Like Greeks, to glory gone!
Swift in their steps, avengers leap
    With their proof armour on!
And hearts beat high with dauntless trust,
    We'll triumph soon or late,
Though they be mouldering in the dust,—
    Brave men of Forty-eight.
                  Hurrah!
    For the men of Forty-eight!

O! when the world wakes up to worst,
    The tyrants once again;—
And Freedom's summons-shout shall burst
    In music on the brain
With heart to heart and hand in hand,
    Ye'll find them all elate,—

And true as ever Spartan band!
　　The Men of Forty-eight.

　　　　　　　　　　　Hurrah!
　　For the Men of Forty-eight.

The Friend of the People, 25 January 1851

A RED REPUBLICAN LYRIC

Smitten stones will talk with fiery tongues,
　　And the worm when trodden will turn,
But cowards, ye cringe to the death fullest wrongs,
　　And answer with never a spurn.
Then torture, oh, Tyrants! the spiritless drove,
　　Old England's helots will bear,
There's no hell in their hatred, no God in their love
　　Nor shame in their death's despair.
　　　　For, our fathers are praying for pauper-pay,
　　　　Our mothers with death's kiss are white!
　　　　Our sons are the rich man's serfs by day,
　　　　And our daughters his slaves by night!

They were few, those grand, hero-hearts of old,
　　Who played the peerless part!
We are fifty-fold, but the gangrene gold,
　　Hath eaten out Hampden's heart.
With their faces to danger, like freemen they fought,
　　With their daring all heart and hand!
And the thunder-deed followed the lightning-thought
　　When they stood for their own good land—
　　　　Our fathers are praying for pauper-pay,
　　　　Our mothers with death's kiss are white!
　　　　Our sons are the rich man's serfs by day,
　　　　And our daughters his slaves by night!

The tearless are drunk with our tears, have they driven
　　The god of the poor man mad?
For we weary of waiting the help of heaven,
　　And the battle goes still with the bad!
Oh! but death for death, and life for life,
　　It were better to take and give—

With hand to throat and knife to knife,
 Then die out as thousands live!
  For, our fathers are praying for pauper-pay,
  Our mothers with death's kiss are white!
  Our sons are the rich man's serfs by day,
  And our daughters his slaves by night!

Rotten-ripe to be hearsed, are earth's long-accursed,
 Why tarries the tyrants' knell?
When the heart of one half the world doth burst,
 To hurry them into hell!
We should not be living in darkness and dust,
 And dying like slaves in the night,
But big with the might of the inward "must,"
 We should battle for Freedom and Right,
  For, our fathers are praying for pauper-pay,
  Our mothers with death's kiss are white!
  Our sons are the rich man's serfs by day,
  And our daughters his slaves by night!

Justice, 1 November 1884

THE LORDS OF LAND AND MONEY

Sons of Old England, from the sod,
 Up-lift the noble brow!
Gold apes a mightier power than God,
 And wealth is worshipt now!
In all these toil-ennobled lands
 Ye have no heritage;
They snatch the fruit of youthful hands,
 The staff from weary age.
O tell them in their Palaces,
 These Lords of Land and Money!
They shall not kill the poor like bees,
 To rob them of Life's honey.

Thro' long dark years of blood and tears,
 We're toiled like branded slaves,
Till Wrong's red hand hath made a land
 Of paupers, prisons, graves!

But our long-sufferance endeth now;
    Within the souls of men
The fruitful buds of promise blow,
    And Freedom lives again!
O tell them in their Palaces,
    These Lords of Land and Money!
They shall not kill the poor like bees,
    To rob them of Life's honey.

Too long have Labour's nobles knelt
    Before exalted "Rank;"
Within our souls the iron is felt—
    We hear our fetters clank!
A glorious voice goes throbbing forth
    From millions stirring now,
Who yet before these Gods of earth
    Shall stand with unblencht brow.
O tell them in their Palaces,
    These Lords of Land and Money!
They shall not kill the poor like bees,
    To rob them of Life's honey.

Massey, *The Poetical Works of Gerald Massey* (London: Routledge, Warne and Routledge, 1861)

OUR LAND

'Tis the Land our stalwart Fore-sires trode,
    Where the brave and heroic-souled—
Gave Freedom baptism of their best blood,
    In the martyr-days of old!
And lives there no remnant of that brave blood,
    Gone down in its pride all-glorious?
O! but to stand as our Hampden stood!
    Or die as he died victorious!
For our rare-old land, and our dear old land,
    With its memories bright and brave!
And sing O! for the hour its Sons shall band,
    To free it of Despot and Slave.

Cromwell is of us! and Shakespeare's thought
    Be -kings us all crowns above!

And Freedom's faith fierce splendours caught,
   From our grand old Milton's love!
And we should be marching on gallantly,
   With their proud stride from glory to glory!
For the Right! In our might, strikingly valiantly,
   Like the free who are famous in story,—
For our rare old land! and our dear old land,
   With its memories bright and brave!
And sing O! for the hour its sons shall band,
   To free it of Despot and Slave.

On Naseby-field of the fight sublime,
   Our old red Rose doth blow!
Would to God, that the soul of our earlier time
   Were stirring with us now!
T'ward the golden clime of the Future, Earth sweeps,
   And the Time trumpets true men to freedom!
In the hearts of Slaves, the mounting god leaps!
   But O! for the men to lead them!
For our rare old land, and our dear old land!
   With its memories bright and brave!
And sing O! for the hour its sons shall band,—
   To free it of Despot and Slave.

What do we lack, that the red, red Wrong
   Should starve us 'mid heaps of gold?
We have brains as broad! we have arms as strong!
   We have hearts as great and bold!
Will a thousand more years' meek suffering, school
   Our lives to a sterner bravery?
No! down and down with their robber rule;
   And trample at once your slavery!
For our rare old land, and our dear old land!
   With its memories bright and brave!
And sing O! for the hour its sons shall band,
   To free it of Despot and Slave.

The Friend of the People, 21 December 1850

THINGS WILL GO BETTER YET

It's all a lie! their Right Divine,
   Their altar grim, their crown and throne!
For them the many shall not pine,
   With souls unfledg'd, and minds ungrown.
Priestcraft may curse, reproving;
   Red-handed kingcraft threat;
But now, thank God! we're moving—
   Things will go better yet.

Old Earth with clouds and thorns is rife!
   Man hath his miseries still!—yet flowers
Make sunshine in the darkest life,
   And that with Heaven this world of ours.
And there be hearts all loving,
   And love shall love beget;
For now, thank God! we're moving—
   Things will go better yet.

From out the brain 'twill wrench a tear
   To count our martyrs by the way;
But bear a hand, my brother dear,
   A glorious remnant lives to-day.
The People, leagued and loving,
   Shall break the Tyrants' neck;
And now, thank God! we're moving—
   Things will go better yet.

The Friend of the People, 18 January 1851

KINGS ARE BUT GIANTS BECAUSE WE KNEEL

Good People, put no faith in kings, nor merchant-princes trust,
Who grind your hearts in mammon's press, your faces in the
   dust,
Trust to your own stout hearts to break the Tyrants dark, dark
   ban,
If yet one spark of freedom lives, let man be true to man,
We'll never fight again, boys, with Yankee, Pole, and Russ,
We love the French as brothers, and Frenchmen too, love us!

But we'll join to crush those fiends who kill all love and liberty,
Kings are but giants because we kneel, *one leap and up go we.*

Trust not the priests, their tears are lies, their hearts are hard
    and cold,
The welcomest of all their flock, are fierce wolves fleeced with
    gold!
Rogues all! for hire they prop the laws that make us poor men
    sin,
Ah! though, their robes are black without, they've blacker souls
    within,
The Church and State are linked, and sworn to desolate the
    land—
Good People, twixt these foxes tails we'll fling a fiery brand!
Who hears the worst that they can wreak that loveth Liberty!
They are but giants because we kneel, *one leap and up go we!*

"Back! tramplers of the many, there, the ambush danger lies,
Beware, or strife's red blood may run, respect a Nations cries,
Think how they taxed the People mad, that old Regime of
    France,
Whose heads like poppies from Death's sythe, fell in a bloody
    dance!
Ah! kill not love, or tear from manhood's crown, the jewels
    longer—
Pluck not God's image from our hearts, because ye are the
    stronger!
Ye plead in vain! ye bleed in vain! ah, blind, when will ye see,
They are but giants because we kneel, *one leap and up go we!*

We've battled for earth's darlings, while they've slunk in
    splendid lair,
With souls that crept like earthworms in dead Beauty's golden
    hair,
A tale of lives wept out in tears their grandeur garb reveals—
And the last sobs of breaking hearts sound in their chariot
    wheels,
But they're quaking now, and shaking now who've wrought the
    hurtling sorrow,
To-day the desolators! but the desolate to-morrow.
Loud o'er their murderous menace, wakes the watchword of the
    free,
They are but giants because we kneel, *one leap and up go we!*

Some brave and patriot hearts are gone to break beyond the
　　wave
And some who gave their lives for love have found a prison
　　grave,
Some have grown grey in watching—some have fainted by the
　　way,
But youth still cherishes within the light of a better day—
Oh! blessings on high-dreaming youth! God's with the dear
　　brave band.
Their spirits breathe of paradise, they're freshest from his
　　hand—
And looking on the People's might who doubts they shall be
　　free!
Kings are but giants because we kneel, *one leap and up go we!*

The Friend of the People, 8 March 1851

THE AWAKENING

How sweet is the fair face of Nature when May
　　With her rainbow earth-born and flower-woven hath spanned
Hill and dale; and the music of birds on the spray
　　Makes Earth seem a beautiful faëry land!
And dear is our First-love's young spirit-wed Bride,
　　With her meek eyes just sheathing in tender eclipse,
When the sound of our voice calls her heart's ruddy tide
　　Up in beauty to break on her cheek and her lips.
But Earth has no sight half so glorious to see,
As a People up-girding its might to be free.

To see men awake from the slumber of ages,
　　Their brows grim from labour, their hands hard and tan,
Start up living Heroes, long dreamt-of by Sages!
　　And smite with strong arm the Oppressors of man:
To see them come dauntless forth 'mid the world's warring,
　　Slaves of the midnight-mine! Serfs of the sod!
Show how the Eternal within them is stirring,
　　And never more bend to a crowned clod:
Dear God! 'tis a sight for Immortals to see,—
A People up-girding its might to be free.

Battle on bravely, O sons of Humanity!
  Dash down the Cup from your lips, O ye Toilers!
Too long hath the world bled for Tyrants' insanity—
  Too long our weakness been strength to our Spoilers!
The heart that through danger and death will be dutiful:
  Soul that with Cranmer in fire would shake hands,
And a life like a Palace-home built for the beautiful.
  Freedom of all her beloved demands—
And Earth has no sight half so glorious to see,
As a People up-girding its might to be free!

Massey, *My Lyrical Life Poems Old and New 2d ed.* (London: Kegan, Paul, Trench, Trübner & Co., 1889)

THE COALITION AND THE PEOPLE

O suffering people! this is not our fight
Who called a holy Crusade for the Right!
The Despots' bloody game our Tricksters play,
And stake our future chance by chance away.
Not Whigs! not Tories! we want English Souls,
Through which there yet reverberates and rolls
Some echo of old greatness; trusty hands
To bear our Banner over Seas and Lands.
Our good Ship may be driving on the rocks;
We need a Compass, and not Weather-Cocks!
We have had Leaders who strode forward all
On fire to serve her at their Country's call;
Who did not stoop, till blind, for place or pelf,
Their whole life burned a sacrifice of Self!
Who faced the spirit of the Storm and Strife
And with an upward smile laid down their life.

But now our Leaders are the coward and cold;
The Gnomes whose daylight is a gleam of gold;
The Dwarfs who sun them in a Despot's smile;
The Quakes who would set our dear green Isle
Spinning their Cotton till the Judgment Hour,
With Ocean turning round for Water-power.

They pander to this Plunderer of the night;
Confused their little sense of Wrong and Right,
And they would bow our England's forehead down
Trustfully in his lap to leave her crown;
See her sit weeping where her brave lie dead;
Blood on her raiment, ashes on her head.
We cannot leave our Land for watch and ward
To these who know not what a gem they guard;
Who would bind us helpless for the Bird of Blood
To swoop on; who would have this famous flood
Of English Freedom stagnate till is stink,
While reptiles wriggle in their slimy drink,
And the frogs reign in darkness; croak all night,
And call the Stars false Prophets of the Light.

O darkened hearts in Homesteads desolate!
O wasted bravery of our vainly great!
The Flower of Men fall stricken from behind:
The Knaves and Cowards stab us bound and blind.
With faces turned from Battle, they went forth:
We marched with ours flint-set against the North.
They shuffled lest their feet should rouse the dead:
We went with Resurrection in our tread.
They trembled lest the world might come to blows:
We quivered for the tug and mortal close.
They only meant a mild hint for the Czar:
We would have surfeited his soul with War.
While they were quenching Freedom's scattered fires,
We kindled memories of heroic Sires.
They'd have this grand Old England cringe and pray,
"Don't smite me, Kings; but if you will, you may."
We'd make her as in those proud times of old,
When Cromwell spoke, and Blake's war-thunders rolled.
They on the passing powers of Darkness fawn;
With warrior-joy we greeted this red Dawn.
To crowned blood-suckers they would bind us slaves,
We would be free, or sleep in glorious graves.

State-Spiders, Here or There, weave webs alike;
These snare the victims, while the others strike.
The Dwarfs drag our great Banner in the mire:
We ask for Men to bear it high and higher.

O stop their fiddling over War's grim revel,
And pitch them from your shoulders to—the Devil.

Massey, My Lyrical Life Poems Old and New

THE FAITH OF THE PHILISTINE

The great Deceiver finds himself decieved:
France's bereaver is of France bereaved:
And England, half converted by his fall,
Thinks there's a God who governs after all!
This is the faith o' the British Philistine;
Failure is damnable; Success divine.

PEACE-AT-ANY-PRICE MEN

You Seven Wise Men of Gotham, who could vote
That England in your bowl must sink or float,
You sorely need a Tonic of Cold Steel,
Who to the Beasts of Prey for Peace would kneel!
Malingerers who can basely maim the might
Of Manhood, and would rather die than fight.
The fear, for Self, makes Cowards, for others, bold:
And love of Country's sapped by lust of Gold.

You, poor white-livered bastards of our race
To rouse some English colour in your face,
Must you on either coward cheek be smitten,
Or have the blood fetched back to them flea-bitten?
Gnash your pale lips for shame! and let the bite
For a moment hide the coward out of sight.
Alas! nor bite would bring, nor blow could start,
True English blood where there is none at heart.

But, we are Peacemen, also; crying for
Peace, peace, at any price—though it be War!

We must live free, at peace, or each man dies
With death-clutch fast for ever on the prize.

Gerald Massey. *My Lyrical Life: Poems Old and New* 2nd series
(London: Kegan, Paul, Trench, Trübner and Co., 1889)

THE SECOND EMPIRE

It had not life enough to die at last,
Nor weight enough to fall; it simply passed:
A Shadow great calamity had cast.

Gone, like a dance of gnats from sunset streams!
We saw it, with these eyes; and now it seems
Dim as a fragment of forgotten dreams.

A mist of blood, it rose up in the night;
A mist of glamour blurred the common light;
A mist of lies, it vanishes from sight.

For Eighteen years we watched where'er life stirred;
Waited and listened, but we never heard
God speak. It went without a warning word!

One flash of Heaven; and all the Pageantry
Of Cloudland crumbles; all the Ephemeræ flee
From the still presence of Eternity!

One ray of risen Liberty hath shone,
And like a name writ in the Sighs breathed on
A Prison Window-pane, the Empire's gone.

Massey, *My Lyrical Life*

JOHN BRIGHT

Thou hast done good work in thy day, John!
Thou wert foremost in many a fray, John!
    Thou shouldst have been first to the end.
But to halt when they sound the advance, John!

Thou art losing a glorious chance, John!
   Of dying the People's Friend!

Once thou wert terribly feared, John!
The enemy spat on the beard, John!
   Of the Rebel so radical then!
And to see how they slaver thee now, John!
Their Model for Statesmen art Thou, John!
   Their man who art Monarch of men!

'Tis Here and 'tis Now that we test, John!
All sympathies for the Oppressed, John!
   Not in far-off lands or the Past.
'Tis Here and 'tis Now We can give, John!
New leave for a people to live, John!
   In a Union with Us that shall last.

But faint hearts have gone far enough, John!
The road is so long and so rough, John!
   That many fall out by the way:
And 'tis dark—for the Stars are withdrawn, John!
Before we can see the fresh Dawn, John!
   That brings in the perfectest day.

The fastest of Friends will now fail us, John!
Worse than our Foes they assail us, John!
   Like fighters of Parthian mould.

And some have got tired with age, John!
Yet the Future must turn its new page, John!
   And the People can never grow old.

Thy hand for a parting shake, John!
Heartily cordial, we take, John!
   If the old ties thou wilt tear.
But Our battle must still go on, John!
Victories have to be won, John!
   Though Thou wilt not be with us there.

Massey, *My Lyrical Life*

THE PRIMROSE DAME

Your Primrose Dame is a likely Lass,
To wile and wheedle the Working Class
 Of their Votes—her end and aim!
A vision of beauty, in by-way or street,
Is the glance of her face, or a glimpse of her feet,—
 When a-foot is the Primrose Dame.

The men used to suffer the brunt of the strife,—
Kissed the children, Courted the Wife,
 And cured the halt and the lame;
But they who once lorded it over the poll
Now send out the women to cadge and cajole,—
 Pray you pity the Primrose Dame!

We're all of One flesh, at Election time,
Whether white-powdered or black with grime,—
 Skim-milk, or *Crême de la crême;*
Open-armed at your door she knocks,
Wants to pry into the Ballot-box,
 Does the promising Primrose Dame.

Soliciting Votes, she is not shy,
Will let you light your pipe at her eye,—
 Kindle your fire with her flame;
But beware of the Snare when you see the smile,
Under the Primrose she can beguile.
 'Tis the Beaconsfield Primrose Dame!

"Refreshments at five, in the Primrose Bower!
You WILL come? You WILL wear it? MY favourite flower?
HIS flower who gave it HIS fame!"
And the touch is of velvet, the look is of love:
But beware of the claw that is sheathed in the glove
 Of the Beaconsfield Primrose Dame.

She will scatter her perfume around you in showers,
Wrung from the lives of our Human Flowers,
 Without thought of shame or blame;
And the Roses of Health, that were ruthlessly torn
From the cheeks of your Children are wantonly worn
 In the Robe of the Primrose Dame.

She simply asks to be mounted astride
The British Lion—thinks she can guide,
   And the rampant animal tame,
If he will only give her his trust;
If he will only kneel down in the dust
   To carry the Primrose Dame.

Her charm for leading the beast by the nose
Is the brazenest image, a GILT primrose,—
   What a meal for an empty wame!
You Flower of Shams, with your counterfeit,
If the Brute should be tempted either to eat,—
   Let us pray for the Primrose Dame!

                    Massey, *My Lyrical Life*

D. F. M'Carthy

THE VOICE AND THE PEN

Oh! the orator's voice is a mighty power,
   As it echoes from shore to shore;
And the fearless pen hath more sway o'er men;
   Than the murderous cannon's roar!
What bursts the chains far o'er the main,
   And brightens the captive's den?
'Tis the fearless pen and the voice of power.
   Hurrah! for the voice and pen!
                 Hurrah!
   Hurrah! for the voice and pen!

The tyrant knaves who deny man's rights,
   And the cowards who blanch with fear,
Exclaim with glee—"No arms have ye,
   Nor cannon, sword, nor spear!
Your hills are ours, with our forts and towers
   We are masters of mount and glen!"
Tyrants beware! for the arms we bear
   Are the voice and the fearless pen!

Hurrah!
Hurrah! for the voice and pen!

Though your horsemen stand with their bridle in hand,
And your sentinels walked around;
Though your matches flare in the midnight air,
    And your brazen trumpets sound;
Oh! the orator's tongue should be heard among
    These listening warrior men;
And they'll quickly say—"Why should we slay
    Our friends of the voice and pen?"
Hurrah!
Hurrah! for the voice and pen!

When the Lord created the earth and sea,
    The stars and the glorious sun,
The Godhead spoke, and the universe woke!
    And the mighy work was done!
Let a word be flung from the orator's tongue,
    Or a drop from the fearless pen,
And the chains accursed, asunder burst
    That fettered the minds of men!
Hurrah!
Hurrah! for the voice and pen!

Oh! these are the swords with which we fight,
    The arms in which we trust,
Which no tyrant hand will dare to brand;
    Which time cannot dim or rust!
When these we bore, we triumphed before,
    With these we'll triumph again!
And the world will say no power can stay
    The voice and the fearless pen!
Hurrah!
Hurrah! for the voice and pen!

The Northern Star and National Trades Journal, 15 February 1851

Edward P. Mead

THE STEAM KING

There is a King, and a ruthless King,
  Not a King of the poet's dream;
But a tyrant fell, white slaves know well,
  And that ruthless King is Steam.

He hath an arm, an iron arm,
  And tho' he hath but one,
In that mighty arm there is a charm,
  That millions hath undone.

Like the ancient Moloch grim, his sire
  In Himmon's vale that stood,
His bowels are of living fire,
  And children are his food.

His priesthood are a hungry band,
  Blood-thirsty, proud, and bold;
'Tis they direct his giant hand,
  In turning blood to gold.

For filthy gain, in their servile chain
  All nature's rights they bind;
They mock at lovely woman's pain,
  And to manly tears are blind.

The sighs and groans of Labour's sons
  Are music in their ear,
And the skeleton shades, of lads and maids,
  In the Steam King's hells appear.

Those hells upon earth, since the Steam King's birth
  Have scatter'd around despair;

For the human mind for heav'n design'd,
  With the body, is murdered there.

Then down with the King, the Moloch King,
  Ye working millions all;
O chain his hand, or our native land
  Is destin'd by him to fall.

And his Satraps abhor'd each proud Mill Lord,
  Now gorg'd with gold and blood;
Must be put down by the nation's frown,
  As well as their monster God.

The cheap bread crew[1] will murder you,
  By bludgeon, ball, or brand;
Then your Charter gain and the power will be vain
  Of the Steam King's bloody band.

Then down with the King, the Moloch King,
  And the satraps of his might;
Let right prevail, then Freedom hail!
  When might shall stoop to right!

The Northern Star and Leeds General Advertiser, 11 February 1843

A NEW CHARTIST SONG

TUNE—"THE BAY OF BISCAY, O!"

Loud roar'd the people's thunder,
  And tyrants heard the storm,
They trembled, and knocked under,
  And gave us mock Reform.[1]
    They felt the electric spark,
    Which bared corruption's ark;
  Rent their veil, they turned pale,
  At the voice of freedom, O!

Then our good ship Britannia,
  Amongst the breakers lay,
Poor bark! we gladly mann'd her,

With Whigs and Gaffer Grey;[2]
  But lubbers all they proved,
  And from the rocks ne'er moved,
There are they, till this day,
On thy rocks, corruption, O!

At length the People's Charter
  Shoots forth its beacon rays!
She deepens now her water,
  The tide around her plays;
    Soon shall her lubber crew,
    Resign her helm to you;
Chartists brave, ye must save,
The good ship, Britannia, O!

The morn of freedom's breaking,
  We hail it from afar:
And for a compass taking,
  Our glorious *Northern Star!*
    We'll soon the breakers clear,
    The port we soon shall near;
Now, we sail, with the gale,
For the Bay of Freedom, O!

Our pilot, brave O'CONNOR[3]
  We soon will get on board,
More sail we'll crowd upon her,
  And get her richly stored;
    Mann'd by a gallant crew,
    Of Chartists staunch and true,
We shall ride, with the tide,
To the port of Freedom, O!

The Northern Star and Leeds General Advertiser, 13 February 1841

CHARTIST SONG

TUNE—MARCH TO THE BATTLE FIELD

Hark! 'tis the trumpet call
  Of liberty is pealing,
Rouse Britons, one and all,

Your majesty revealing;
Rouse from your leaden sleep,
　Death is in your slumber,
Rise like the mighty deep,
　Its billows loud outnumber.

Chorus:

Press round the standard, press,
　Ne'er for lucre barter,
Your wives and children's happiness,
　Stand firm for freedom's Charter.

Press round our standard true,
　Again, behold 'tis flaunting
Defiance to the despots few,
　And all their idle vaunting;
Whig and Tory wrath we'll brave,
　And boldly bid defiance,
To courtly fool and priestly knave,
On heaven's our sole reliance.

Chorus:

Press round the standard, press,
　Ne'er your free rights barter,
Universal happiness,
　Is in our glorious Charter!

　Nought but freemen's rights we claim,
　　All men's rights respecting,
　Liberty! thy sacred name!
　　Thy shrine alone protecting;
Swear by freedom's holy name,
　By her to stand or fall man,
Spurn a coward vassal's chain,
　Your watchword one and all man.

Chorus:

Press round the standard, press,
　Ne'er your free rights barter,

Universal happiness,
  Is in our glorious Charter!

The Northern Star and Leeds General Advertiser, 8 May 1841

THE BRAVE OLD KING

AIR—"THE BRAVE OLD OAK"

A song for the King, the brave Old King!
  The King of the poor white slaves;
There's none in the land that more nobly doth stand
  'Gainst the power of the Poor Law knaves.
His manly heart ever took the part
  Of the poor and the oppress'd;
This is better far than the jewell'd star
  Which gleams on a despot's breast.

    Chorus:

Then here's to the King, the good Old King!
  And long may he live and reign.
A true pattern is he of what Monarchs should be:
  We shall never see his like again!

Tho' in prison strong for opposing wrong,
  In bondage sore confin'd;
He has stood like a rock, spite of bolt and lock,
  The friend of humankind.
A Briton so bold, that power nor gold
  Could never turn away—From the path of right;
  For 'tis his delight,
And he walks in it night and day.
    Then here's to the king, etc.

Then ye millions who toil for the lords of the soil,
  And the lords of the dread steam king,
Your gratitude show to the tyrants' foe,
  And your cheerful tribute bring.
One heart and one mind, let King Richard find,

Till to freedom we him restore,
And justice be done by the "Altar and Throne"
    To the "Cottage of the Poor."
        Then here's to the king, etc.

The Northern Star and Leeds General Advertiser, 6 January 1844

J. M'Owen

FATHER! WHO ARE THE CHARTISTS?

Millions who labour with skill, my child,
On the land—at the loom—in the mill, my child.
        Whom bigots and knaves
        Would keep as their slaves;
Whom tyrants would punish and kill, my child.

Millions whom suffering draws, my child,
To unite in a glorious cause, my child.
        Their object, their end
        Is mankind to befriend,
By gaining for all equal laws, my child.

Millions who ever hath sought, my child,
For freedom of speech and of thought, my child,
        Though stripp'd of each right
        By the strong hand of might,
They ne'er can be vanquish'd or bought, my child.

Millions who *earnestly* call, my child,
For freedom to each and to all, my child;
        They have truth for their shield,
        And never will yield
Till they triumph in tyranny's fall, my child.

And they've sworn at a Holberry's grave,[1] my child,
(That martyr so noble and brave, my child)
        That come weal or come woe,

Still *onward* they'll go
Till Freedom be won for the slave, my child!

The Northern Star and Leeds General Advertiser, 10 February 1844

H. R. Nicholls

THE PARLIAMENT

AIR—"THE ONE-HORSE CHAY"

All the world's in town arriving,—
Some by rail, and some are driving,
Lords, ladies, manufacturers, and farmers not a few;
For the wisdom of the nation
Is met in convocation;
Now the Parliament's assembled, I wonder what 'twill do!

Our lordly legislators,—
They don't like agitators,
For they make the people think, if nothing else they do;

And 'tin-pot' legislation
Is spoilt by agitation;
Now the Parliament's assembled, I'll tell you what 'twill do.

Of religion spouting,
But education scouting,—
And soul-saving bishops, endowing one or two;
But to me it very odd is,
They don't try to save our bodies
And let our souls alone—it's the best thing they could do.

Of landed interest talking,
But labour interest baulking,—
The cotton lords and millocrats, no doubt, will have their due;

But those who work the cotton,

Of course, are quite forgotten,
Or told, that to emigrate 's 'the best thing they can do.'

Lord John[1] 'bout nothing spoutin',
Which part he is out and out in,—
Using many words, with ideas very few;
Will cry reform is *nil*,
To get on, we must stand still,
And to do nothing, is the best thing we can do.

All progression shirking,
All retrenchment burking,—
Of "the British Lion" speaking, and "Protection" too;
But if Hume[2] reform proposes,
They cry with fingers to their noses,
'Don't you wish that you may get it? you will have it when you
do!'

Now the people knowledge gainin',
Will soon be very plain in,—
Expressing their opinion of this bribed and bribing crew;

Some day they will assemble,
And make 'both houses' tremble—
For they'll kick 'em to the Devil—and 's the best thing they can
do!

The Friend of the People, 8 February 1851

Thomas Noel

THE PAUPER'S DRIVE

There's a grim one-horse hearse in a jolly round trot,
To the churchyard a pauper is going, I wot;
The road it is rough and the hearse has no springs;
And hark to the dirge which the sad drive sings:
Rattle his bones over the stones!
He's only a pauper, whom nobody owns!

O, where are the mourners? Alas! there are none—
He has left not a gap in the world now he's gone—
Not a tear in the eye of a child, woman, or man;
To the grave with his carcass as fast as you can:
    Rattle his bones over the stones!
    He's only a pauper, whom nobody owns!

What a jolting, and creaking, and splashing and din!
The whip how it cracks, and the wheels how they spin!
How the dirt, right and left, o'er the hedges is hurled!
The pauper at length makes a noise in the world!
    Rattle his bones over the stones!
    He's only a pauper, whom nobody owns!

Poor pauper defunct! he has made some approach
To gentility, now that he's stretched in a coach!
He's taking a drive in his carriage at last;
But it will not be long, if he goes on so fast!
    Rattle his bones over the stones!
    He's only a pauper, whom nobody owns!

You bumpkins! who stare at your brother conveyed—
Behold what respect to a cloddy is paid!
And be joyful to think, when by death you're laid low,
You've a chance to the grave like a gemman to go!
    Rattle his bones over the stones!
    He's only a pauper, whom nobody owns!

But a truce to this strain; for my soul it is sad,
To think that a heart in humanity clad
Should make, like the brutes, such a desolate end,
And depart from the light without leaving a friend!
    Bear soft his bones over the stones!
    Though a pauper, he's one whom his Maker yet owns.

Patrick Scott, *Victorian Poetry 1830 to 1870* (London:
Longman Group Limited, 1971)

Peter Pindar

ODE TO TYRANTS

Who, and what are ye, scepter'd bullies—speak,
That millions to your will must bow the neck,
And, ox-like, meanly take the galling yoke?
Philosophers your ignorance despise;
E'en FOLLY, laughing, lifts her maudlin eyes,
And freely on your wisdoms cracks her joke.
How dare ye on the men of labour tread,
Whose honest toils supply your mouths with bread;
Who, groaning, sweating, like so many hacks,
Work you the very clothes upon your backs?
   Clothes of calamity, I fear,
   That hold in every stitch a tear.
Who sent you?—Not the Lord who rules on high,
Sent you to MAN on purpose from the sky,
Because of wisdom it is not a proof:
Show your credentials, SIRS; if he refuse,
Terrific gentlemen, our smiles excuse,
BELIEF most certainly will keep aloof.
Old virtuous, rugged Cato, on a day,
Thus to the SOOTHSAYERS was heard to say:—
"AUGURS, by all the gods it is a shame,
"To gull the mole-eyed million at this rate:
"Making of gaping blockheads such a game,
"Pretending to be hand and glove with FATE!
"On guts and garbage when you meet,
"To carry on the holy cheat,
"How is it ye preserve that solemn grace,
"Nor burst with laughter in each other's face."
"Thus to your courtiers, SIRS, might I exclaim—
     "In wonder's name,
"How can ye meanly, grovelling, bow the head
"To pieces of gilt gingerbread?

"Fetch, carry, fawn, kneel, flatter, crawl, tell lies,
"To please the creature that you should despise?"
Tyrants, with all your power and wide dominion,
Ye ar'n't a whit like GOD in my opinion:
Though you think otherwise, I do presume;
Hot to the marrow with the ruling lust,
Fancying your crouching subjects so much dust,
Your lofty selves the mighty sweeping broom.
Open the warehouses of all your brains;
Come, Sirs, turn out—let's see what each contains;
Heavens, how ridiculous! what motely stuff!
Shut, quickly shut again the brazen doors,
Too much of balderdash the eye explores;
Yes, shut them, shut them; we have seen enough.
Are these the beings to bestride a world?
To such sad beasts, has God his creatures hurl'd?
Men want not tyrants—overbearing knaves—
Despots that wish to rule a realm of slaves;
Proud to be gazed at by a reptile race:
Charm'd with the music of their clanking chains.
Pleas'd with the fog of STATE, that clouds their brains,
Who cry, with all the impudence of face,—
"Behold your GODS!—down, rascals, on your knee;
"Your money, miscreants—quick, no words, no strife;
"Your lands, too—scoundrels, vermin, lice, bugs, fleas;
"And thank our mercy that allows you *life!*"
Thus speak the HIGHWAYMEN in purple pride,
On Slavery's poor gall'd back so wont to ride.
Who would not laugh to see a TAILOR bow
Submission to a pair of satin breeches?
Saying—"O BREECHES, all men must allow
"There's something in your aspect that bewitches;
"Let me admire you, BREECHES, crowned with glory:
"And though I made you, let me still *adore* ye;
"Though a *rump's* humble servant, form'd for need,
"To keep it warm, yet, Lord, you are so fine,
"I cannot think you are my work indeed—
"Though merely mortal, lo! you seem divine."
Who would not quick exclaim, 'The Tailor's mad?'
Yet TYRANT ADORATION is as bad.

The Chartist Circular, 9 November 1839

Joseph Radford

THE CHARTER

When thrones shall crumble and moulder to dust,
  And sceptres shall fall from the hands of the great,
And all the rich baubles a Monarch might boast,
  Shall vanish before the good sense of a state;
When Lords, (produced by the mandate of Kings),
  So proud and dominant, rampant with power,
Shall be spoken of only as by-gone things
  That shall blast this part of creation no more,
Based firm upon truth, the Charter shall stand
The land-mark of ages—sublimely grand!

When class-distinctions shall wither and die,
  And conscious merit shall modestly bear
The garlands wrought by its own industry,
  The proper rewards of labour and care;
When man shall rise to his station as man,
  To passion or vice no longer a slave;
When the *march of mind* already begun,
  Shall gathering roll like a vast mountain wave,
The Charter shall stand the text of the free,
Of a Nation's rights the sure guarantee.

So long as tyrannic oppression is found
  To come as a blight o'er the face of the earth;
To spread its devastating influence round,
  And nip "patient merit" e'en in its birth;
So long as we see in meagre array,
  The demons of want and misery and woe,
In their direst forms stalk forth at noon-day,
  Spreading havoc and death in their track as they go!
The Charter shall shine the pole-star bright,
The hope of these victims of "might against right".

So long as Justice impartially spreads
   The savour of truth o'er discord and strife;
So long as kindly benevolence sheds
   Her halo divine on the dark path of life;
So long as the thrice-hallow'd sacred fires
   Of "love of country" burns in the breast;
So long as the impulse virtue inspires
   Shall lead to relieve and support the oppress'd;
So long shall the Charter be deeply engrav'd
On the high-beating hearts of millions enslav'd!

Birmingham

The Northern Star and Leeds General Advertiser, 2 January 1841

William Rider

THE LEAGUE

Who are that blustering, canting crew,
Who keep the cheap loaf in our view,
And would from us more profit screw?
      The League.

Who cry "Repeal the curs'd Corn Law,"
And would their workmen feed with straw,
That they may filthy lucre paw?
      The League.

Who wish to gull the working man,
And *burk* the Charter,[1] *if they can,*
With their self-aggrandising plan?
      The League.

Who deal in sophistry and cant—
Of common sense evince the want—
And strive the Charter to supplant?
      The League.

Who meet defeat at every turn,
From the Chartists, strong and stern,
Yet from it wisdom will not learn?
                    The League.

Who have receiv'd their final fall,
This afternoon, in our Cloth Hall,
And there not one more meeting call?
                    The League.

Leeds, 30 March 1841

The Northern Star and Leeds General Advertiser, 3 April 1841

David Ross

A CALL TO THE PEOPLE

Britain, long thy sons have cherish'd
   The remembrance of thy fame;
In thy cause brave hearts have perish'd
   To restore thy former name.

Labour's claims were once respected;
   Labour then could life maintain;
But the poor, too long neglected,
   Groan beneath oppression's chain.

By what plea doth man endeavour
   Thus his brother to oppress?
All were equal born; then never
   Deign your tyrants to caress.

Despots, though in temples dwelling,
   May not hope to chain the mind;
This, all other power excelling,
   Yet will free the human mind.

Kings, by warrior bands attended,
  Tremble at its growing power;
While our cause, by truth defended,
  Strengthens with each coming hour.

All the power of pride elated
  Hath against our cause been hurled;
But, immortal, yet 'tis fated
  To give freedom to the world.

Sons of labour! dread no longer
  All the efforts of your foes:
Once united, you are stronger
  Than the tyrants you oppose.

Though in dungeon depth is buried
  Hearts that beat in freedom's cause,
Yet the flag which such have carried
  Soon will win the world's applause.

By the love ye bear each other,
  By the knowledge you obtain,
Once unite as friend and brother—
  This will freedom's battle gain.

Then your children will be taken
  From the life-consuming mill,
And your shouts of joy awaken
  Every pulse to rapture's thrill.

At the sickly loom no longer
  You will toil for felon fare;
When the people prove the stronger
  Nature's blessings all will share.

Then for you the earth its treasure
  In abundance will bestow;
Life will thus be crown'd with pleasure,
  And each heart with joy o'erflow.

Brighter than the dawn when breaking
  O'er the wild unfettered sea,

Will be the hour when all awaking
    Shall determine to be free.

Leeds

The Northern Star and Leeds General Advertiser, 30 September 1843

William S. Villiers Sankey

ODE

Men of England, ye are slaves,
Though ye quell the roaring waves—
Though ye boast, by land and sea,
Britons everywhere are free.

Men of England, ye are slaves,
Bought by tyrants, sold by knaves;
Your's the toil, the sweat, the pain,
Their's the profit, ease and gain.

Men of England, ye are slaves,
Beaten by policemen's staves;
If their force ye dare repel,
Your's will be the felon's cell.

Men of England, ye are slaves;
Ev'n the House of Commons craves
From the Crown, on bended knee,
That its language may be free.

Men of England, ye are slaves—
Hark! the stormy tempest raves—
'Tis the nation's voice I hear,
Shouting "Liberty is near."

The Northern Star and Leeds General Advertiser, 29 February 1840

TO WORKING MEN OF EVERY CLIME

Working men of every clime,
Gather still, but bide your time,
Bide your time, and wait a wee,
Yours will be the victory.

Britain's sons, whose constant toil
Plies the loom and tills the soil,
Lift the voice for liberty,
Yours will be the victory.

Toil-worn sons of Spain advance,
Give the hand to those of France,
Join you both with Italy,
Yours will be the victory.

Serfs of Poland, gather near,
Raise, with Austria's sons, the cheer,
Echo'd far through Germany,
Yours will be the victory.

Danish workmen, hear the cry,
Scandinavia's quick reply,
Workmen, "panting to be free,"
Yours will be the victory.

Dutchmen, linger not behind,
Working men should be combined,
Russian slaves themselves will see
Yours will be the victory.

Europe's workmen, one and all,
Rouse ye at your brethren's call,
Shouting loud from sea to sea,
Yours will be the victory.

Kings and nobles may conspire,
God will pour on them his ire;
Workmen shout, for ye are free,
Yours is *now* the victory.

The Northern Star and Leeds General Advertiser, 28 November 1840

RULE BRITANNIA!

Let Britain's heralds take their stand,
  And loudly through the isle proclaim,
This is the Charter of the land;
  While million voices shout the same.
Hail, Britannia! Britannia's sons are free!
Suffrage guards their liberty.

The distant isles have heard the cry;
  Born high upon the swelling gale,
And in one general burst reply
  As freedom's thrilling voice they hail—
Hail, Britannia! Britannia's sons are free!
Suffrage guards their liberty.

The nations, that in silent shame
  Had pined beneath the tyrant's yoke,
Have caught from thee the generous flame,
  And from their limbs the fetters broke.
Hail, Britannia! Britannia's sons are free!
Suffrage guards their liberty.

The Northern Star and Leeds General Advertiser, 14 November 1840

SONG

AIR—"YE MARINERS OF ENGLAND"

Ye working men of England,
  Who plough your native soil,
Whose hands have reared her fabrics
  With unabated toil;
Though your labours clothe her nobles,
  The Monarch on the throne,
Yet bereft, ye are left,
  In slavery to groan;
While the wealthy revel proudly,
  Still in slavery ye groan.
In battle field contending,
  With the might of England's foes,

Your fathers won those laurels
  Which twine with England's Rose;
Yet when ye sought the Commons' House,
  Your Suffrage rights to own,
Still bereft, ye were left,
  In slavery to groan.
While purse-proud voters pass you by,
  And ye in slavery groan.

They boast of England's freedom,
  And toast it o'er their wine,
While millions of her bravest sons,
  In want disfranchised pine;
But the nation is degraded,
  While ye, her sons are known,
Thus bereft, to be left,
  In slavery to groan,
While the millions are disfranchised,
  And still in slavery groan.

Yet, working men of England,
  Give way not to despair,
For your banner yet shall proudly
  Float high upon the air;
Your rights shall be conceded,
  The bugle shall be blown,
To the fame, of your name,
  When none in slavery groan—
When ye have won your freedom,
  And none in slavery groan.

The Northern Star and Leeds General Advertiser, 25 April 1840

Benjamin Stott

SONG FOR THE MILLIONS

How long will the millions sweat and toil,
  To pamper the lordlings' bastard brats;
How long will they till the fruitful soil,

To be starved by the base aristocrats?
　　How long will they bear the galling yoke,
　　Ere their bones shall burst, their chains be broke,
　　And vengeance come down like a thunderstroke?

The spirit of freedom yearns and bleeds,
　　And liberty lies in patriots' graves;
Whilst the monster tyrant's ear unheeds
　　The suffering wail of weeping slaves;
　　　　But shall mankind for ever bear
　　　　The stings of woe, and grief, and care,
　　　　And live and die in dark despair?

Forbid it heaven, and all the powers
　　That rule the universal world;
'Twere better that this globe of ours,
　　'Mid lightning's flashes, swift were hurl'd,
　　　　And with it all the human race,
　　　　Into the gulf of endless space,
　　　　Further than mortal ken can trace.

Bondsmen and slaves in every clime,
　　Your voices raise in freedom's cause;
Despots, be wise; be wise in time,
　　Remember it is Nature's laws
　　　　That make men equal; and dare ye,
　　　　In hellish conclave met, agree
　　　　To alter Nature's wise decree?

Vain is your wish, your strong desire
　　Can never! never! be obtained;
Ye cannot quench fair freedom's fire,
　　Though ye of blood a deluge rain'd
　　　　Seek in the rolls of lasting fame;
　　　　There shall ye find each honour'd name.
　　　　Whose memory feeds the sacred name.

Oh! may that flame burn fierce and bright,
　　Within the breasts of all mankind;
May knowledge pour a flood of light
　　From out the intellectual mind;
　　　　A light, that shall illume the earth,

Whose genial rays shall soon give birth
To glorious liberty, that boon of worth.

The Northern Star and Leeds General Advertiser, 12 March 1812

SONG FOR THE MILLIONS

Beware! ye white slaves of old England, beware!
    Your dastard oppressors are fiendish and base;
Their spies are abroad, to betray and ensnare—
    To bring you to ruin, to death, and disgrace.
They are thirsting for blood, and impatient to spoil
    The prospects of freedom which all now enjoy;
They have soldiers to crush you who live by your toil,
    Then beware of the infamous traitor and spy!

Be firm and unite, but be cautious in words,
    On your prudence depends the success of your cause:
Remember, policemen have bludgeons and swords,
    And unjust protection from despotic laws.
The press is corrupt, and knaves they can find
    Who will perjure their souls, and swear truth is a lie,
Then, producers of wealth, be not wilfully blind,
    But beware of the infamous traitor and spy!

'Tis true that your sufferings are grievous and great,
    And death, from starvation, you constantly fear;
While a proud, pampered priesthood would teach you to wait
    For that comfort in heaven they rob you of here.
'Tis true ye are goaded by insult and wrong,
    But justice will come; be united and wise;
The weak shall not ever be slaves to the strong;
    Then beware of the tyrants, their traitors, and spies!

Celestial freedom! the birthright of all,
    Inert in our bosoms, inhaled by our breath;
Thy spirit abhors both oppression and thrall,
    We still live in hope for thee even to death.
Oh! let thy bright presence enliven our land;
    The free-born will despots and dungeons despise;

They will purge the fair earth from slavery's brand,
   And exterminate tyrants, and traitors, and spies!

Manchester

The Northern Star and Leeds General Advertiser, 2 July 1842

SONG FOR THE MILLIONS

Friends of Freedom, swell the strain
That peals across th' Atlantic main,
And echoes wide o'er hill and plain,
      Arousing men to Liberty.
Your every moral power awake,
Bestir yourselves for Freedom's sake;
Base Slavery's chains shall snap and break
      Before your Godlike energy.

Lift up your faces from the dust,
Your cause is holy, pure, and just;
In Freedom's God put all your trust,
      Be he your hope and anchor.
Give to the world your firm decree,
That Britons will—they will be free—
Shout, shout for glorious Liberty!
      It will succeed and conquer.

Vain tyrants, that would make us slaves,
Go look upon the patriots' graves,
And study there, ye dastard knaves,
      The folly of your knavery.
What! think ye to subdue the mind,
Which God hath given to mankind?
Ye surely will for ever find
      Men will not suffer slavery.

Though ye have prisons to immure
The poor, and friends unto the poor,
Yet think not basely to allure
      The flock from they who lead them.
Vain are your dungeons, idly vain.
The rack, the torture and the chain;

Ye neither can nor shall restrain
      Our strong desire for freedom.

We ask for rights by Nature given,
Sanctioned and ratified by Heaven,
For which our forefathers have striven
      On the battle-field and wave;
We wish to make no man our foe,
For all are equal born we know,
And all must surely, surely go
      To the republic of the grave.

The Northern Star and Leeds General Advertiser, 24 September 1842

James Syme

LABOUR SONG

Toil, brothers, toil; sing and toil,
  From earliest dawn till dark.
What matter, though kings and priests should spoil;
You have nothing to do but work.

Go form the richest fabrics,
  And the costliest robes of gold,
To deck the legal plunderers,
  Whilst you're shivering with the cold.

Sing, brothers, sing, sing and toil,
  Though ragged and scant of bread;
You are honoured—the palace deigns to spoil
  From the workman's lowly shed.

Toil, brothers, toil; let the anvil ring
  With clanging blows, and strong;
Go forge the ponderous bars, and sing
  (As you pant and sweat) a song.

Then sing, brothers, sing, "the good and great,"
  Who tenant the gay saloon,

Who "graciously" stoop from their high estate,
    And rob you. Blissful boon!

Toil, brothers, toil, sing and toil;
    Draw not the avenger's blade,
Though perjured legislators spoil
    Your famishing children's bread.

Raise palace homes upon the land,
    Send navies ocean o'er;
The sickle wield with sturdy hand,
    The sparkling mine explore.

Toil, brothers, toil, from dawn to dark;
    Let not the heart complain,
Though you have hardly aught, save work;
    The idler all the gain.

Then toil, brothers, toil, sing and toil,
    Let not a curse be said,
Though mitred knaves, and princes, spoil
    Each comfort from your shed.

Sing, brothers, sing, I'd have you sing,
    But let your ditties be
Such anthems as can only ring
    From spirits that are free.

Oppression's funeral dirge go sing,
    And peal the dying knell
Of public plunder and each courtly thing.
    Such songs would suit you well.

The Northern Star and Leeds General Advertiser, 26 December 1840

Sir.—The following stanzas were suggested by the Accidental perusal of a Whig recommendation to the sons of toil to "sing" at their labour, and thereby render it "almost a pastime."

This song was sent to the "feelosophers," who perhaps only retailed the idea; but as they have taken no notice of it, I make bold to send it to a journal which I constantly read, and which rears its proud front despite of all the attempts of creatures like unto these "Chambers" to destroy its influence.

                                             I am, Sir,
                                yours respectfully,
                                   JAMES SYME."

William Thom

DREAMINGS OF THE BEREAVED

The morning breaks bonnie o'er mountain an' stream,
An' troubles the hallowed breath o' my dream!
The gowd light of morning is sweet to the e'e,
But, ghost-gathering midnight, thou'rt dearer to me.
The dull common world then sinks from my sight,
An' fairer creations arise to the night;
When drowsy oppression has sleep-sealed my e'e,
Then bright are the visions awaken'd to me!

Oh! come, spirit mother, discourse of the hours,
My young bosom beat all its beating to yours,
When heart-woven wishes in soft counsel fell,
On ears—how unheedful prov'd sorrow might tell!
That deathless affection—nae trial could break,
When a' else forsook me *ye* wouldna forsake,
Then come, oh! my mother, come often to me,
An' soon an' for ever I'll come unto thee!

An' thou shrouded loveliness! soul-winning Jean,
How cold was thy hand on my bosom yestreen!ᵃ
'T was kind—for the loweᵇ that your e'e kindled there,
Will burn aye, an' burn, till that breast beat nae mair.
Our bairniesᶜ sleep round me, oh! bless ye their sleep,
Your ain dark-e'ed Willie will wauken an' weep;
But blythe in his weepin' he'll tell me how you,
His *heaven-hamed*ᵈ mammie, was "dautin' his brow."ᵉ

Tho' dark be our dwallin'—our happin'ᶠ tho' bare,
An' night closes round us in cauldness an' care;
Affection will warn us—an' bright are the beams
That halo our hame in yon dear land of dreams.
Then well may I welcome the night's deathy reign,
Wi' souls of the dearest I mingle me then,

The gowd[g] light of morning is lightless to me,
But, oh, for the night we' its ghost revelrie!

[a] Last night
[b] Flame
[c] Children
[d] Whose home is in heaven
[e] Patting his forehead
[f] Patting his foehead
[f] Covering
[g] Gold

THE MITHERLESS BAIRN

When a' ither[a] bairnies[b] are hushed to their hame,
By aunty, or cousin, or frecky[c] grand-dame;
Wha stan's last an' lanely an' naebody carin'?
'T is the puir[d] doited[e] loonie[f]—the mitherless bairn!

The mitherless bairn gangs[g] till[h] his lane bed,
Nane[i] covers his cauld[j] back, or haps[k] his bare head;
His wee, hackit[l] heelies[m] are hard as the airn,[n]
An' litheless[o] the lair o' the mitherless bairn!

Aneath[p] his cauld brow, siccan[q] dreams tremble there,
O' hands that wont[r] kindly to kame[s] his dark hair!
But mornin' brings clutches, a' reckless an' stern,
That lo'e nae[t] the locks o' the mitherless bairn!
Youn sister, that sang[u] o'er his saftly-rocked bed,
Now rests in the mools[v] whaur her mammie is laid;
The father toils sair[w] their wee bannock[x] to earn,
An' kens[y] nae[z] the wrangs o' his mitherless bairn!

Her spirit, that pass'd in yon hour o' his birth,
Still watches his wearisome wand'rings on earth,
Recording in heaven the blessings they earn,
Wha couthilie[a1] deal wi' the mitherless bairn!

Oh! speak him nae harshly—he trembles the while—
He bends to your bidding, and blesses your smile!
In their dark hour o' anguish, the heartless shall learn
That God deals the blow for the mitherless bairn!

William Thorn, *Rhymes and Recollections of a Handloom Weaver*,
2nd ed. (London, 1845)

In hardy Scotland, it is not always a sure sign of poverty in its sons and daughters that they are to be seen tripping it bare-footed from April till Christmas. It is choice; but when necessity carries the matter a little farther into the winter, the feet break up in gashes, or "hacks;" hence hackit heelies.

[a] Other
[b] Children
[c] Coaxing
[d] Poor
[e] Confused
[f] Boy
[g] Goes
[h] To
[i] None
[j] Cold
[k] Covers
[l] Chapped
[m] Heels
[n] Iron
[o] Comfortless
[p] Beneath
[q] Such
[r] Were accustomed
[s] Comb
[t] Love not
[u] Sung
[v] Mould
[w] Sore
[x] A little bread
[y] Knows
[z] Not
[a1] Kindly

James Vernon

SONNET TO WILLIAMS AND BINNS

Williams and Binns[1], the youthful patriots,
　Have sternly dared the tyrant's iron frown,
　With manly fortitude—such as shall crown
Them with a people's heartfelt thanks, mid notes
Of unexampled gratitude—from throats
　Whence emanate a nation's voice, and show
　The people's strength, that lays in justice low,
And sets up truth, the bane of all despots,
Like opening flowers in some unsheltered spot,
　They bend beneath the bitter pelting storm;
Still spring's rude blast will shortly be forgot.
　Its rage is past—it ceases to deform.
Soon you will struggle through life's mingled doom,
Knowing that after death 'tis yours to bloom.

South Mollon, 2 February

The Northern Star and Leeds General Advertiser, 13 February 1841

John Watkins

LINES ON SHELL, KILLED AT NEWPORT

Who fought for freedom, more than life?
Who gave up all, to die in strife?
   The young, the brave, no more a slave,
        Immortal Shell!
        That died so well,—
He fell, and sleeps in honour's grave.

They shot him, shot the father's son—
Too soon his honest race was run.
   The "red-coat" fired—poor Shell expir'd
        Freedom! he cried,
He spoke, and died.
   He gain'd the freedom, he required.

Oh, horrid was the wound that bled!
And piteous was his look when dead!
   He died a martyr for the Charter.
        He died in pain,
        But not in vain:
Who would not life for freedom barter?

They laid him in his timeless tomb.
Oh, weep not for his happy doom:
   But, on the sod, lets kneel to God,
        And may his spirit
        Our hearts inherit,
   That we may break the despot's rod.

Battersea, near London

The Northern Star and Leeds General Advertisers, 26 September 1840

SONNET

Chartists! what strive ye for? for liberty!
Most glorious strife! more noble as more hard.
  'Twas liberty inspir'd the British Bard
Who surnam'd our Britannia—"The Free!"
Byron! chiefest of poets! yes, 'twas he.

But when, oh Britons, when will you succeed?
When will the many overcome the few?
  "Must ye yet toil to starve, or fight or bleed?
Blood to the tree of freedom is as dew,
But it should flow from tyrants, not from you.

A victory gain'd by blood is never kept—
Vow, then, that yours shall be a bloodless fight
  And virtue's eyes will shine, that long have wept.
God waits to help you, for your cause is right,
And, to succeed, you have but to Unite!

The Northern Star and Leeds General Advertiser, 29 April 1842

EXTRACT FROM THE PLAY OF JOHN FROST

(Scene, A dungeon—Frost reading)

"Blessed are the merciful, for they shall obtain mercy."
From whom shall they obtain it?—not from man!
Man curses man; cruel e'en his mercy.
Me, merciful, they recommend to mercy,
And what do I obtain?—not that, not justice!
I sought for mercy for the suff'ring poor,
And am condem'd for't—aye, for that
I'm sentenc'd to be hang'd, be drawn, and quarter'd—
My sever'd limbs to be disposed of[1]—how?
Sold, strewn, or cook'd, as pleases our good Queen!
To pity poor men's woes is treason now.
The loyal laugh at them, are thank'd and knighted.
God, thou art merciful! Have mercy on me!
Oh those who have more need of it than I,
Because they've none on me, nor on the poor.
Oh, God! if 'tis expedient one man perish

For thy poor people's sake, I'll be that man:
If I have erred, 'twas with no bad intent;
But strictest judgment they have dealt on me.
Oh may my death atone my sins in life.
Oh, hear my prayer, Oh God! And pardon me.

(Enter Jailor)

JAILOR. Her Majesty most graciously has mercy—
She will not hang you, but transport you, Sir.

FROST. Transport me!
I'd rather die—I'd rather far be hang'd.

JAILOR. At your pleasure, Sir;
But you will be transported, Sir—not hang'd.
I thought you would have liked to hear it, Sir.

(Exit Jailor.)

FROST (solus)
Transported!—'tis to drag on death alive.
Such mercy is the worst of cruelty.
The fiends alone can call it mercy.
Oh, 'tis sardonic! transport! aye, indeed!
Transport in penal flames!—transported, ha!
They'll next call hell,—heaven—devils, too.
They'll christen angels—so, indeed, they are,
Compar'd with those who make their hell of England.
Alas for me!—what shall a good man do?
Vice reigns on earth and virtue is her victim.
They seiz'd me, immured me—the very priests,
That pray God's pity on poor prisoners,
Made me a prisoner—was't to pray for me?
I was betray'd by my own counsellors,
And men, I saved, witness'd against me falsely,
Condemn'd their friend to shambles to be slaughter'd
More like a beast for market than a man.
And now Victoria's mercy for me is—
What?—banishment to earth's remotest bounds,
Far out of hearing of redress, or pity—
There to be chain'd with felons 'neath the sun,
A keeper o'er me with a whip of wire,

And when I groan with unhabitual toil,
Or faint with thirst, and hunger, or disease,
To have the whip scourge off my blistered skin,
And be worse tortur'd for my cries and shrieks.
Nay, when worn nature sinks in torpid sleep,
And dreams of former life stir thoughts of home,
To be awak'd and goaded to my doom,—
I whose whole course of life hath run contrary,
So that my fate will make itself more felt.
I to spend life's latter days thus—thus nameless,
It is too dreadful for my mind to bear,
How can my body then?—it must not be!
They cannot mean it, sure—a moment so—
With such companions and such overseers,
In such an irresponsive wilderness,
Where man is authoriz'd to torture man,
And so exults in his most savage power
That wildest beasts grow tame and lose their terrors
Compar'd with him, arm'd with his racking engines,
A moment of such life were like whole years.
And must I go with memory and spend
The last grey remnant of my being thus?
I shall go mad, or worse, become a fiend—
And this they call their mercy—royal mercy!
Be merciful, indeed, and give me death—
Oh, let me die while yet I am a man—
Give me some chance of leaving earth for heaven.

The Northern Star and Leeds of General Advertiser, 2 January 1841

THE CORN LAWS AND EMIGRATION

Because our lords have taxed the staff of life,[1]
The working man, his children, and his wife
All slave together, yet they must not eat—
Toil gives an appetite, but brings no meat!
The price of bread by law is kept so high,
That what we earn suffices not to buy.
But, why is this? what makes our bread so dear?
Far cheaper 'tis abroad than it is here!
Yes, but a tax is laid on foreign grain,

To make our home-grown corn its price maintain;
And half-fed men may toil, and starve, and die,
That idle lords may lift their heads on high.
We might buy cheap, but landlords want great rents,
To spend in keeping grand establishments.
Their feasts, their fancies, jewels, balls, and plays,
The poor man's nakedness and hunger pays.
The tenant says, if corn comes duty free,
'Twill bring down prices here, and ruin me:
Taxes and rents in England are so high,
I cannot sell so cheap as you could buy.
Pensions, and perquisites, all other prices
Must come down too, save luxuries and vices.
The honest husbandman must emigrate,
And leave poor peasants to increase the rate,
Unless our lords consent to live on less,
And pride succumb to humble happiness!

The Northern Star and Leeds General Advertiser, 1 January 1842

C. Westray

TO THE CHARTISTS

On, countrymen, on to the fight,
   The struggle for freedom most dear,
Hurl down on the tyrants the blight,
   Of the hearts their oppression doth sear.

Forget not the honest and brave,
   Who in tyrant Whig's dungeons are cast,
And indignantly spurn the base slave,
   Who with slander their fair fame would blast.

Be not lured by the treacherous smile
   Of base traitors, who seek but your fall;
They'll employ every base, Whig-like guile,
   To divert you from Liberty's call.

Sons of Albion stand firm to your posts—
  Respond to fair liberty's sigh—
That despite of the tyrant's red hosts,
  Your Charter you'll have, or you'll die.

The Northern Star and Leeds General Advertiser, 20 February 1841

THE VOICE OF FREEDOM

Heard ye that soul-inspiring sound,
  Borne swiftly on the ev'ning gale,
Diffusing gladness o'er the land,
  Stilling the mourning orphan's wail.

Joy to the starving poor oppress't.
  Those glorious whisperings do bring;
Throughout the breadth of Albion's Isle
  Its heartfelt cheering accents ring.

Its whisper'd murmurs low and soft,
  When first it struck upon the ear
Of tyrants and their courtly horde,
  Them smote with pallid, coward fear.

But now that voice is like the roar
  Of Afric's mighty forest king;
And British slaves who dare be free,
  Our Tyrants' pealing death-dirge sing.

That sound is freedom's glad'ning voice,
  Proclaiming truth's eternal reign;
When tyrant despots dare not load
  The freeman's limbs with serf-like chains.

The Northern Star and Leeds General Advertiser, 5 November 1842

Thomas Martin Wheeler

FREEDOM AND THE CHARTER

TUNE—"BRIGHT ARE THE BEAMS OF THE MORNING SKY"

Though bright are the beams of dear woman's eye,
  Though rapture her lips can impart,
Yet brighter the glance of dear liberty,
  And sweeter its charms to the heart.
Its joys are a fountain of pleasure,
  A source from whence happiness flows;
Then who would not taste of this pleasure,
  As the honey bee sips of the rose

Then the toast, then the toast, be our freedom,
  Let each breast that is manly approve;
Then the toast, then the toast, be our freedom,
  And nine cheers for the cause that we love.

Raise, raise the cause of freedom on high,
  Let each heart that is trusty approve;
The offering thus hallowed by liberty's sigh,
  Out-rivals the charms e'en of love.
Then raise high your voices in transport,
  Our Charter its joys shall impart;
The hours thus devoted to freedom,
  Yield the only true balm to the heart.

Then the toast, then the toast, be our Charter,
  Let each breast that is manly approve;
Then the toast, then the toast, be our Charter,
  And nine cheers for the cause that we love.

The Northern Star and Leeds General Advertiser, 15 May 1841

THE CHARTIST BOLD

TUNE—"FIRM AS OAK"

Oh, firm as oak and free from fear
   The Chartist bold should be;
His arm is for his country dear,
   To achieve her liberty.

Come weal, come woe,
Still on we go,
Our Charter to attain;
Our cause is just,
In God we trust.
We soon shall see our country free.
We soon shall see our country free.

Our Charter we know, will lay tyranny low,
And union from discord flow;
Then unite, unite, unite,
The Charter to attain. Unite, unite,
The Charter to attain.

Though tyranny's despotic band
   Have chained our patriots brave;
Though persecution's iron hand
   Hath brought them to the grave;

Come weal, come woe,
Still on we go,
Our Charter to attain;
Our cause is just,
In God we trust.
We soon shall see our country free.
We soon shall see our country free.

Our Charter we know, will lay tyranny low,
And union from discord flow;
Then unite, unite, unite,
The Charter to attain. Unite, unite,
The Charter to attain.

Kensington

The Northern Star and Leeds General Advertiser, 31 July 1841

Thomas Wilson

A SONG FOR THOSE WHO LIKE TO SING IT

The hand of oppression is stretched forth to slay
   The young babe of freedom and light;
But knowledge has driven the darkness away,
   That hid from the people their might;
And the people will rise with the might of the just,
And pride and oppression shall sink to the dust.

The voice of the bigot is upraised to ban,
   The souls of the noble and free;
But his poisonous breathing can now only fan,
   The fire of young liberty;
And the people will rise with the might of the just,
And pride and oppression shall sink to the dust.

The purse-proud have joined in the effort to quell,
   The determined and resolute shout,
Which the universe echoes as tyranny's knell—
   'Tis the voice of the banded and stout;
For the people will rise with the might of the just,
And pride and oppression shall sink to the dust.

The Northern Star and Leeds General Advertiser, 29 October 1842

John Athol Wood

THOU ART A SELF-DEGRADED SLAVE

If thou canst view, with tearless eye,
   The millions doomed to toil and die;
To bear with bitter scoffs, and sneers,

With hopes deferred o'er ling'ring years;
To pine in misery and grief
   Throughout their lives; nor know relief—
The while a self-entitled "great,"
   Consume the wealth the poor create,
And curse them with a pauper grave—
   Thou art a vile, a heartless slave.

If thou canst bear—with patience too—
   That any upstart idle crew
Of useless drones; should dare deprive
   The workers of their human hive,
Of all the honey-garnered store,
   They've toiled through many a wear hour,
T' obtain; that in a future day—
   When time has wrought their strength's decay—
From work they may cessation have;
   Thou art a craven heartless slave.

If thou canst see vile class-made laws
   With wide, distended, rav'nous jaws—
That seek within each monstrous maw,
   T' entrap the wretched struggling poor;
Who from the hardness of the times,
   By want, are driven into crimes;
And punished—while the wealthy man,
   Vile deeds enact with safety can,
And minds of purest mould deprave—
   Thou art indeed a heartless slave.

If thou canst see a *royal thing*
   A self-entitled Queen or King,
Attired in blood empurpled robe,
   And gems from mines far o'er the globe,
With luxury on every hand,
   And power supreme at *its* command,
While—candour must the truth impact—
   There's black corruption in *its* heart;
And know that bread the people crave,
   Without regret, *thou art a slave.*

If thou canst see God's fecund earth,
   That wealthy mine of priceless worth,

A wild uncultivated waste,
  To suit some shallow lordling's taste
For breeding game; while not a Son
  Of Toil, his hand dare lay upon
A hare, or else the vulture "law"
  May pounce on him with talon'd claw,
And transport him across the wave—
  Contented, *then thou art a slave.*

If thou canst see this "Child of Toil"
  Denied his right to share the soil,
To plough it up, to sow the seed,
  To reap its fruits, for time of need;
An outcast driv'n from door to door,
  Houseless, wretched, starved, nay more,
Reviled, and mercilessly slain,
  By every Mammon loving Cain—
And yet no pity for him have,
  Thou art a wretch, a thing, a slave.

If thou canst see the causes whence
  A thousand evils spring—and hence,
Reflecting on the sterling worth
  Of honest hearts, crushed down to earth;
Whilst wretches thrive, who cringe and bend,
  Who fawn and flatter though the end
Be e'er so vile—yet will not give
  A hand to help the suff'rers; live
And rescue thus the true and brave,
  Thou art a vile degraded slave.

The Friend of the People, 29 March 1851

David Wright

BRITISH FREEDOM

Are not the People Free—.PITT

Yes, we are free! to plough the sea,
    And dig the earth for treasure,
And when we do, the ruling few
    Can take our gains at leisure.

We're free to fight with all our might,
    In every Whiggish battle,
And when we do, the ruling few,
    Treat us like slaves or cattle.

And free we're born, to sow the corn,
    And free, when ripe, to reap it,
And when we do, the ruling few,
    Are free to come and eat it.

We're free to weep, when tyrants sleep,
    And starve when they are feasting,
And when we do, the ruling few,
    Feed us with scorn and jesting.

We pay the tax, laid on our backs,
    And seldom try to stop it;
And when we do, the ruling few,
    Can take by force, and pocket.

And thus you see, that we are free,
    To labour for starvation;
Because they take all that we make,
    To pay their d—d taxation.

Aberdeen, 12 May 1841

McDovall's Chartist and Republican Journal, 29 May 1841

Notes

"A Chester Gaol"

Poem refers to events in Chester in August 1839, particularly the trial of Stephens, MacDouall, Bradley, and four Chartist workers from Ashton: Compson, Mitchell, Davis, and Higgins. They were accused of treason due to their involvement in an armed uprising. All were sentenced to prison for a period of one to one and a half years and served their terms in the Chester County jail. The poem may have been written by one of the condemned Chartists just mentioned.

1. *The Northern Star* (1838–51)—The principal Chartist newspaper, published first in Leeds and then in London. Its circulation reached fifty thousand a week by 1839.

2. *they tax the bread we eat*—Refers to the corn laws that levied heavy taxes on imported grain so as to maintain high domestic prices; these laws were introduced in 1815 and finally repealed in 1846.

3. *Convention*—Chartist General Convention of the Industrious Classes that met in London on 4 February 1839.

4. *Russell*—Lord John (1792–1878). Whig prime minister (1846–52 and 1865–66). As home secretary under the Melbourne administration, he ruthlessly pursued the Chartists and opposed the claims of the Charter and the National Petition. Was actively opposed to both new legislation and universal suffrage that might have improved the condition of industrial workers.

5. *Lord Melbourne*—William Lamb, second viscount (1779–1848). Member of the House of Lords, prime minister (1835–41).

6. *Brougham and Lyndhurst*—Lord Henry Brougham (1778–1868). Publicist, Whig, parliamentary figure, critic. Lord John Lyndhurst (1772–1863), Tory, member of parliament, political ally of Brougham, although they were from opposing parties.

7. *McDouall*—Peter Murray. Popular Chartist agitator and publicist, by profession a doctor. Published *McDouall's Chartist and Republican Journal* from Manchester in 1841. Born in western Scotland where he practiced medicine. Joined the Chartists in 1838; the following year was a delegate to the convention from Ashton. Under prosecution many times. Rewards were posted for his capture and his description was distributed throughout London. Fled to France for two years, returned to England in 1845.

8. *Campbell*—Sir John (1802–1878). Main representative of state prosecution at the Chester trials in October 1839.

9. *Gurney*—Sir John (1768–1845). Presiding judge at the court at the same session. Well-known for his severity toward the Chartists.

10. *Or stay in Chester Gaol*—At the conclusion of their term of imprisonment, Chartists often had to pay bond money to assure the court that they would maintain good behavior in the future.

11. *The Rights of Man*—Name of a pamphlet written by Thomas Paine (1791–92) in which the principles of a democratic republic are expounded. Was generally very popular among the Chartists.

12. *Poor Law*—New Poor Law Amendment Act of 1834 forbade all outdoor relief in money or food. Only relief offered to the poor was admission to the new workhouses. These were called "Poor Law Bastilles." Were run in such a manner as to frighten away everyone who could possibly survive without accepting this form of public relief. (For more detail, see chap. 12, "Attitude of the Bourgeoisie," in Frederick Engels's book, *The Condition of the Working Class in England*.)

13. *O'Connell*—Daniel. (1775–1847). Was active in the movement in the 1830s that attempted to repeal the new Coercion Act for Ireland, which restricted all political activity. Was also an advocate of the emancipation of Ireland.

"The Judges Are Going to Jail"

This poem was reprinted in *The Northern Star*. It concerned the trial of John Frost—former magistrate, one-time mayor of Newport (South Wales), national Chartist leader, chairman at the General Convention, and one of the outstanding spokesmen of the Chartist movement that included William Jones—watchmaker and Chartist orator; and Zephenia Williams—atheist, mine agent, and radical leader. These were the leaders of the Newport Rising in South Wales, on 4 November 1839. The three main leaders—Frost, Williams, and Jones—were arrested, and within two months were sentenced to death.

1. *Lord Denman*—Judge active in many judicial proceedings against the Chartists.
2. *Little Johnny*—Lord John Russell. See n.4 to "Chester Gaol."
3. *Beaks*—Term of contempt for judges.

"Air"

Example of a Chartist marching song. Clearly marked rhythm and one-line refrains are the distinctive characteristics of this genre. A few lines resemble slogans. "Vive La Chart" and "Raise the brand of liberty" are examples.

"How to Be a Great Lord"

Poem was reprinted by the *The Northern Star* from another newspaper with a democratic orientation. Similar reprints were common in the practice of Chartist newspapers. Sometimes they reprinted writings from newspapers with an anti-Chartist orientation if these could be useful to them.

"The State Pauper's Soliloquy"

State paupers was a pejorative term used by aristocrats when referring to the Chartists.

"The Pauper's Drive"

Poems of a similar nature, devoted to the bitter fate of the pauper, were common in early Chartist poetry. Are a direct continuation of pre-Chartist, workers' poetry.

"What Is a Peer?"

Is not related directly to Chartist literature. Was originally published in 1831 in the *Poor Man's Guardian*, published by Henry Hetherington—a leader of the unstamped campaign, a signatory of the People's Charter, and a radical and Chartist until his death in 1849. The poem enjoyed great popularity among Chartists and was often reprinted in Chartist publications, for example, *The Northern Liberator*, 18 April 1840.

"American Stripes"

A poem written in response to the remark placed in *The Glove* on 23 March 1844. In general, the Chartists paid a great deal of attention to the plight of black slaves in America and to the activities of the abolitionists. Chartist writers continually printed in their publications the lines of John Greenleaf Whittier, an American poet, as well as other poet-abolitionists. A considerable number of articles and poems written by the Chartists were devoted to the struggles of slaves for their freedom.

"The Hermit"

Poem was published anonymously, but has been suggested that it was written by Ernest Jones. Represents one of the rare examples of antireligious poetry written by Chartists.

Crito

Pseudonym of a comparatively unknown Chartist poet from Bolton, Lancashire.

F.

"TO THE CHARTISTS OF WALES"
   1. *Cambrian*—refers to Wales.

J. W. C.

"RALLY AGAIN, BOYS"
   1. *each storm we encounter*—Reference to the severe judgment that the government meted out to the Chartists in 1842.

S. J.

"PRESENTATION OF THE NATIONAL PETITION"
   1. *Strand*—Chartist National Petition that contains 3,317,752 signatures, presented by T. S. Duncombe in Parliament; rejected by 287 to 49 on 2 May 1842.
   2. *ye shall not be heard your grievances to show*—After the refusal of Parliament to accept the Chartist petition, Duncombe asked that at least representatives from the petitioners be heard. The great majority of Parliament refused Duncombe's suggestion.

T. Z. Y.

"THE CONTRAST"
1. *Lord Johnny.* Lord John Russell, home secretary.
2. *O'Connor—Feargus (1794–1855).* According to G. D. H. Cole, "Feargus O'Connor was unquestionably the best-loved, as well as the most-hated, man in the Chartist movement. . . . all over England he had an immense hold upon the people" (*Chartist Portraits*, p. 300). Perhaps the best known of the Chartist leaders. Helped to edit and publish various principal Chartist publications including *The Labourer* and the most influential, *The Northern Star.* Was a advocate of a Land Scheme, which proposed that the only possible way of raising wages for industrial workers was to remove surplus factory labor from the manufacturers by giving workers free land. In 1850 O'Connor once again introduced a motion in Parliament in favor of the Chartist National Petition. It was defeated and, ultimately, so was the movement itself. O'Connor died after several years of confinement in a madhouse. Thousands of workers held a public funeral for him at Kensal Green, and he was mourned throughout Great Britain.
3. *Stephens*—Joseph Rayner (1805–79). Advocate of industrial reform, Chartist, and minister, expelled in 1834 from the Wesleyan Connexion, for advocating the separation of church and state. A number of his sermons and lectures were published as pamphlets. Is quoted as having said that he was "a revolutionist by fire, a revolutionist by blood, to the knife, to the death." Early on advocated the use of physical force against the evils of British industrialism in the 1830s and 1840s. In August 1839 was imprisoned and not released until the following year. Was active in factory reform. Played an active part in the agitation that led to the amendments of the Factory Acts of 1850 and 1853. Published *Stephen's Monthly Magazine*, *The Ashton Chronicle*, and *The Champion*.

W. B.

"TO THE POETS OF AMERICA"
Poem dedicated to American abolitionists and writers.
1. *Garrison*—William Lloyd (1805–79). Editor of the newspaper, *The Liberator*, an ideological leader of the abolitionists.
2. *Child*—David (1794–1874). English democratic poet.
3. *Chapman*—Maria (1806–85). English democratic poet.
4. *Pierrepont*—John (1785–1886). English democratic poet.
5. *Bryant*—William Cullen (1794–1878). American journalist and poet.
6. *Whittier*—John Greenleaf (1807–92). American poet and abolitionist.
7. *Montgomery*—James (1771–1854). English democratic poet.
8. *Cowper*—William (1731–1800). English democratic poet.
9. *Campbell*—Thomas (1777–1844). English democratic poet.
10. *Moore*—Thomas (1779–1852). English democratic poet.

John Arnott (n.d.)

Chartist member of the Society of Fraternal Democrats and a popular poet.

"A SONG ADDRESSED TO THE FRATERNAL DEMOCRATS"
On 22 September 1845, at a dinner held to celebrate the first French Republic of 1792, a radical party emerged under the title of Fraternal Democrats. It soon

became the focus for English, German, and Polish socialists, including Marx, Engels, George Julian Harney, and a newcomer to British radicalism, Ernest Jones—perhaps the most famous literary figure in the Chartist movement. The Fraternal Democrats embraced foreign republicanism. Feargus O'Connor attacked this society and wrote in *The Northern Star* in 1847 that Chartists have "nothing whatever to do with any foreign movement."

Bandiera

Almost certainly a pseudonym for Gerald Massey publishing in Harney's periodicals.

George Binns (1816–48)

Chartist agitator and poet, born and raised in Sunderland. Together with James Williams, Binns ran a bookshop in Sunderland that was a center for Chartist organizing in the district. While running this literary center, Binns continued his activities as a Chartist agitator. Williams and Binns were imprisoned for sedition in the summer of 1840. Binns was exiled to New Zealand after this release from prison in 1842, where he died an early death from consumption. As a speaker and writer of Chartist hymns and lyrical and emotional poems, he was very popular in the northeast. Was evidently influenced by Byron, romantic heroic sensibilities, and Christian symbolism—the latter being a fairly common motif among Chartist poets.

"TO THE MAGISTRATES WHO COMMITTED ME TO PRISON UNDER THE DARLINGTON CATTLE ACT"
Binns was tried at a Durham judicial session for his Chartist activity in April of 1840 and was sentenced to six months in prison, in solitary confinement. Binns refused to be represented by a defense attorney and mounted his own defense. The main points of his speech served as the basis for this poem.

"FLOWERS AND SLAVES"
Written in a small town several miles from Durham, published during Binn's imprisonment.

John Henry Bramwich (1804–46)

Leicester Chartist and "stockinger-poet," i.e., a knitter of stockings. His mother was a weaver and could barely sustain her two children. At the age of nine Bramwich began working in a factory. Joined the infantry at seventeen, and served in the army for sixteen years, which included service in the West Indies. Returned to England and entered a textile factory. Bramwich developed a lung disease due to his work. Bedridden, he began to write verses, realizing he had little time to live. In a letter shortly before his death he wrote: "A slave without lungs is worth nothing on the British slave market. I assure you you have to be Sampson and Goliath together to work with contemporary knitting [stocking] machines. I regard myself as a person killed by the system. I am not alone: thousands share my fate. Millions have already died without understanding anything."
His first poems appeared in 1841 in the publication, *The Extinquisher*, and thereafter appeared regularly in other Chartist publications. Many of his verses

express religious motifs, and his poetry is often similar to religious hymns. Poems of this sort were widespread among the Chartist poets, the rhythm resembling that of religious hymns. Examples of this sort of poetry include early works by Linton and Massey. The hymn, "Great God Is this Patriot's Doom" by Bramwich, was composed on the occasion of Samuel Holberry's public funeral.

L.T. Clancy (n.d.)

Chartist poet, author of a collection of poems, *Scraps for the Radicals*, published in *The Northern Star.*

"IMPROMPTU"
Poem in the collection, *Scraps for Radicals.*

1. *Conference*—Refers to a National Convention in Birmingham on 27 December 1842. Joseph Sturge, a Quaker free trader and Birmingham alderman who represented the radical middle classes, suggested excluding from the rules of the association the word *Charter,* explaining that this name after the 1842 uprisings was linked to violent revolutionary acts. Workers did not want to reject this name, and when the vote was taken, Sturge was defeated. Sturge then led a minority of the radical middle classes from the hall to found a Complete Suffrage Union and his supporters now dropped the use of the term *Universal Suffrage* in favor of the term, *Complete Suffrage.* According to Engels: "The workers hooted with derision and quietly went their own way. From this moment Chartism became a purely working-class movement, and was free from all the trammels of bourgeois influence." From then on, he concludes, "the Radical section of the middle class fell under the domination of the Liberals, and now [played] a very miserable role indeed on the political scene" (See chap. 9, "Working-class Movements," in *The Condition of the Working Class.)*

Charles Cole (n.d.)

Little-known worker-poet. Signed his works, "a Labour Mechanic." His works appeared in the Chartist newspaper, *The Friend of the People,* originally called *The Red Republican.*

Thomas Cooper (1805–1892)

Son of a painter. Became a master bootmaker. Was largely self-educated. In 1827 became a teacher and Methodist preacher. In 1841 joined the Chartists. Started to sign his poems, Thomas Cooper, Chartist. The Chartists had begun to set up their own chapel or mechanics' institutes to educate the workers. Many of these were short-lived. The most outstanding example of this sort of intellectual endeavor was found at Leicester, where Cooper, in 1841 at the Shakespeare Room, established an adult evening and Sunday school, using the Bible, Channing's *Self Culture,* and other such tracts as textbooks. The classes were named after great Chartist heroes—Sydney, Marvell, Milton, Cartwright, and Cobbett, among others. They wrote their own Chartist hymns, read Shakespeare and Burns, and heard Cooper lecture on Milton. Later Cooper held Chartist camp meetings, marches (with Chartist hymn singing), and advocated physical force. In May 1843, he was accused of inciting the workers to riot, and sentenced to two years' imprisonment. The revolutionary urgings of leftist Chartists were foreign to Cooper. And when he was released from prison he took a reformist position and in the 1850s joined the Christian Socialists and broke with the Chartist workers' movement. Was a publisher and literary critic. His publications included *Cooper's Journal, The Rushlight,* and *The Extinguisher.* In 1872 he wrote his autobiography.

"THE LION OF FREEDOM"
Written on the occasion of the freeing of Feargus O'Connor from prison on 30 August 1841, and which was celebrated as a holiday of sorts. *The Northern Star* published a notice announcing the order of the procession to celebrate O'Connor's release: "O'CONNOR / Will Leave The Castle At One O'Clock Precisely, / Accompanied By / THE MARSHALL AND COMMITTEE, / Who Will Conduct Him, To a / TRIUMPHAL CAR! / Built Expressly For The Purpose, / When the trumpets shall sound the advance, / THE PROCESSION / will then proceed in the following order: / Marshals on Horseback / Committee of Release / Demonstration, / Two and two, wearing White and Green / Ribbons, and carrying a splendid Flag / Members of Chartist association / Two and two, wearing Green Ribands / Brass Band / Delegates from other towns, two and two. The song, "The Lion of Freedom," written for the occasion by Cooper, was sung and became one of the most popular Chartist songs.

"SONNETS ON THE DEATH OF ALLEN DAVENPORT"
Davenport died on 29 November 1846.

Allen Davenport (1775–1846)

London Chartist and shoemaker. Born in a small village to poor peasants. One of ten children. Became a soldier and later studied the bootmaking trade. By 1805 was attracted to Thomas Spence's ideas concerning workers' ownership of land. Davenport wrote one of the first biographies of Spence in 1836. In 1837 a rival party to the London Working Men's Association (LWMA) began to form around Harney, Bronterre O'Brien, and O'Connor. In January, with the help of Davenport, Harney began the East London Democratic Association, to appeal to the more depressed trades of London—in opposition to the more middle-class LWMA. By the spring of 1838 Harney and Davenport's group and the LWMA split. In 1839 he became a Chartist. Edited many Chartist periodicals and newspapers. First poetic attempt was in 1814. Was a contributor to the *Poor Man's Guardian* in the 1830s where a considerable quantity of political verses were printed. Was a poet by the time he joined the Chartists. Sometimes signed his Chartist verses "Alphus" and "Economicus" and the initials "A.D."

"IRELAND IN CHAINS"
Written in the style of the Marsellaise and devoted to a common theme—the liberation of Ireland. Davenport was a supporter of the independence of Ireland and wrote: "I should like her to be a free and independent nation. Her sufferings ought to be a sufficient reason for her redemption."

Ebenezer Elliott (1781–1849)

"REFORM"
   1. *Abaddon*—Destroyer, or angel of the bottomless pit. Rev. ix, 11. "And they had a king over them which is the angel of the bottomless pit, whose name in the Hebrew tongue of Abaddon."

2. *Mammon*—False god of riches and avarice.

3. *MAN to Mercia*—Henry Brougham, the Lord Chancellor. Supported the new and despised Poor Law. Endorsed Malthus's objections to a "permanent fund" for the poor. In a famous speech Lord Brougham made a distinction between the "people" and "the populace—the mob." This speech caused an uproar among radicals.

"THE REVOLUTION OF 1832"
Probably refers to the Reform Bill of 1832, a moderate bill that reformed the worst abuses of the political system, giving more working families the franchise and separate representation to some of the larger industrial towns.

"HYMN"
1. *Caxton*—William (1422?–91). English printer who introduced the printer's art into England by the latter half of the fifteenth century. For the Chartist essayist, poet, or pamphleteer, the written word was as powerful as any army of soldiers.

"PRESTON MILLS"
A textile manufacturing town in Lancashire where, beginning in the summer of 1853, a series of strikes began at the mills. By late October, all the mills in the town were closed by the mill owners. In late April 1854, the strike collapsed.

Alfred Fennel

"THE RED FLAG"
1. *Haynau*—Julius Jacob (1786–1853). Austrian general who suppressed the revolution in Italy in 1848 and in Hungary in 1849.

2. *Czar*—Nicholas I.

3. *The betrayers of France Rome's chains again bind*—Refers to the march of the French armies against the revolutionary Romans in 1849.

Edwin Gill (n.d.)

Chartist from Sheffield. His works appeared in *The Northern Star* in the early 1840s.

"THE CHARTER FOR EVER SHALL WEATHER THE STORM"
1. *humbug*—This is how O'Connor and other Chartists referred to the Anti-Corn Law League.

2. *Tyrannical rocks*—Tories.

3. *Treacherous blasts*—Whigs.

4. *No surrender—Charter and no surrender*—Very popular slogan of the Chartists.

George Julian Harney (1817–97)

One of the main leaders of the left wing of the Chartists. Organizer of the Society of Fraternal Democrats, subeditor of *The Northern Star* in 1843, and member of the National Charter Association, and publisher of many Chartist newspapers. Excellent speaker. Born in Kent. From age sixteen took part in a social struggle. Allied himself with Henry Hetherington in opposition to the government's newspaper stamp law, passed to suppress the radical press. Harney helped Hetherington publish his unstamped newspaper, *Poor Man's Guardian*, was imprisoned three times, and soon emerged as a national and radical leader of the Chartist movement in the late 1830s. Harney met Frederick Engels at *The Northern Star* office in Leeds, and through him became acquainted with foreign republican exiles. Founded the London Democratic Association and in 1845 the Society for Fraternal Democrats, the first international association of Chartists. In 1848 tried to save the faltering Chartist movement by founding *The Red Republican* and *The Star of Freedom*. Later he became a moderate and middle-class reformist.

"ALL MEN ARE BRETHREN"
Here Harney imitated Walter Scot's "Lady of the Lake," which started with the lines: "Hail to the Chief who in triumph advances! / Honour'd and bless'd be the ever-green Pines!" All Men Are Brethren was the motto of the Fraternal Democrats. In 1849 it was replaced by the slogan, Proletarians of All Countries Unite.

William Hick (n.d.)

Little-known Chartist from Leeds, author of *The Chartist Song Book*. Belonged to a Chartist teetotaler's society. Was attracted by Feargus O'Connor's Land Plan.

"THE PRESENTATION OF THE NATIONAL PETITION AND THE MOTION OF MR. DUNCOMBE"
Refers to the 2 May 1842 presentation of the Chartist National Petition presented by T. S. Duncombe to Parliament.
1. *Duncombe*—Thomas Slingsby (1796–1861). Radical member of the House of Commons who supported the Chartists.
2. *the House*—House of Commons in the English Parliament.
3. *Alfred the great*—King of the West Saxons (849–901). General, lawmaker, philosopher, historian, and writer.
4. *fustian jackets*—O'Connor referred to workers in his speeches using this term. Often used by Chartists instead of *factory proletariat*.

Thomas Hood (1799–1845)

English poet and humorist. Born in London. Editor of *Hood's Magazine* and various other periodicals. In his *Condition of the Working Class in England*, Engels wrote: "Thomas Hood, the most talented of the present generation of English humorists, like all humorists, has strong sympathies with suffering humanity . . . but his character lacks all dynamic energy. Early in the year 1844 . . . he wrote a fine poem called 'The Son of the Shirt,' which wrung many compassionate but ineffectual tears from the daughters of the bourgeoisie" (see chap. 83 "The Proletariat," in *The Condition of the Working Class in England*.) The poem first appeared in the Christmas edition of *Punch* in 1843.

Iota

Pseudonym for one of the Chartists arrested in the Newport Uprising, Monmouthshire, Wales, November 1839. The main work of this poet consisted of a collection of sonnets dedicated to this uprising and to its three principal leaders—John Frost, Zephaniah Williams, and William Jones.

"SONNETS DEVOTED TO CHARTISM"

1. *Newport*—On the night of 3 November and 1839 4, Frost, Williams, and Jones led some 7,000 colliers and ironworkers on Newport, South Wales, at the beginning of what was to have been a concerted rising in the valleys to capture key towns and establish a Chartist republic. The march was badly handled and organized, and after a short battle at the Westgate Hotel, the Chartists were dispersed by a few dozen soldiers. Twenty-four people were killed or died from their injuries (more than twice the death toll at the well-known "Peterloo Massacre" in Manchester, 16 August 1819), 125 were arrested, and 21 were charged with high treason, including Frost, Williams, and Jones. The cases were heard in Monmouth on 10 December 1839.

2. *Shell*—Young Chartist killed by soldiers during the Newport uprisings.

Ebenezer Jones (1820–60)

One of the most interesting Chartist poets. Had a significant influence on English poetry of the later periods, especially on William Morris and Dante Gabriel Rossetti, and on the Chartist poet William Linton. His most interesting collection is called *Studies of Sensation and Event*. The book originated in the Chartist journal, *The Labourer*, reviewed by Ernest Jones.

Ernest Jones (1819–69)

Publisher, orator, and writer. Perhaps the most famous and well educated of the Chartist writers. Was born into an upper-class family. Over the course of his life he proved to be more literate than most of his fellow Chartist poets and writers. Ruined his health and finally his life in the cause of Chartism.

Became a leading strategist and ideologist of the working-class movement. Tried to steer Chartism into the direction of giving political power to the working classes. Was more working-class oriented than many of his fellow Chartists and mistrusted middle-class radicalism. His views made him popular for a time with Marx and Engels who regarded Jones as their most promising advocate in Great Britain. Jones led the left-wing faction of the Chartists in the 1840s. In 1847 he began *The Labourer* with O'Connor. His first novel was *The Confessions of a King*.

Jones wrote romances in prose and verse, novels, pamphlets (including *Capital and Labour* in 1867, and *Democracy Vindicated* in 1867), and much poetry. His juvenilia in verse were published by his parents in 1830 when Jones was eleven. Some of his *Chartist Songs and Fugitive Pieces* were published with music, e.g., "The Song of the Lower Classes"—later, "Song of the Low"—with music by John Lowry.

In 1848 he was sentenced to two years in prison for revolutionary activity. When he was released he started *Notes to the People*, which contain some of his best prose and verse. While he was in prison his wife and children were maintained by the Chartists of Halifax, where he stood in the general election of 1847, securing 280 votes.

Toward the end of the Chartist movement, Jones called for a convention in Manchester in May 1852 to rally the remnants of the Chartists, but this failed.

From 1852 to 1858 he published a national broadly based weekly—*People's Paper.* Finally, he helped form the Political Reform Union, which led to the Reform Act of 1867.

"OUR SUMMONS"
Appeared in *Chartist Songs and Fugitive Pieces,* first published in 1846.

"A CHARTIST CHORUS"
Published many times, this is about the influence of O'Connor's utopian Land Plan.

"OUR DESTINY"
From *Chartist Song and Fugitive Pieces* and in another collection called *The Battle Day and Other Poems* by Jones. The cycle of poems is called, "The Cry of the Russian Serf to the Czar."

"OUR WARNING"
From *Chartist Song and Fugitive Pieces,* first published in 1846.

"OUR CHEER"
Also from *Chartist Song and Fugitive Pieces.* Reprinted under the titles, "Our Rally" and "The Italian Exile to His Countrymen," in *The Battle Day and Other Poems.*

"A SONG FOR THE PEOPLE"
1. *sister-isle*—Ireland.

"THE MARCH OF FREEDOM"
First published in *The Labourer,* this poem relates to revolutionary events in Europe in 1848.
1. *a cigar*—Soldiers armed themselves with cigars to light the fuses of bombs similar to hand grenades.
2. *Ferdinand and Frederick*—Refers to Austrian Emperor Ferdinand 1 (1793–1875) and the Prussian King, Frederick William IV (1795–1861).
3. *Ziska*—Jan (1360–1424). Bohemian general and leader of the Hussites. Leader of the popular revolutionary army during the peasant wars in Czechoslovakia.
4. *Hussites*—Followers of John Huss (1369–1415), Bohemian religious reformer. Executed by the Catholic reaction.
5. *Bakounine*—Mikhail (1814–76). Russian anarchist.
6. *Sorrowing Sister*—Ireland.
7. *Erin*—Ireland.

"THE SONG OF THE GAGGERS"
1. *Lilliput*—Imaginary country in Swift's *Gulliver's Travels,* country of people six inches tall.
2. *Brobdingnaq*—Country of giants in *Gulliver.*

"BONNIVARD"
Written by Jones in July 1848 while in prison. First published in 1851 in Jones's *Notes to the People.* Francois Bonnivard was a Swiss nationalist and republican (1493?–1570). By order of the Duke of Savoy, Bonnivard was imprisoned in the

Castle of Chillon from 1530 to 1536. Byron's poem, "The Prisoner of Chillon" (1816), was inspired by Bonnivard.

1. *the stone*—According to historical legend, Bonnivard, chained to the wall by a long chain, tread a path into the stone floor.

"PRISON BARS"
Written by Jones while still in prison in 1848. Published in 1851 in *Notes to the People*.

"HYMN FOR LAMMAS-DAY"
The poem later was called, "The Song of the Day's Labourer." Lammas-Day was a popular holiday of the harvest. Celebrated on 1 August.

"WE ARE SILENT"
Contents of the poem related to the reactionary period after the defeat of the revolutionary forces throughout Europe and England in 1848–49. With this defeat, the Chartist movement began its decline.

"FAREWELL OF THE NEW RHEINISH GAZETTE"
1. *Ferdinand Freiligrath* (1810–76). German poet. Member of the Union of Communists. Jones's poem was published in 1849. Freiligrath eventually gave up his revolutionary politics.

"BREAD"
1. *Pierre Dupont* (1821–70). French poet and songwriter of working-class origin. Wrote "Song of the Bread" in 1846 and "Song of the Workers" in 1846. Very popular among French workers.

"THE PRISONER TO THE SLAVES"
1. *From my cell*—Written in prison.

"THE FISHERMEN"
Poem was written in 1848 but not immediately published since Jones was then arrested.

1. *the fisher of France*—Alphonse Marie Louis De LaMartine (1790–1869). French poet and political figure.

2. *the fisher of Russia*—Russian Czar, Nicholas 1.

3. *the Austrian fisher*—Von Metternich (1773–1859). Austrian statesman who led the post-Napoleonic political reaction in Europe.

"EXTRACT FROM THE NEW WORLD"
Extract from Jones's long poem, written while in prison.
1. *Franklin*—Benjamin (1706–90).

"THE SONG OF THE LOW"
An earlier title of this poem was called "The Song of the Lower Classes." Reprinted from J. Saville's *Writings and Speeches of Ernest Jones*.

Eugene La Mont (n.d.)

Popular Chartist poet. Died in 1844. Chartist poets dedicated several poems to him, the best of which was written was by James Syme. The last stanza reads:

"But thine, La Mont, and names like thine / Shall live in hearts that heaven illumes, / And wafted to a niche divine, / Outlive the wreck of tombs."

"THE LAND OF THE BRAVE AND THE FREE!"
Poem was also printed in the *Chartist Circular*, 7 August 1841.

Jonathan Lefevre (n.d.)

Relatively little-known Chartist poet who lived in Bristol.

"THE ENSLAVED"
Poem written on 11 March 1840, the day the leaders of the Chartist uprising in Wales—Frost, Williams, and Jones—were sentenced to life imprisonment at hard labor in Australia.

William James Linton (1812–97)

One of the great Chartist poets, radical intellectuals, and publicists. Was by trade a wood engraver, one of the most distinguished engravers of his time. Used the pseudonymn, "Spartacus," a Roman gladiator and leader of a massive slave rebellion in the first century B.C.

His poems were published in almost all the Chartist magazines and newspapers. Linton published *The National*, *The English Republic*, and *The Northern Tribune*, as well as a large collection of poetry. In 1839 printed the *Hymns for the Unenfranchised* in *The National*. From 1840 to 1847 his works were printed in *The Northern Star*, *The Labourer*, and the Irish newspaper, *The Nation*.

In 1849 he published a long poem dedicated to the revolutionary events in Great Britain and Europe called *The Dirge of Nations*. The height of his activity was from 1851 to 1853, during which time he wrote his well-known collection of poems, *Rhymes and Reasons Against Landlordism*, which, together with Jones's works, is one of the best examples of Chartist poetry.

During the last years of his life Linton lived in the United States. In 1871 he printed a pamphlet in defense of the Paris Commune and a biography of the American abolitionist poet John Greenleaf Whittier (1807–92).

In 1895 his biography, *Memories*, was published.

"LABOUR AND PROFIT"
Poem was very popular and often reprinted by the Chartists.
   1. [Sir] *Richard Arkwright* (1732–92). English inventor. Considered inventor of a spinning machine used on a wide scale. Became extremely wealthy.
   2. *Hargreave*—James (?–1778). Inventor of the spinning jenny in 1764. English weaver from Blackburn.
   3. *Crompton*—Samuel (1753–1827). English inventor of a needle machine in 1799, which utilized the designs of Arkwright's and Hargreave's inventions.
   4. *Radcliffe*—William (1760–1841). Inventor of a cleaning machine.
   5. *Peels*—Robert (1750–1830). Manchester textile owner. Father of Robert Peel, English prime minister (1834–35 and 1841–46).
   6. *Cobden*—Richard (1804–65). English statesman and economist. Manufacturer and leader of the Free Traders and Anti-Corn Law League.
   7. *Cannot Toil be cheaper?*—Goal of getting rid of the Corn Laws, which Free Traders struggled for, was the reduction of the wages of industrial workers.

"THE LAMENT OF THE PRESENT"
Poem dedicated to the delivery of the Chartist Petition by Parliament on 10 April 1848, and to the period of reaction that followed the defeat of this petition three days later when many Chartists were arrested.

"FOR ROME!"
Poem written during the defense of Rome in 1849 under the leadership of Giuseppe Garibaldi (1807–82).
    1. *Mazzini's vow*—Giuseppe Mazzini (1805–72). Italian revolutionary and author. One of the principal ideologists of the Italian revolution in 1848.

"IN THE JESUITS' BURIAL GROUND"
Epigram of the collection, "Modern Monumental Inscriptions," published in *The English Republic*.
    1. *Barrot*—Camille Odillon (1791–1873). French statesman prominent as a liberal monarchist under the July 1830 monarchy who supported Louis Philippe. Directed the party of the "dynastic left." From 1839 Barrot demanded the "broadening of the bases of the monarchy" by an electoral reform. Head of the first ministry called by President Louis Napoleon on 20 December 1848 and also minister of justice. Was dismissed in October 1849.

"ON THE TOMB OF GENERAL EUGENE CAVAIGNAC"
    1. *The brother of the Republican*—Eugène Cavaignac (1802–57). Suppressor of July uprising of the Paris proletariat. His brother, Godefroy Cavaignac (1853–1905), was a French bourgeois republican.

"FOR A SMALL COLUMN IN MEMORY OF THE AFFLICTION OF M. THIERS"
    1. *Thiers*—Louis Adolphe (1797–1877). French historian and president of the French republic (1871–73).

"UNDER A STATUE OF ALPHONSE DE LAMARTINE"
    1. *Poet and Orator*—Alphonse De Lamartine (1790–1869). Poet and political figure.

"ANOTHER FOR LORD JOHN"
    1. *The Body of Moses*—Opera refers to the biblical story of the archangel Michael who, with an army of loyal angels, victoriously warred against Lucifer, Rev. xii, 7–9. "And there was war in heaven: Michael and his angels fought against the dragon; and the dragon fought and his angels and prevailed not. . . . and the great dragon was cast out, that old serpent, called the devil.

"RHYMES AND REASONS AGAINST LANDLORDISM"
Collection published in *The English Republic* and *The Friend of the People* under the title, "Rhymes for the Landlorded."

"FROM THE CENTRE UPWARDS"
    1. *Russell-Castlereagh*—Robert Stewart (1769–1822). British Tory statesman. Effected the union of England and Ireland in 1801. Lord John Russell (1792–1878), prime minister (1846–52 and 1865–66).

"REVENGE"
   1. *Agent*—agent who collected the rent for the landlord.

"EMIGRANTS"
Poem dedicated to the emigration after the Irish famine.

"IRISH HARVEST SONG"
   1. *Fitzgerald*—Edward (1763–98). Led the uprising in 1798 in Ireland. Was wounded at his arrest and died in prison.

Robert Lowery (n.d.)

Tailor, writer, and Chartist activist. Was originally trained as a seaman. Became lame during his early voyages and was forced to take up less arduous work. Was linked with the revival of unionism in 1834 and helped to organize a local branch of the Grand National Consolidated Union. Lowery was initially a spokesman for physical force and armed insurrection in 1839—the year of rioting in various parts of Wales, in Birmingham and, on 4 November in Newport. Was considered a great orator. Later, like other Chartists after the failure of Chartism in the late 1840s, Lowery moved away from working-class struggles. Became a full-time worker and lecturer for the middle-class temperance movement.

Gerald Massey (1828–1907)

Born into a poor family. At eight he began working in a textile factory. In 1847 he published his first collection called *Original Poems and Chansons*. The revolutionary events of 1848, and in particular the activity of the Chartists, influenced Massey's awakening interest in the working class. On 10 April 1848, Massey attended the Chartist demonstration on Kensington Common, followed by the Chartist petition being delivered to Parliament by Feargus O'Connor.
   Massey was the bookkeeper of the Christian Socialist workshops. After the events of 1848, devoted his energies to his literary output. Published a monthly magazine called *The Uxbridge Spirit of Freedom*. Massey allied himself with Julian Harney and wrote for *The Red Republican* and other radical journals. According to John Plummer, a staymaker in Kettering, the writings of Massey during the year of revolution, 1848, were "most in accordance with the general tone of opinion entertained by the majority of working men of the present day." Toward the end of his life Massey moved away from radical, Chartist politics and followed the pre-Raphaelites.

"SONG OF THE RED REPUBLICAN"
Poem that introduced the first number of Harney's magazine, *The Red Republican*, and to some extent became the banner poem of that publication. Poem was first published in *Cooper's Journal*, 15 June 1850.

"LOVERS' FANCIES"
Example of Massey's early romantic verse.

"THE MEN OF 'FORTY-EIGHT'"
Dedicated to the men who participated in the revolutionary struggles of 1848. Very popular in progressive circles even today. The modern writer Jack Lindsay

used the poem's title for his own historical novel called *The Men of Forty-Eight*, where the poem itself was used as an epigraph.

"A RED REPUBLICAN LYRIC"
Often reprinted in Chartist and post-Chartist publications, for example, *The Republican* (1850).

"JOHN BRIGHT"
Manchester Quaker, radical manufacturer who ended up opposing factory reform and factory legislation. Voted against the Ten Hours a day legislation in 1844.

Edward P. Mead

Called "Commodore," popular Chartist lecturer and poet, from Birmingham, often printed in *The Northern Star.*

"THE STEAM KING"
Almost entirely reprinted in Engels's *The Condition of the Working Class in England* in chap. 7, "The Proletariat." Engels writes that the poem gives the workers' "own point of view concerning the factory system."
1. *the cheap bread crew*—Refers to the Anti-Corn Law League. Led largely by middle-class radicals under the slogan, "Cheap Bread." Net effect of their efforts was to lower the wages of the agrarian workers.

"A NEW CHARTIST SONG"
1. *Reform*—refers to the Reform Bill of 1832.
2. *Gaffer Grey*—Charles Earl Grey (1764–1845). Government Whig figure. Member (1830–34) of Parliament. Responsible for Parliamentary Reform of 1832.
3. *O'Connor*—Feargus (1794–1855). One of the Chartist leaders, head of the most militant wing of the Chartists in the beginning of the movement. In the early 1830s O'Connor gained an Irish seat in Parliament. In September 1835, founded the Marylebone Radical Association. The following year O'Connor was elected to the London Working Men's Association, which in 1837, drafted the Six Points. Out of this radical trade union/artisan movement, which in May 1838 published the *People's Charter*, Chartism was born. In November 1841, he helped to start *The Northern Star*, first published in Leeds by Joshua Hobson. In the general election of July 1847, he was elected for a seat from Nottingham, thus becoming the first and last purely Chartist member of Parliament. O'Connor is considered the principal architect of the Land Plan. (For more details, see note to Thomas Wheeler.)

J. M'Owen (n.d.)

Chartist poet from Sheffield, published only a few poems in *The Northern Star.*

"FATHER! WHO ARE THE CHARTISTS?"
1. *Holberry's grave*—Samuel Holberry, Radical Sheffield Chartist. Was sentenced to four years' imprisonment with hard labor in March 1840, as a result of the Newport uprising. Was also accused of participating in an attempted rising in Sheffield in January 1840. Died in prison on 21 June 1842, at the age of twenty-seven, as a result of the conditions suffered therein. Was considered a martyr by

Notes

the Chartists, and his funeral in Sheffield turned into a demonstration attended by an estimated fifty thousand workers.

H. R. Nicholls (n.d.)

Little-known Chartist poet whose poems appeared in Harney's *The Friend of the People*, Ernest Jones's *Notes to the People*, and Thomas Cooper's *Cooper's Journal*.

"THE PARLIAMENT"
1. *Lord John*—John Russell, home secretary and later prime minister.
2. *Hume*—Joseph (1777–1855). English middle-class radical.

Joseph Radford (n.d.)

Little-known Birmingham Chartist poet whose verses appeared in *The Northern Star*.

William Rider (n.d.)

Veteran Chartist radical from Leeds, closely involved with *The Northern Star*. Probably wrote most of the leading articles after 1849. Advocate of the Chartist faction called "physical force." Argued that moral means of struggle were a waste of time. By 1839 Rider belonged to the left wing of the Chartists, the London Democratic Association, headed by George Julian Harney. While the National Convention was deliberating strategy, the association urged militant action such as a general strike. Was a member of the Chartist Convention. Frustrated at the convention's inability to organize for militant actions, Rider publicly renounced his position of delegate, declaring that among the members of the Convention, "You will not find even eight honest men."

"THE LEAGUE"
Refers to the Anti-Corn Law League. Organized by Manchester factory owners, it set as its goal the removal of all laws that limited the import of grain products. According to Engels, in his *Condition of the Working Class*, the Anti-Corn Law League "resulted in a loosening of the bonds which linked the Radical elements in the bourgeoisie with the proletariat. The workers soon realised that they would gain little from the repeal of the Corn Laws, which would, however, be very beneficial to the middle classes" (chap. 9, "Working-Class Movements"). The league was a federation of societies that had developed from the original association, founded by the Manchester manufacturers in 1839. More and more league agitators became revolutionary in tone.
1. *And burk the charter*—Leaders of the league tried to enlist Chartists in the struggle against the Corn Laws that had the effect of weakening the Chartist movement. However, many Chartists no longer trusted the middle classes, especially since the riots of 1842, including the "Plug Riots" in August, and the Chartist trials in October, when the middle classes offered no support.

David Ross (n.d.)

Teacher at the elementary school at Leeds. Joined the Chartist movement in 1841. Considered one of the best Chartist orators. Collaborated with *The Northern Star* and *The National Reformer*.

Williams S. Villiers Sankey (n.d)

One of the most popular Chartist poets.Chosen as a delegate from Edinburgh to the General Chartist Convention. The M.A. he put after his signature possibly meant Master of Arts, since he was also a medical doctor. His poetry is characterized by its lyrical quality. As a rule he wrote his verse from widely known songs. Shelley's poetry had a great influence on Sankey. This is seen especially in "Ode," which resembles Shelley's "Song to the Men of England" (1819). The first stanza of Shelley's poem reads: "Men of England, wherefore plough / For the lords who lay ye low? / Wherefore weave with toil and care / The rich robes your tyrants wear?"

Benjamin Stott (n.d)

Chartist poet, member of the Manchester Organization of the Chartists. In 1842 published the collection called "Songs for the Millions" in *The Northern Star.* In 1843 these songs came out in a separate booklet in Middleton.

James Syme (n.d.)

Scottish Chartist who lived in Edinburgh.

"LABOUR SONG"
Was reprinted later by the Scottish *Chartist Circular* (28 August 1841). The philosophers of whom Syme speaks with such contempt were the Chambers brothers, publishers of a philanthropic and liberal magazine, *Chambers Magazine.*

William Thom (1798–1848)

Scottish Chartist and weaver. Lamed in childhood, Thom worked in a hand-weaving factory at the age of ten. Was self-educated. Some of his verse appeared in local newspapers and later in Chartist journals. To support his family Thom played his flute in the street and often begged for money. Began a short-lived journal called the *Inverury Gossamer.* For a while was part of a literary circle in London and his verses became popular. Thom, however, could not stand the relatively comfortable life—"I was encased in a carpeted room—with a fire and sound windows—Lord man, how it contrasts with the dank dark den . . . hopeless hell of a Dundee weaving shop." Returned to Dundee and died a few weeks later, leaving his wife and children destitute.

James Vernon (n.d.)

London Chartist worker-poet. Arrested with many other Chartists after April 1848. Because he was often subjected to forced labor, he suffered from paralysis and was at times bedridden. His verses were published in *The Northern Star* and in separate booklets, one called *J. Vernon: The Afflicted Muse* (South Molton, (n.p.) 1842).

"SONNET TO WILLIAMS AND BINNS"
1. *Williams and Binns*—James Williams and George Binns: Chartist leaders. Jointly ran a bookshop in Sunderland. Published tracts, handbills, and poems from their shop until their arrest for sedition in the summer of 1840.

John Watkins (1792–1831).

Popular Chartist agitator, publicist, poet, and lecturer. His lectures were published in *The Northern Star*. Devoted all his energy to Chartist struggles and was an advocate of physical force. Imprisoned for the dissemination of seditious literature. Watkins wrote a great number of pamphlets, two songs—"John Frost" and "Griselda"—and the long poem, "The Golden Age." Like many Chartist poems, his works were often dedicated to particular persons and events.

"LINES ON SHELL, KILLED AT NEWPORT"

Dedicated to the 1839 Newport Uprising and the murdered Chartists. Shell is George Shell—eighteen-year-old—Chartist shot at Newport. Left his parents a letter on his way to the insurrection, a letter that ultimately appeared in most Chartist publications. The letter reads as follows: "Dear Parents—I hope this will find you well, as I am myself at this present. I shall this night be engaged in a glorious struggle for freedom, and should it please God to spare my life, I shall see you soon; but if not, grieve not for me. I shall have fell in a noble cause. My tools are at Mr. Cecil's and likewise my clothes. Farewell—Yours truly, George Shell."

"EXTRACT FROM THE PLAY OF JOHN FROST"

In 1840 Watkins wrote a play about Frost—a Chartist leader of the Welsh uprising in 1839. The work attracted many Chartist poets and writers, but not a single publisher agreed to publish Watkins's play, which was finally published only at Watkins's own expense. Excerpts of the play appeared in *The Northern Star* in 1841 and was produced by independent workers' collectives. Watkins himself wrote: "This drama is not so much intended to illustrate the characters of the dramatic personae in it, nor the insurrection at Newport, on which the plot turns, as it is an attempt to illustrate Chartism itself. Nevertheless, the writer has selected the chief victim to be the hero, and, so far as one not personally known to him could know him, he has endeavoured to make a true portrait of him, likewise of Shell" (*The Northern Star*, 10 April 1841).

1. *My severed limbs to be disposed of*—At first Frost had been sentenced to death and to quartering after death.

2. *Transport you*—Upon the intercession of the Chartists, the death sentence was changed to "transportation for life" (this meant permanent exile to Australia, sometimes to New Zealand, and was often a death sentence since many prisoners died en route). Most of the national leaders, scores of local leaders, and hundreds of followers of the Chartist movement were tried and imprisoned. Between June 1839 and June 1840, at least 543 Chartists were detained for periods of between a few weeks and a few years.

"THE CORN LAWS AND EMIGRATION"

Under this title, Watkins planned a cycle of poems, of which only two were completed.

1. *Because our lords have taxed the staff of life*—Reference to introduction of the Corn Law in 1815.

Thomas Martin Wheeler (1811–62)

London Chartist and poet. Born to a carpenter's family. In 1825 was an apprentice to a draper, and became what was known as a woolcomber, among the most economically depressed workers in the country. In addition to low wages, the work was dirty, unhealthy, and overcrowded. Traveled around England by foot, trying ten different professions. In 1839 was attracted to Owenism and had his poems published in Owen's newspaper, *The New Moral World*. In 1840 became a Chartist and joined a political section of *The Northern Star*. In 1842 Wheeler was chosen general secretary of the National Chartist Association. In 1848 went to the National Convention. Was also active in the Anti-Corn League. Helped O'Connor organize the Chartist Land Plan in the 1840s. The plan organized small farming projects available to working people, a way of escape or at least a form of competition that would keep up urban wages. The Chartist Land Plan was launched first at the National Convention in April 1845, and formalized in December at a special convention called in Manchester. For a while, Wheeler became secretary of this Chartist Land Plan, but realized the unreliability of it. From 1852 to 1853 Wheeler collaborated with Ernest Jones's *The People's Paper*. Wheeler was also president of the British Industrial Association, a trade union organization. Wrote several poems and two novels: *Sunshine and Shadow* and *Light in the Gloom*. Died at the height of his power.

Thomas Wilson (n.d.)

Chartist from Leeds. In 1839 was arrested for Chartist agitation and condemned to four months' imprisonment.

John Athol Wood (n.d.)

Chartist poet. His poems were printed in the early 1850s in *The Friend of the People*, *The Red Republican*, and *Notes to the People*.

Bibliography

Periodicals

The Champion. London, 18 September 1836–26 April 1840. Edited by John and James Paul Cobbett, 1838; also James Whittle, 1839?

The Charter. London, Nos. 1–60, 27 January 1839–15 March 1840. Edited by William Carpenter and William Hill.

The Chartist. London, Nos. 1–23, 2 February–7 July 1839.

The Chartist Circular. 1858 [2 issues only, nos. 6 and 9]. Edited by Ernest Jones.

The Chartist Circular. Glasgow. Nos. 1–146, 28 September 1839–9 July 1842. Edited by William Thomson.

Cooper's Journal: or, Unfettered Thinker and Plain Speaker for Truth, Freedom, and Progress. London, nos. 1–30, 5 January–26 October 1850. Edited by Thomas Cooper.

The Democratic Review of British and Foreign Politics, History and Literature. London, vols. 1–11, June 1849–September 1850. Edited by G. Julian Harvey.

The English Republic. London, Leeds, Brantwood, 1851 and 1854–55 monthly; 1852–53 weekly. Edited by William James Linton.

The Extinguisher. Leicester, 1841. Edited by Thomas Cooper.

The Labourer: A Monthly Magazine of Politics, Literature, and Poetry. London, Northern Star Office, vol.I, 1847; vol. II, 1847; vol. III, 1848. Edited by Feargus O'Connor and Ernest Jones.

McDouall's Chartist and Republican Journal. Manchester, Nos. 1–27, 3 April–2 October 1841. Edited by Peter Murray McDouall. [Nos. 22–27, *McDouall's Chartist Journal and Trades Advocate*]

The Northern Liberator. Newcastle-upon-Tyne, 21 October 1837—26 April 1840. Edited by Augustus Hardin Beaumont until February 1838; then Thomas Ainge Devyr.

The Northern Star and Leeds General Advertiser. Leeds, 18 November 1837–23 November 1844. Edited by William Hill, November 1837–July 1843; Joshua Hobson, July 1843–November 1844. [Continued as] *The Northern Star and National Trades Journal*. London, 30 November 1844–13 March 1852. Edited by George Julian Harney, 1845—summer 1850; William Rider, G. A. Fleming, 1850–52.

Notes to the People. London, vols. 1–11, 1851–52. Edited by Ernest Jones.

The People's Paper. London, 8 May–4 September 1858. Edited by Ernest Jones.

The Poor's Man's Guardian and Repealer's Friend. London, nos. 1–14, 3 June–, 1843.

The Red Republican. London, Nos. 1–24, 22 June–30 November, 1850. Edited by George Julian Harney. [Continued as] *The Friend of the People*. London, vols. I–II, nos. 1–24, nos. 1–33, 14 December 1850–26 July 1851.

The Star of Freedom. 8 May 1852–27 Nov. 1852. Edited by George Julian Harney.
Stephen's Monthly Magazine of Useful Information for the People. Manchester, January–October 1840. Edited by Joseph Rayner Stephens.

Anthologies

Auden, W. H. *Nineteenth Century British Minor Poets*. New York: Delacorte Press, 1966.

Benet, William Rose, and Cousins, Norman. *The Poetry of Freedom*. New York: The Modern Library, 1945.

Bold, Alan, ed. *The Penguin Book of Socialist Verse*. Harmondsworth, Middlesex: Penguin Books, 1970.

Chapman, Abraham. *Black Voices: An Anthology of Afro-American Literature*. New York: New American Library, 1968.

Culler, A. Dwight, ed. *Poetry and Criticism of Matthew Arnold*. Boston: Houghton Mifflin Company, 1961.

Hayward, John. *The Oxford Book of Nineteenth Century English Verse*. Oxford: Oxford University Press, 1964.

Hughes, Langston, and Bontemps, Arna. *The Poetry of the Negro: 1746–1949*. New York: Doubleday and Company, Inc., 1949.

Hutchinson, Thomas, ed. *Shelley Poetical Works*. New York and London: Oxford University Press, 1970.

Kovalev, Y. V., ed. *An Anthology of Chartist Literature* [Introduction translated in *Victorian Studies* vol. II (1958) and in Communist Party of Great Britain "Our History" no. 17 (Spring 1960)]. Moscow: Foreign Languages Publishing House, 1956.

Marshall, William H., ed. *Lord Byron: Selected Poems and Letters*. New York and Boston: Houghton Mifflin Company, 1968.

Scott, Patrick. *Victorian Poetry 1830–1870*. London: Longman Group Limited, 1971.

Bibliography

Thompson, Dorothy, and Harrison, J. F. C. . *Bibliography of the Chartist Movement, 1837–1976*. Sussex: The Harvester Press, 1978.

Contemporary Printed Books

Cooper, Thomas. *Poetical Works of Thomas Cooper*, London: Hodder and Stroughton, 1877. *The Purgatory of Suicides: A Prison-Rhyme in Ten Books*, 3rd ed. London: Chapman and Hall, 1853.

Elliott, Ebenezer. *The Poetical Works of Ebenezer Elliott*. Edited by Edwin Elliott. vols. 1 and 2. London: Henry S. King and Co., 1876.

Jones, Charles Ernest. *The Battle Day and Other Poems*. London: G. Routledge and Co., 1855.

Chartist Poems. London: [n.p.], 1846.

Chartist Songs and Fugitive Pieces. London: [n.p.], 1846.

Linton, William James. *Prose and Verse Fifty Years: 1836–1886*. 12 vols. *Claribel and Other Poems*. London: Simpkin and Marshall and Co., 1865.

Lovett, William. *The Life and Struggles of William Lovett.* London: George Bell and Sons Ltd., 1920.

Massey, Gerald T. *The Ballad of Babe Christabel, With Other Lyrical Poems.* New York: J. C. Derby, 1854.

———. *My Lyrical Life Poems Old and New.* 2nd series. London: Kegan, Paul, Trench, Trubner and Co., 1889.

———. *The Poetical Works of Gerald Massey.* London: Routledge, Warne and Routledge, 1861.

———. *Voices of Freedom and Lyrics of Love.* London: J. Watson, 1851.

Thom, William. *Rhymes and Recollections of a Hand Loom Weaver.* 2nd edition. London: Smith, Elder and Co., 1845.

Books and Articles on the Chartist Movement, Chartists, and Related History

Ashton, Owen R. "Chartism and Popular Culture: An Introduction to the Radical Culture in Cheltenham Spa, 1830–1847." *Journal of Popular Culture.* vol. 2, no. 4 (Spring 1987).

Buckley, Jerome Hamilton. *The Victorian Temper.* Cambridge: Harvard University Press, 1969.

Chesterton, G. K. *The Victorian Age in Literature.* New York and London, Oxford University Press, 1966.

Cole, G. D. H. *Chartist Portraits.* New York: Macmillan Publishing Co. Inc., 1965.

———. *A Short History of the British Working Class Movement 1789–1927.* London: George Allen & Unwin Ltd., 1948.

Collins, Philip. *Thomas Cooper, The Chartist: Byron and the 'Poets of the Poor.'* Nottingham: University of Nottingham Press, 1969.

Dickens, Charles. *Letters of Charles Dickens to the Baronness Burdett-Coutts.* Edited by Charles C. Osborne. London: John Murray, 1931.

Engels, Friedrich. *The Condition of the Working Class* in England. Translated and edited by W. O. Henderson and W. H. Chaloner. Stanford: Stanford University Press, 1958.

Epstein, James, and Thompson, Dorothy, eds. *The Chartist Experience.* London: Macmillan & Company Ltd., 1985.

Hauser, Arnold. *The Social History of Art.* vol. 4. New York: Vintage, 1958.

Hill, Christopher. *The Century of Revolution 1603–1714.* New York: W. W. Norton & Company, Inc., 1961.

———. *The World Turned Upside Down.* New York: Penguin, 1972.

Himmelfarb, Gertrude. *The Idea of Poverty. England in the Early Industrial Age.* New York: Vintage, 1985.

Hollis, Patricia, ed. *Class and Conflict in Nineteenth-Century England 1851–1850.* London and Boston: Routledge and Kegan Paul, 1973.

Hovell, Mark. *The Chartist Movement.* Edited by T. F. Tout. Manchester: Manchester University Press, 1925.

James, Louis. *Fiction for the Working Man 1830–1850.* London: Oxford University Press, 1963.

Jones, David. *Chartism and the Chartists.* New York: St. Martin's Press Inc., 1975.

Kovalev, Y. V. "The Literature of Chartism." *Victorian Studies.* vol. II (December 1958): 124–38.

Linday, Jack. *Charles Dickens: A Biographical and Critical Study.* London: Dakers, 1950.

Lockwood, Helen Drusilla. *Tools and the Man.* New York: Columbia University Press, 1927.

Plummer, Alfred. *Bronterre: A Political Biography of Bronterre O'Brien 1840–1864.* London: George Allen & Unwin Ltd., 1971.

Rosenblatt, Frank. *The Chartist Movement In its Social and Economic Aspects.* Part 1. New York: Columbia University Press, 1916.

Royle, Edward. *Radical Politics 1790–1900: Religion and Unbelief.* London: Longman Group Limited, 1971.

———. *Chartism.* 2nd ed., London: Longman Group Limited, 1980.

Saville, John. *Ernest Jones: Chartist. Selections from the Writings and Speeches of Ernest Jones.* London: Lawrence and Wishart Ltd., 1952. *The Red Republican and The Friend of the People.* 2 vols. New York: Barnes & Noble Books, 1966.

Searby, Peter. *The Chartists in Wales.* Essex: Longman Group UK Limited, 1986.

Semmel, Bernard. *Jamaican Blood and Victorian Conscience: The Governor Eyre Controversy.* Boston: Houghton Mifflin, 1963.

Silver, Harold. *English Education and the Radicals 1780–1850.* London and Boston: Routledge and Kegan Paul, 1975.

Simon, Brian. *Studies in the History of Education, 1780–1870.* London: Lawrence and Wishart, 1960.

Thompson, Dorothy. *The Chartists.* New York: Pantheon Books Inc., 1984.

———. *The Early Chartists.* London and New York: Macmillan Press, 1971.

Thompson, E. P. *The Making of the English Working Class.* New York: Random House Inc., 1966.

Vaughan, Michalina, and Archer, Margaret Scotford. *Social Conflict and Educational Change in England and France 1789–1848.* Cambridge: Cambridge University Press, 1971.

Vicinus, Martha. *The Industrial Muse.* New York: Harper and Row Publishers, 1974.

Webb, R. K. *The British Working-Class Reader 1790–1848.* New York: Augustus M. Kelley, 1971.

Weisser, Henry. *British Working-Class Movements and Europe: 1815–48.* Manchester: Manchester University Press, 1975.

Williams, Gwyn A. *Rowland Detrosier: A Working-Class Infidel 1800–34.* York: St. Anthony's Press, 1965.

Novels about Chartists

Disraeli, Benjamin. *Sybil, or the Two Nations.* 1845. New York: Viking Penguin, 1980.

Gaskell, Elizabeth. *Mary Barton.* 1847. New York: Viking Penguin, 1970.

———. *North and South.* 1855. New York: Oxford University Press, 1982.

Kingsley, Charles. *Alton Locke, Tailor and Poet.* 1850. New York: Oxford University Press, 1983.

Eliot, George. *Felix Holt, the Radical*. 1866. New York: Penguin Books, 1972.

NOVELS SET OR WRITTEN DURING THE CHARTIST ERA
Dickens, Charles. *Barnaby Rudge*. 1841. New York: Penguin Books, 1973.
———. "The Chimes," in *Christmas Books*. 1844. New York: Penguin Books, 1971.
———. *Hard Times*. 1854. New York: Harper and Brothers, Publishers, 1960.
———. *The Old Curiosity Shop*. 1840–41. New York: Oxford University Press, 1951.

Index of Poem Titles